THE MONETARY AND FINANCIAL SYSTEM

CIB ASSOCIATESHIP SERIES

THE MONETARY AND FINANCIAL SYSTEM

B. Julian Beecham, FCIB

Third edition of *Monetary Economics* (renamed *The Monetary and Financial System*) originally published as *Longman Exam Guide*, in 1986

Pitman

To my students

Pitman Publishing
128 Long Acre, London WC2E 9AN

A Division of Longman Group UK Limited

First published in 1986
Second impression with amendments 1986
Second edition 1988
Third edition 1990
Reprinted 1991

British Library Cataloguing in Publication Data

Beecham, B. Julian
The monetary and financial system. – 3rd.ed.
1. Monetary system
I. Title II. Beecham, B. Julian 1927–. Monetary economics
332.4

ISBN 0 273 03245 3

Typeset by Medcalf Type Ltd, Bicester, Oxon
Printed and bound in Great Britain

Contents

Preface

This book is one of the Pitman Publishing series of textbooks which are written to cover the post-Wilkinson syllabi of the Associateship exams of the Chartered Institute of Bankers (CIB).

The book has been designed as the most direct route to meeting the requirements of the Monetary and Financial System (MFS) examination paper of the CIB. The MFS exam paper will consist of eight questions, covering eight of the ten subject areas of the syllabus, from which you will be expected to select and answer four questions in the essay or detailed note form. The old Monetary Economics syllabus has been altered (1990) in order to give the subject a greater practical and institutional bias. The new syllabus is distinctly divided into ten sections to focus attention on the individual subject areas. However, you should not regard each section as being totally self-contained; it is in the nature of the subject that a full understanding of one area of the syllabus demands knowledge of other areas, and the questions set in the examinations will inevitably reflect this.

Chapter 1 provides pointers on how best to use your private study time in preparing for the examination. It also gives suggestions on examination technique, i.e. on how you actually conduct yourself during the examination itself. Adherence to both should help you to achieve success in the examinations you take. Chapters 2 to 11 are arranged in sequence with the layout of the MFS syllabus. Each chapter begins by stating the requirements of the syllabus for the topic covered in that chapter. This is followed by a section which briefly defines the technical terms involved and which gives an overview of the topic area in question, to help you get started. Then follow two sections dealing with the essential theories and principles connected with the topic; one dealing with their explanation and the other with their application to the UK MFS. These sections are backed up by approximately six examination questions recently set in that topic area, together with outline answers. There then follows a full specimen answer to a carefully chosen recent examination question: this is to help you improve your technique in how best to answer the question, the whole question and nothing but the question. Finally, each chapter ends with advice on how to take a step further in keeping yourself fully abreast of movements in the subject matter of each topic. The format of the book provides wide margins so that you may update your copy with the relevant information as it comes to light. The text in each chapter is divided into sections and sub-sections, giving you an opportunity to think upon and digest what you have been reading before proceeding further.

The general thrust of the examination will be direct, seeking precise and up-to-date information and understanding – and that could make the questions difficult for those candidates who have learned out-of-date material, instead of concentrating on acquiring a finely-focused perspective of the *evolving* practices of the monetary and financial system of a developed aeconomy. I believe that this book, and the series as a whole, will help you establish a well-grounded understanding of the required knowledge and exam techniques which will help you to do your best in the exams you take. Good luck!

B. Julian Beecham, FCIB
Cardiff

Acknowledgements

My grateful thanks to:

Nick Douch for constructive criticism, and the Chartered Institute of Bankers and Peter Gutmann, for kind permission to use the Monetary Economics *Examiners' Reports*, Monetary Economics *Syllabus, Updating Notes* and Waterlow Publishers Ltd for permission to use Signpost articles from *Banking World*.

The Bank of England for permission to refer to articles in their *Quarterly Bulletins* and published papers, and *Financial Times* for allowing the use of their London Money Market Rates table.

And to Enid, my wife, for her invaluable assistance.

B. Julian Beecham
Cardiff
1990

CHAPTER 1

Study Techniques

If you *know* where you're going, you're halfway there.

A careful use of your private study time in preparation for the examination, and a well-practised examination technique, are perhaps the two most important requirements for examination 'success'.

Preparation

1. Make sure that you fully know, and have in your possession, the latest CIB syllabus for the Monetary and Financial System, or the syllabus for the examination you plan to sit.
2. Create study time within your weekly activities. Discipline yourself to stick to the study time. Within the study time allocate time to *all* subjects within the course you are studying. Set study targets and endeavour to achieve them so that you cover the whole syllabus: few things corrupt character more than leaving things *half* done. This last point is even more important where students are taking examinations by correspondence course and by private study.
3. Read as much as you can about each topic from the quality daily and weekly newspapers, banking magazines and other learned journals and bulletins. Watch and listen to appropriate programmes on the television and radio. These activities will help you to update your knowledge and to understand technical terms more fully. They will also help you appreciate the context in which to place your essays, home assignments and answers to examination questions.
4. When you come to write essays or home assignments, you should first collect all the relevant data and information from the references suggested by your tutors. Make good use of the college and public libraries. Your opening paragraph should clearly state what the scope of the essay/assignment is and how you intend to meet it. It is extremely helpful to make an answer plan, in which you identify the main points to be covered. Arrange these points in a cohesive form *before* you begin to write the essay/assignment: this will give your essay a clear structure. Write one paragraph on each point, using headings if you feel this makes the answer clearer. Keep a dictionary handy to avoid spelling mistakes. Also avoid bad grammar, emotive language and unnecessary repetition. Wherever appropriate bring the points you have made together in a conclusion. Remember to answer the question, the whole question and nothing but the question!
5. Read the chief examiner's reports and *Signpost* articles carefully to find out which topics usually cause most problems and why!
6. Read any article that the chief examiner might write or refer to about the subject.
7. Design your overall study programme in such a way that you leave time for *revision* before the examination: this is vitally important.

Examination technique

1. In the examination room, keep calm and read the question paper through and spend five to ten minutes deciding which questions you are going to answer. Use time too to make sure you understand *exactly* what the examiner is asking. Spot and underline the key words/phrases on each question you have chosen to answer, so that you may write precise answers to the specific points in the questions.
2. Allocate your time to the required number of questions.
3. Tackle first the question which you can answer best – build up confidence.
4. Prepare an answer plan for each question you answer by setting down the main points and arranging them in their logical order *before* beginning to write in detail. Do not waste time in copying the question on the answer book, simply state the number of the question you intend to answer.
5. Be brief and relevant – you will get no marks for irrelevant material, however well it is expressed. Draw the attention of the examiner to key words and phrases in your answers by underlining them.
6. If there is more than one part to a question, make sure you answer all parts.
7. Answer the right number of questions. If you are required to answer four, then the examiner will mark the first four you have done and will ignore anything else.
8. Finally, read what you have written, correct as necessary, and cut out anything which does not make sense.

Overall

Remember, this is not a subject you can memorise or swot; it is one that requires understanding which can be acquired only by application throughout the course. Last-minute cramming alone almost certainly spells disaster.

CHAPTER 2

Money and Inflation

Syllabus requirements

- The nature and functions of money and liquidity.
- The meaning and measurement of the value of money including a simple understanding of the use of indices in measuring changes in money's value.
- The causes and the problems of inflation.
- The composition of the 'narrow' and 'broad' money in the UK.
- Alternative measures of money in a modern economy (and in the UK in particular).
- The index-linking of financial assets.

Getting started

Money is anything which is generally and instantly accepted in payment for purchases and in settling debts. It is generally accepted because it is the legal tender (notes and coins) or a representative of notes and coins (demand deposits with financial institutions). Since money is accepted in exchange for all things, it measures the values of all things, by comparing their prices: values measured in terms of money are called prices. Thus money performs its essential functions to enable money-based economies to function smoothly. It makes specialisation possible by making exchange possible and by streamlining the activities of banking and financial institutions. Therefore it makes possible a higher standard of living in advanced money economies.

Since money measures the value of all other things, it follows, therefore, that other things measure the value of money. If money purchases less of other things than it did, say, last year, then its value, its instant purchasing power, has fallen. Conversely, if it purchases more than it did in the past, its value has risen. Thus the value of money is *inversely* related to the prices of other things, i.e. the general price level, as measured by, say, a retail prices index: when the retail prices index rises (inflation), the purchasing power of money falls, and vice versa. The main cause of inflation is too much money chasing too few goods. Inflation erodes the value of money and, by doing so, it strikes at the heart of money economies. Therefore the authorities of money economies try to control the supply of money in the economy mainly by controlling the spending ability of the general public. If and when they succeed, the cancerous growth of inflation is rooted out of the monetary and financial system, and money, once again, begins to perform its functions satisfactorily.

In sophisticated economies, where the banking and financial system is well-developed, the monetary authorities make a distinction between 'narrow' and 'broad' money aggregates. Whereas the narrow money aggregate is the sum total of instant purchasing power in the economy, i.e. the total of cash, sight deposits, unused overdrafts and credit cards, the broad money aggregate is the sum total of the total instant purchasing power *plus* the total of potential purchasing power in the economy, i.e. narrow money *plus* easily, but not instantly, encashable financial assets. The potential purchasing power is instant purchasing power, but one stage removed. The distinction between narrow and broad money measures assists the authorities in devising appropriate policies to control whichever type of the money supply is getting out of hand. It is not the money, but the uncontrolled supply of money which is the root of all evil in money economies.

Functions of money

The commodity which possesses general acceptability can perform at once all the *functions* of money, viz:

1. *Medium of exchange*: it splits exchange, first, into a process of sale of one's goods and services for money, and second, into a process of purchase of the goods and services wanted in exchange. It facilitates buying and selling by overcoming the problems of barter. It acts as wealth with liquid purchasing power, giving its possessor the freedom of choice in the satisfaction of wants, and enabling him to save and lend easily. From this function arises the definition of the 'narrow' money: the sum total of instantly spendable money balances.
2. *Store of value*: it enables wealth to be stored up indefinitely without deterioration in value, except in times of rapidly rising inflation. It can then be exchanged, now and in the future, without loss in purchasing power, for other goods. From this and the previous function of money arise, the definition of 'broad' money: the sum total of instantly spendable money balances (narrow money) *plus* stored money balances which can be spent instantly with no or little financial loss.
3. *Unit of account or standard of value*: it measures the values of all other things because they are exchanged for it. 'Price' is the value of a good in terms of money; by comparing the prices of various goods their values can be compared. As the unit of account, it enables accounts to be kept, costs to be assessed precisely and choices to be made between competing projects by comparing the costs and returns from each. This function helps explain the economic concept of 'opportunity cost'; the true cost of a good is the alternative good which was not bought.
4. *Standard for deferred payments*: it enables contracts to be fulfilled in the future to be assessed now, thereby equating present and future values. The equation of present and future values is crucial to lenders making loans to borrowers who contract to repay an agreed sum regularly over several months or even years.

Importance of money to advanced economies

By performing all its functions, money makes possible division of labour and specialisation; division of labour presupposes exchange: money helps in the payment of rent, wages, profit and interest; as a store of value and a standard of deferred payments, money enables investment of capital in plant, machinery, etc.; it streamlines the activities of banking and financial institutions as financial intermediaries, safely linking lenders to borrowers; it makes possible a higher standard of living in advanced money economies, via its four functions; it has a dynamic role as well; governments control its supply to achieve economic aims.

Bank deposits

In countries where banking and financial systems are not developed, coins and paper money (bank notes) form the major proportion of their total money supply. In countries with highly developed monetary and financial systems, deposits with banks and other financial institutions are also an important component of the money supply. The *sight* bank deposits are deposits which can be withdrawn on demand, either in part or in full. Sight or demand deposits are clearly money since they possess the major characteristics of money, being generally acceptable, divisible and transferable by cheque and other means; they also perform all the functions of money.

Types of money

There are three main types of money:

1. *Primary money*
   It comprises money which is the liability of monetary authorities, e.g. notes and coins, and the operational deposits of commercial banks with the central bank. Primary money is the ultimate means of payment, therefore it is also known as 'high powered' money. Only an injection of high powered money into the bank and building society deposits in the UK – as you will see later on – sparks off the credit-creation process by these financial institutions.
2. *Secondary money*
   It consists of the primary money claims which the UK public can make against its deposits with banks and building societies. It compromises the deposit liabilities of banks and building societies. The credit-creation process generates an increase in the secondary, or 'low powered' money; low powered money does not of itself trigger the credit-creation process.
3. *Near money*
   It comprises financial assets of the public which can be cashed quickly with little or no financial loss, e.g. building society shares and deposits, Treasury bills (issued by the authorities for short-term borrowing), certificates of deposit (issued by financial institutions) which are held as investments and not as means of payment.

   You should now be able to see the relationship between money and near money and the narrow and broad definitions of money supply: the narrow definition of money comprises solely spending money, and the broad money definition comprises the transaction-based spending money *plus* the savings-orientated near money.

The near money assets have two functions:

1. To earn interest and to act as a store of wealth. Thus they are attractive to those who are able to save. In most cases, money yields no interest and therefore, unlike near money, provides no hedge against inflation.
2. To be fairly quickly convertible into cash, without significant risk of loss, either of interest or of capital. It may therefore be attractive to plan to make larger payments out of near money assets rather than out of money.

The technical definition of 'liquidity' separates money from near money: money *is* liquid purchasing power and can be directly exchanged for goods and services, whereas near money is *not* liquid purchasing power. If near money is to be used directly to purchase goods and services, it must first be converted into money, i.e. cash; this requirement of conversion into cash, with the consequent risk of monetary loss, differentiates near money assets from money. Near Money is money, one stage removed.

Liquidity spectrum

It is absolutely essential to understand that the concept of money is very closely linked with the concept of liquidity. A liquid asset is one that can instantly be turned into cash without risk of loss. On the one extreme of the liquidity spectrum we have money with instant liquid purchasing power, viz, notes and coins and sight deposits with financial institutions. In the middle we have near money assets which have a definite money value but which do not directly function as a medium of exchange. On the other extreme, we have 'non-money', i.e. physical assets which are least liquid in their ability to act as a medium of exchange, e.g. houses, business premises, lands. The conversion of such assets into money will involve marketing costs, inconvenience and often waiting. The concept of liquidity spectrum is a scale on which financial and other assets are placed in order of their liquidity, measured by the liquidity standard of money, because money, by definition, is liquidity.

In the liquidity spectrum, it would be wrong to draw absolute dividing lines between various types of money and other financial assets because there *is* substitutability, especially at the margin, between various types of money and specified financial assets. The more complex, sophisticated and stable the financial institutions a country has, the greater variety of financial assets available to the public and the greater the degree of substitutability there is likely to be among these financial assets.

As financial innovation becomes more sophisticated, so many near money assets, become available, e.g. the higher interest deposits, with banks and building societies which are generally available, like sight deposits, on demand and without financial penalty.

The value of money

The value of money is its purchasing power, i.e. the goods and services it obtains through exchange. Therefore a fall in the value of money is the same thing as a general rise in prices and vice versa. Thus the value of money changes *inversely* with changes in the general price level. A major cause of the fall in the value of money is inflation, as you'll see below.

Index numbers and the value of money

In most countries the changes in the value of money are measured by a number of statistical devices, known as *index numbers*. These attempt to measure changes in the purchasing power of money over given periods.

Retail price index (RPI)

The RPI, published by the Department of Employment, is commonly used in the UK to measure changes in the value of money, and therefore real incomes, over a given period. It is based on the 'weighted' prices of a 'basket of goods' and services, which are seen as reflecting average expenditure patterns in UK households. The 'weighting' given to each item in the 'basket' is related to the share of the household's expenditure in purchasing it. If the purchase price of the basket in a given month is say, 10 per cent higher than on the base date, then it is assumed by the public, trade unions, employers and the government that the value of money in the UK has fallen by 10 per cent; the same sum of money buys 10 per cent less now than it did on the base date. Such a general assumption can be misleading. Large groups of the population will have different expenditure patterns and may not be fully affected by changes in the prices of the goods in the basket. For example, a rise in mortgage rates or 'motor tax' will not affect those with no mortgage debt or motor cars. Consumption patterns change at different levels of income or with individual tastes.

The RPI has two other major drawbacks in this respect: first, its difficulty in assessing changes in the quality of goods purchased now and in the base year. For example, it is difficult to compare the current prices of, say, television sets with those of 10 or 15 years ago, because this product, like many others, has been considerably improved over the years. This improvement is partly reflected in the current higher prices which may not, therefore, reflect a 'true' fall in the real value of money incomes. Second, its difficulty in assessing the effects of changes in tastes or demand. Higher prices may, in part, reflect an increased preference by society for certain goods and services, resulting in increased demand, rather than a fall in the real value of money incomes.

One important point to note in connection with index numbers is that all price indices suffer from statistical errors, imprecision and misrepresentation. Due to these drawbacks, changes in the value of money cannot be measured *precisely*. It is useful to be fully aware of this fact.

Theories of the value of money

There are several theories of the value of money; however, Fisher's Equation has become the more important because of the preoccupation of most governments in recent years with controlling the money supply in order to maintain the real value of money.

Fisher's equation

This equation attempts to show the link between the quantity of money in the economy and the level of prices. It maintains that the level of prices is directly proportional to the quantity of money in circulation and therefore if the growth in the money supply is not controlled prices will rise (causing the value of money to fall).

According to this equation, $MV = PT$, where

M = quantity of money (cash and chequeable accounts) in circulation
V = velocity of circulation (the rate of turnover of M), i.e. the speed with which money is circulating through the economy in a given period; an increase in V implies an increase in M, because both increase spending
P = general price level (or a price index, say, RPI)
T = total number of transactions during a given time period.

The equation further claims that in the short term, V and T are constant; therefore any increase in M is reflected in a proportional increase in P.

Drawbacks of Fisher's equation

1. There is no one generally acceptable definition of M.
2. The equation is a truism: total spending (MV) must equal total sales (PT).
3. Increase in P may also be caused by the excess of demand over supply, even though M is stationary.
4. V and T are not constant: changes in the demand for money are reflected in changes in V, to which this supply-based equation pays insufficient attention. During the upswing of the economic activity, when prices are rising, an expansion of credit may increase

the money supply, thus the increase in the money supply is the *result*, not the cause, of rising prices, as the equation maintains.

Inflation, deflation and the value of money

The phenomena of *inflation* and *deflation* cause changes in the value of money.

The outward sign of **inflation** in an economy is a sustained increase in the general price level. But the reason for a rise in prices is increased total spending relative to the supply of goods and services on sale: too much money chasing too few goods and services. Thus inflation is caused by either an excess of the money supply, or an excess of demand in the economy. The group of economists called the 'monetarists' maintain that it is the excess of money supply which causes rising prices: 'inflation is always and everywhere a monetary phenomenon' (Friedman). Another group of economists, the 'Keynesians' (after the famous English economist, J. M. Keynes), maintain that when the total money demand in the economy exceeds the available or potentially producible output, an inflationary gap develops, and that generates rising prices. The net result of inflation on the value of money is to decrease its purchasing power.

There are four major causes of inflation.

1. High demand for loans from financial institutions mainly banks and building societies in the UK, which, when granted and spent, increase money supply (see Ch.5). The resulting increase in demand pulls up the prices of consumer and capital goods. This in turn increase the demand for more bank loans, which pulls up prices still more. The cause of this type of inflation is *demand pull*. Demand pull can also be triggered by a sharp and significant rise in the demand for exports, with the result that too much money is chasing too few goods in the domestic economy.
2. Heavy government spending to reflate the economy, in order to bring it out of deep recession, can also create inflation: prices will rise if the increased output does not match increased aggregate demand.
3. A successful and continuous demand for higher wages will cause businessmen to raise prices continuously in order to recoup their higher labour costs. The rise in prices then triggers off demand for still higher wages. This cause of inflation is called *cost push*: prices are pushed up, at least initially, by higher labour costs.
4. An inflationary psychology which motivates people to spend savings quickly in order to avoid a further decline in the purchasing power of their money. This will increase the general price level, owing to increased total spending relative to the goods and services available in the market.

Since the purchasing power of money is *inversely* related to the level of general prices, inflation, by eroding the value of money, causes a loss of confidence in money's ability to perform its functions satisfactorily. Money's ability to perform its functions is affected to different degrees at various levels of inflation; therefore the *rate* of inflation is crucial.

(a) With the inflation rate up to about 2.5 per cent p.a. (creeping inflation), money fulfils all its functions.

(b) As the rate of inflation increases, the 'store of value' is the first function to suffer: no one wants to hold on to savings in wasting assets. Non-financial assets (antiques, old master paintings) begin to be preferred over financial assets. Savers demand a rate of interest at least equal to the rate of inflation.

(c) The 'unit of account function' is next to suffer: adjustment to business accounts (inflation accounting) are needed to enable meaningful comparisons over time.
(d) With further increases in the inflation rate, the next function to suffer is the 'standard of deferred payments': upward adjustment clauses are built into future calculations of debt contracts (e.g. rent agreements) to avoid debtors gaining at the expense of creditors.
(e) Finally, and rarely, if the inflation rate reaches astronomical levels (hyper-inflation), the 'medium of exchange' function suffers: people begin to revert to barter, and the authorities revalue (up value) the unit of money (e.g. 1 unit of new money = say, 1000 units of the old money) to make buying and selling more manageable.

Deflation is a phenomenon which causes a decrease in the general price level, due to a decrease in total spending relative to the supply of goods and services on the market. Deflation increases the value of money i.e. its purchasing power. It benefits, in the short term, those on fixed incomes and creditors. In short, unchecked deflation can cause businesses to decline, unemployment to rise and incomes to fall. In practice, however, when prices fall producers reduce production and retailers carry less stock and the demand for labour and therefore money incomes fall. The consequent reduction in spending leads through unsold stocks to a further lowering of output and a further increase in unemployment. Thus unchecked deflation through a chain reaction, gives momentum to a downswing in economic activity. Deflation has not really occurred in Britain since the 1930s.

Disinflation and reflation

Under inflation, the general price level rises and therefore the value of money falls. The authorities may take *disinflationary* or *deflationary* measures, viz. increase in interest rates and taxes, decrease in government spending and imposition of credit restraints, to keep the rise in prices and incomes in check. Without such disinflationary measures the rate of inflation could reach astronomical levels, i.e. become hyper-inflation.

Under deflation, the general level of prices falls and therefore the value of money rises. Unhindered deflation would, in theory, reduce prices and profits to zero! The authorities may take *reflationary* measures, i.e. measures which are the *reverse* of deflationary measures, to counteract the damaging effects of deflation on the economy. Reflationary measures aim directly to increase aggregate expenditure in the economy.

The relationship between: (a) inflation and disinflation; and (b) deflation and reflation is shown in Fig. 2.1.

Legal tender

While money is something which people will generally accept in settlement of debts, legal tender is what the law says they must accept if it is offered. Legal tender may be *limited* legal tender, i.e. people must accept it if offered, but only up to specified limits of payment; on the other hand it may be *unlimited* tender, i.e. it must be accepted in settlement of debts of any amount.

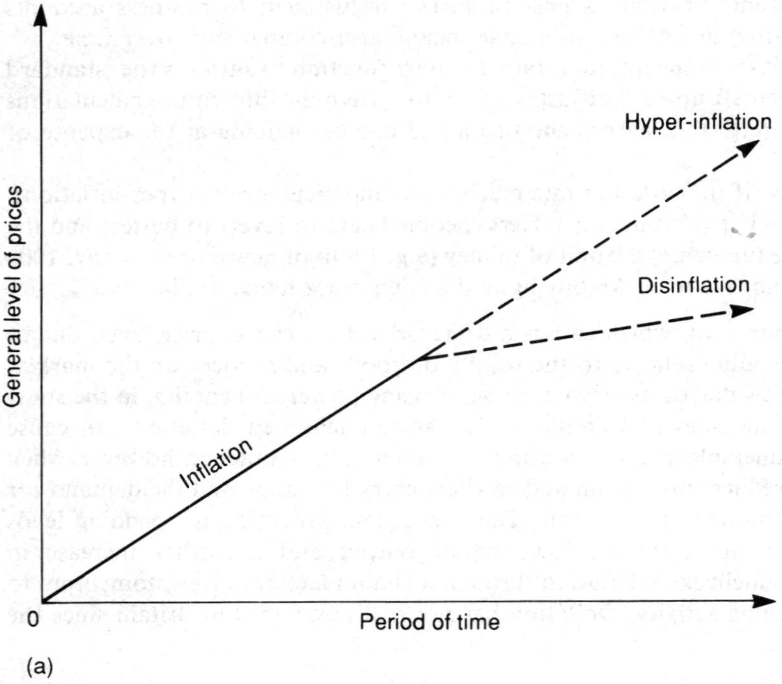
General level of prices
Hyper-inflation
Disinflation
Inflation
0
Period of time
(a)

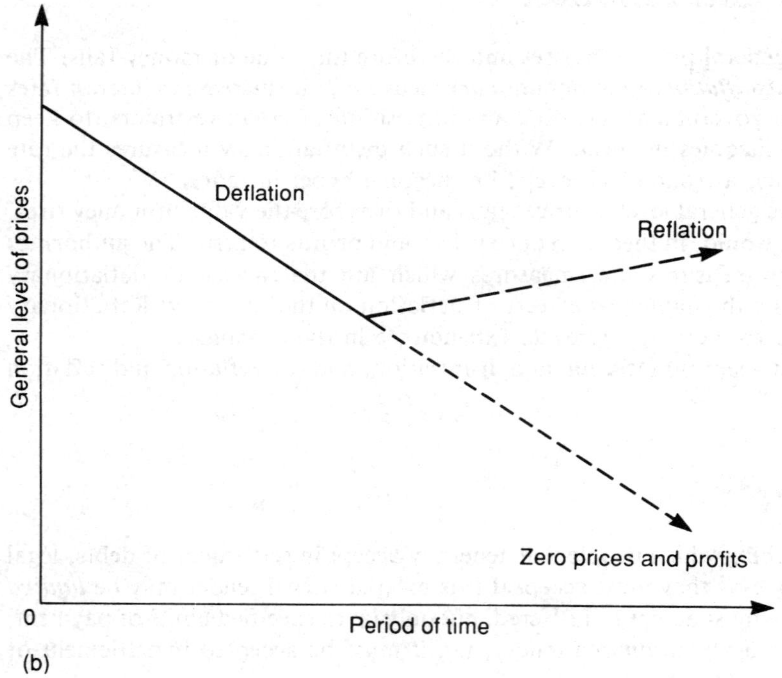
General level of prices
Deflation
Reflation
Zero prices and profits
0
Period of time
(b)

Fig. 2.1

Bank and building society deposits

The chequeable sight deposits in Britain, as in other countries with highly developed banking system, are an important feature of the money in the economy. The medium of exchange in Britain consists of notes and coins and chequeable current accounts. The leading building societies also provide full chequeing accounts payable on demand which therefore must be regarded as money (see Ch.3).

The *near money* assets in Britain include postal orders, money orders, bills of exchange, bank and building society short notice deposits, national savings securities except National Savings Certificates and Save As You Earn contracts – these are too illiquid. Treasury bills, local authority deposits, certificates of tax deposit (for the corporation tax paid in advance by business companies), certificates of deposit (sold by banks and building societies to large depositors), and National Savings Bank accounts.

Official monetary aggregates in Britain

The meaning, measurement and control of money are inter-related concepts. If the monetary authorities (the Treasury and the Bank of England) do not know precisely what money is, and what forms it can take, then they will not be able to measure it, nor will they be able to control its supply.

In the UK, as in most other countries, a distinction is made between 'narrow' and 'broad' measures of money. The *narrow* money measures include those assets which represent immediate purchasing power, i.e. those assets which perform the medium of exchange function of money. Narrow money comprising *immediately* available purchasing power might well understate the *potential* purchasing power in the economy, given the existence of liquid assets which could quickly, and without the risk of significant financial loss, be converted into cash; hence the need for *broad* money measures.

On 29 June 1989, the Bank of England announced changes in the then monetary aggregates in the UK. The reasons for the changes and the components of the altered aggregates are given later in this chapter; however a description of the contents and the logic of introduction of the aggregates as at 29 June 1989, is given below.

In order to understand why there are so many official definitions of money, you must first and foremost understand the concept of the liquidity spectrum (see p.6). The various aggregates differ in their composition and in their response to changes in interest rates, incomes and inflation.

M2

M2 = non-interest bearing component of M1, *plus* private sector interest-bearing *retail* sterling bank deposits, *plus* private sector holdings of *retail* building society shares and deposits, *plus* National Savings Bank *ordinary* accounts. M2 is a narrow measure of money.

Sterling *retail* deposits include:

(a) All non-interest-bearing sight deposits.
(b) All other deposits (regardless of size and maturity) on which cheques may be drawn or from which standing orders, direct debit mandates or other payments to third parties may be made.
(c) Other deposits of less than £100,000 having a maturity of less than one month. Deposits

of £100,000 and over, or with maturities over one month are held mainly as investment and are therefore not sufficiently liquid.

(d) All shares and deposits with building societies which are within one month of maturity.
(e) All deposits with the National Savings Bank ordinary account.

The monetary logic underlying the introduction of M2 is to provide a monetary aggregate that comprises the 'transaction' balances of the private sector in modern times, an aggregate which is neither so narrow as to be confined to notes and coins and current accounts, nor so broad as to include large investment balances.

M0

M0 = notes and coins in circulation with the public, *plus* till money of banks, *plus* bankers' operational deposits with the Bank of England. The rationale for its introduction in 1983 was principally the same as for the introduction of M2: i.e. that a great proportion of M1 was made up of interest-bearing sight deposits which are *not* transaction deposits but rather investment deposits. M0 further emphasises the distinction which the authorities have drawn between, on the one hand, 'narrow' money or transaction balances, which they believe respond unambiguously and consistently to changes in short-term interest rates, and, on the other hand, 'broad' money, or private sector liquidity, which has particular relevance for decisions about fiscal and funding policies – these official policies relate to tax revenue, public spending and borrowing activities. M0 is the only targeted monetary aggregate at present (see Ch.7).

M4

M4 = M3 *plus* private holdings of building society shares and deposits and sterling CDs *less* building society holdings of bank deposits, bank CDs and notes and coins. M4 is the newest broad money aggregate, introduced in May 1987. It seems that the monetary authorities will be paying particular attention to the behaviour of M4 (see below).

M5

M5 = M4 *plus* holdings by the private sector (excluding building societies) of money market instruments (bank bills, Treasury bills, local authority deposits), certificates of tax deposit (receipts of tax paid in advance), national savings instruments (excluding certificates, SAYE and other long-term deposits. The inclusion of sterling commercial paper issued by banks and building societies with less than five years to maturity as a component of M5 is under consideration of the authorities. M5 represents the broadest definition of money stock in the economy.

The restructuring of the broad monetary aggregates

In May 1987, the Bank of England announced the restructuring of broad money aggregates. The necessity for this arose because of the difficulties of targeting broad money (broad money has not been targeted for 1987/88) against a background of deregulation (see Ch.4) and innovation within the financial system. The impact of increased competition on measures of broad money will be spurred further by the Building Societies Act 1986, which came into effect on 1 January 1987. The Act opens up the possibility that some building societies may opt to become banks.

Therefore a new broad money aggregate covering banks and building society sterling deposit liabilities to the non-bank, non-building society private sector and that sector's holdings of notes and coins, was needed. Hence the authorities introduced M4. M4 is conceptually equivalent to M3 in that, notwithstanding the inclusion of notes and coins which are the liabilities of the public sector, it is institutionally based.

Narrow and broad money comprises a liquidity spectrum of financial assets, often closely related with a high degree of substitution between them, therefore M1, M2, M3, M4 and M5 can be regarded as representative points on the spectrum.

The effects on monetary aggregates of Abbey National Building Society's conversion into a bank

Abbey National became a public limited company in July 1989, and was classified a 'retail bank', under the 1987 Banking Act. From the end of July onwards its figures have been included within balance sheet totals of the banks. The inclusion of Abbey National's deposits (£32 billion, at the end of 1988) has inflated the total bank deposits by around 11 per cent, although there was no change in the composition of the sterling assets of the combined bank and building society sector. According to the Bank of England there is no statistical technique that could deal with the discontinuity caused by the reclassification of Abbey National as a bank. It has led the Bank to review the principal monetary aggregates.

M2, M4 and **M5** aggregates are unaffected by the Abbey National conversion because banks' and building societies' contributions are included in each aggregate.

M0 is affected to a small extent. Abbey National kept operational deposits with the Bank in connection with the clearing of effects. After its conversion into a bank, these deposits have been classified as bankers' operational deposits, within M0.

M1, M3 and **M3c** were expected to suffer the most distortions because they excluded building society deposits. If more societies were to become banks in the future, these aggregates would have become too distorted to be useful in discerning monetary trends in the economy. Hence the authorities stopped their publication. Although M1 as a whole is not published, its non-interest-bearing component (**'nib' M1**) is published: NibM1 is unlikely to be influenced significantly because building societies do not in practice take significant amounts of non-interest-bearing deposits.

A new monetary aggregate, **M4c** will be introduced, which will be similar in concept to M3c. It will include M4 *plus* foreign currency deposits held with UK banks and building societies by the rest of the UK private sector.

In addition to the conversion of the Abbey National, other developments, such as new financial products introduced in recent years by banks, building societies and other financial institutions, call for a re-examination of the definition of the broad money aggregate, **M5**. The Bank therefore published a discussion paper in the autumn of 1989, for comments by interested parties.

At the time of writing, the following is the position of the monetary aggregates:

MO – very small change;
NibM1 – no significant change; will continue to be published (definitional change possible);
M2 – unaffected (definitional change possible);
M3 – publication ceased;

M3c – publication ceased;
M4 – unaffected;
M4c – will be introduced;
M5 – unaffected (definitional change possible).

Since money is 'claims' against somebody, it is useful to know against whom the holders of narrow and broad money assets have claims. Using the monetary aggregates announced by the Bank of England on 29 June 1989, Table 2.1 shows the institutions whose liability each component of the narrow and broad money is.

Table 2.1

	Narrow money	Broad money
Liability of:		
Bank of England		
Notes	M0, NibM1, M2	M4, M5
Bank's operational deposits	M0	
Treasury		
Coins	M0, NibM1, M2	M4, M5
Treasury bills		M5
CTDs		M5
National Savings Bank ordinary accounts	M2	
National Savings instruments		M5
Commercial banks		
Sight deposits	NibM1, M2	M4, M5
Retail deposits (less than £100,000, and less than one month to maturity)	M2	M4, M5
Time deposits		M4, M5
CDs		M4, M5
Foreign currency deposits of UK residents		M4c
Bank bills		M5
Sterling commercial paper		M5
Building societies		
Retail shares and deposits (less than £100,000, and less than one month to maturity)	M2	M4, M5
Non-retail shares and deposits		M4, M5
Foreign currency deposits of UK residents		M4c
CDs		M4, M5
Sterling commercial paper		M5
Local authorities		
Deposits		M5

Shortcomings of monetary aggregates

Even as things stand, none of the aggregates covers specifically the usage of unused overdraft or other loan facilities and credit cards as means of liquidity by companies and individuals, and as parts of transaction money. Examination questions asking for the shortcomings of the monetary aggregates would expect the inclusion of this information in the answers.

The spread of cash dispensers and debit and credit cards especially has reduced the amount of cash which people hold, and this gives a downward bias to M0, i.e. it is less likely to overshoot even a lower target range. There, M0's usefulness as a monetary target is considered by the financial markets, as doubtful. The reasons for M0 to be the only targeted monetary aggregate (since the Budget of 1987/88) are given in Chapter 7.

Recent examination questions

The following six questions taken from past papers give an indication of the type of questions you may encounter on 'Money' and 'Inflation'. You could usefully spent ten minutes or so on each question, trying to identify the main points you would use in your answers, before turning to the section on 'outline answers' which follows.

Question 1

(a) What is meant by index-linking of financial assets? Include some examples of index-linked assets in your answer.
(b) To what extent is index-linking likely to succeed in curbing inflation? How else might governments attempt to deal with the problem.

Question 2

Since 1984 the UK monetary authorities have set a target for the growth of the monetary aggregate M0, also known as the 'wide monetary base'.

(a) Define M0 and explain the reasons for its introduction.
(b) Is the behaviour of M0 alone sufficient to provide a clear picture of monetary conditions in the UK?

Question 3

(a) What attributes must an asset possess in order to be considered liquid?
(b) To what extent do the following possess the attributes referred to in (a) necessary for them to be considered liquid:
  (i) Treasury bills;
  (ii) gilt-edged stock;
  (iii) bank notes;
  (iv) building society term shares;
  (v) certificates of deposit issued by a commercial bank?
(c) Classify the assets set out in (b) above according to whether they are included in the measures of the money stock in the UK.

Question 4

Compare and contrast the principal liabilities of commercial banks and building societies with particular reference to the following:

(a) money as a medium of exchange;
(b) money as a store of value;
(c) the control of money supply.

Question 5

(a) Distinguish between 'narrow' and 'broad' measures of money.
(b) Tabulate the relevant liabilities of the central bank, commercial banks, and building

societies according to whether they feature in narrow and broad money definitions. Indicate in this table the money supply definitions in which these liabilities appear.

(c) Apart from the liabilities considered in (b), what other items are included in the money supply?

Question 6

Some of the functions of money are performed by other liquid assets. What are these assets? Why are they held in preference to bank notes and bank deposits in the performance of these functions?

Outline answers

Answer 1

(a)
- Inflation erodes the capital value of financial assets.
- Index-linking gives full protection against the effects against of inflation by linking the capital value in line with increases in prices as (usually) measured by the retail price index.
- Index-linking of the rate of return on securities etc., brings the rate of interest into line with the rate of inflation.
- Examples of index-linked assets in the UK:
  (i) certain gilt-edged stock
  (ii) certain National Savings Certificates
  (iii) (also) the pensions of civil servants.

(b)
- Index-linking, by encouraging the public to save safely, curbs inflation.
- Index-linking, however, only attacks the symptoms and not the roots of inflation.
- Experience world-wide shows that index-linking becomes institutionalised, making it more difficult for the economy to return to a low rate of inflation.
- Government may take the following measures to deal with the roots of the inflation problem:
  (i) Control money supply growth:
  (ii) Discourage spending by the public and private sectors via fiscal measures (e.g. higher taxes, lower spending limits for the local and central governments).
  (iii) Introduce, in the short term, a prices and incomes policy to keep wages, profits and prices in check.
  (iv) Keep the exchange rate of the currency, via central bank intervention, at a level high enough to curb the price rises of imported goods, yet not so high as to discourage exports by overpricing them (see Ch.8).

Answer 2

(a)
- M0 comprises notes and coins in circulation, till money and banks' operational deposits with the Bank of England.
- M0 is a very narrow measure of the money supply, therefore it is confusing to term it the 'wide monetary base'.
- M0 was introduced because:
  (i) M1, the traditional measure of narrow money, became unreliable owing to the inclusion of a large and volatile element of interest-bearing deposits.

(ii) M0, as an alternative, seemed to offer a less distorted and less misleading indicator of changes in narrow money, and a guide to inflation.

(b)
- Although M0's credibility has been questioned since its introduction in 1983: M0 grows much more slowly and remains mostly within its target range.
- No *single* monetary aggregate can fully encapsulate monetary conditions and provide a correct basis for controlling the complex relationships between monetary growth and prices and incomes, because there is substitutability between the components of various monetary aggregates.
- M0 is too narrow as a money supply aggregate and its behaviour cannot provide a comprehensive view of the purchasing power in the economy.

Answer 3

(a) Attributes of liquidity:
- Quickly convertible into means of payments; such conversion is without risk of monetary loss.

(b) (i) Treasury bills – quickly convertible into means of payments (i.e. through secondary markets), but suffer from risk of loss: their value during their 91-day life fluctuates in line with short-term interest rate movements.

(ii) Gilt-edged stock – maturities vary, from five to 15 years to undated, but all marketable. Significant risk of loss in value because of their long maturities and high responsiveness to interest rate movements. Those close to maturity are liquid.

(iii) Banknotes – most liquid: instant purchasing power without any risk of monetary loss. Inflationary loss irrelevant to this concept of liquidity because it relates to an asset maintaining its value in money, not 'real', terms.

(iv) Building society term shares – illiquid (except those nearing maturity): cash tied up for the term, or available on demand with significant penalty.

(v) Certificates of deposit – generally regarded as liquid: issued for short maturities (maturities may range from three months to one year); easily marketable in secondary money markets; risk of loss due to interest rate changes is similar to that of Treasury bills. Those close to maturity are liquid.

(c)
- Treasury bills included in M5.
- Gilt-edged stock not included in any measure of money.
- Bank notes included in all measures of money.
- Building society term shares not included in any measure of money.
- Certificates of deposits included in M4 and M5. Those held by overseas residents are excluded from any measure of money.

Answer 4

(a)
- Only bank current accounts (not cheques) may be classed as medium of exchange: available as a *direct* means of payment.
- The cheques received by depositors from a building society may be used as a direct means of payment but these cheques are drawn upon a *bank current* account of the building society. Recent changes in money transmission services may blur the distinction between bank current accounts and building society ordinary accounts.
- All other bank and building society accounts do not act as medium of exchange: they have to be converted into cash or chequeable current accounts before performing the medium of exchange role – it is the *cash* which is withdrawn on

demand that constitutes the medium of exchange, not the bank deposit from which it is withdrawn.

(b) • Bank current accounts are not a store of value: they earn little or no interest. This is changing fast.
- All other banks and building society accounts are a store of value: they all earn, albeit differing, rates of return; the term deposits generally earn the highest rate of return; they provide a 'real' rate of pre-tax returns.
- Inflation rates higher than rates of returns tend to undermine their role as a store of value.
- Money in bank current accounts suffers from erosion in purchasing power during inflationary times.

(c) • Define M4 measure of the money supply.
- Traditionally the authorities have sought to control only bank deposits (together with notes and coins) in controlling the money supply.
- There is close substitutability between bank and building society deposits, hence the introduction of the wider monetary aggregates, M4 and M5.
- Define M5.

Answer 5

(a) Narrow money is held for *transactions* (medium of exchange function) purposes and consists of assets which may be used for immediate spending.
- Broad money definition comprises the above *plus* assets which act as a *store of value*, but which are still liquid enough to be turned into cash quickly and without significant loss.

(b) (According to narrow and broad money as they stood in June 1989.)

	Narrow	Broad
Central bank liabilities		
Notes and coins	M0, M1, M2	M3, M4, M5
Operational deposits	M0	
Commercial bank liabilities		
Sight deposits	M1, M2	M3, M4, M5
Retail deposits (under £100,000 with less than a month to maturity)	M2	M3, M4, M5
Time deposits		M3, M4, M5
CDs		M3, M4, M5
Foreign currency deposits of UK residents		M3c
Building society liabilities		
Retail shares and deposits	M2	M4, M5
Non-retail shares and deposits		M4, M5
CDs		M4, M5

(c) *Other items included*

Money market instruments

CTDs

National Savings instruments (excluding NSCs and SAYEs and other longer-term deposits)

Answer 6

Briefly explain the concept of the liquidity spectrum, emphasizing the substitutability at the margins between real and near money assets.

- Near money assets perform the store of value function of money and, once removed, the means of exchange function.
- Near money assets held by the UK non-bank and bank sectors: postal orders, money orders, bills of exchange, building society deposits, National Savings securities and accounts, Treasury bills, local authority deposits, certificates of tax deposits, certificates of deposits, gilt-edged securities, money at call and short notice, and interest-bearing deposits with banks.
- Reasons for holding near money assets in preference to bank notes and current accounts with banks:
  (i) Bank notes and current accounts with banks generally earn no interest, therefore inflation erodes their actual purchasing power – unattractive as a store of value.
  (ii) Near money assets provide a hedge against inflation, and sometimes a 'real' increase in the rate of return, therefore more attractive as a store of value.
  (iii) Most near money assets can be converted into cash or chequeable accounts fairly quickly and without significant loss of interest or capital, therefore larger payments can be planned easily and without financial loss in terms of near money assets.

A tutor's answer

The following question, in view of there being so many measures of money at present, is highly relevant. The answer highlights the fact that in a sophisticated modern economy there are many financial assets which perform some, if not all, the functions of money. Also that there is such substitutability among these assets in the public's mind as to make it impossible to give one unambiguous definition of money as a whole in modern economies. The specimen answer should help you to assess the scope of the question, to make a relevant answer plan and to write within the scope of the question.

Question

(a) Explain briefly why a country's monetary authorities consider the behaviour of the money supply to be important.
(b) Discuss the problems which arise in modern economies in defining the money supply.

Answer plan:
(a) To control inflation:
- monetarist's analysis
- expectation of future inflation rate
- exchange rate
- economic growth rate.

(b) Some assets:
- perform some of the functions of money
- have varying degrees of liquidity
- have substitutability.

Specimen answer

(a) If the money supply grows faster than the growth in output then, other things being equal, there will be too much money in the economy chasing too few goods. This will lead to an increase in the general price level (e.g. RPI in the UK). Rising prices are a symptom that the economy is suffering from inflation.

The monetarists use Fisher's Equation to explain the above analysis: $MV = PT$, where M = quantity of money; V = velocity of circulation of M; P = general price level; T = total number of transactions. Since V and T are assumed to be stationary, an increase in M will be reflected by an increase in P, because $P = MV/T$.

The corrosive effects of inflation badly damage the national economy. Rising prices cause employees to ask for higher wages, lenders to ask for higher interest returns and landlords to ask for higher rents. In such circumstances, the profit margins of business firms are depressed, which causes a reduction in investment, and that leads to an increase in unemployment.

High priced domestic goods are difficult to sell abroad, whereas comparatively lower priced imports increase. This leads to deficit on the balance of trade, which, in time, leads to a fall in the foreign exchange value of the national currency. Thus a country with a rate of inflation higher than the inflation rates of its trading partners, will find that its currency buys less both domestically and internationally.

Inflationary psychology motivates the inclusion of anticipated inflationary increase clauses into contracts for wages, loans and rents: inflationary psychology materializes inflationary *expectations*.

In extreme cases, unchecked growth in inflation leads to hyperinflation (e.g. in Weimar Republic Germany during 1922/23). Hyperinflation means that the citizens will refuse to accept the national legal tender in settlement of debts.

It is for the above reasons that the control of the money supply has been an important aspect of economic policy in major countries for many years.

(b) In modern economies there exists a diversity of assets which can be called money because each performs *some* of the functions of money, because such assets have *varying degrees of liquidity* – (e.g. *near money* assets perform the store of value, but not the medium of exchange, function of money). It is therefore difficult to establish precisely where the line should be drawn in defining money.

Nevertheless, a distinction is usually made in developed economies between narrow and broad definitions of money. *Narrow* money (e.g. M0 in the UK) stresses money's means of exchange function; *broad* money definitions extend beyond cash and bank deposits and include liabilities of several other financial institutions (e.g. M4, in the UK includes the sterling balances with the banks and building societies). The issue, however, is to what extent should financial instruments not included (e.g. unused overdraft facilities) in even the broadest definition of money (e.g. M5, in the UK) also be included in money aggregates monitored by the authorities, because there exists considerable *substitutability* between various assets.

There are two main reasons why it is difficult to provide an unambiguous definition of money supply in a modern economy. First, in the developed economies the banking and financial institutions are sufficiently sophisticated to be able to create a growing variety of financial assets which are capable of performing some, if not all, of the traditional functions of money. Second, in the eyes of the public, there is substitutability especially at the margins, among these financial assets.

A step further

If you wish to obtain up-to-date information on changes of definition of the various monetary aggregates, then the *Quarterly Bulletin of the Bank of England* and the *Financial Times* are invaluable sources. Read carefully 'Measures of Broad Money' in the *Bank of*

England Quarterly Bulletin, May 1987. There are also many useful articles on money which can be found in *Banking World* of The Chartered Institute of Bankers, and in the past editions of the *Financial Times*. These articles can be located by using the *Financial Times Monthly Index* in your college or public libraries. Fairly frequently you will find articles in the daily quality newspapers interpreting the definitional changes of monetary aggregates. Sometimes there are excellent programmes on the television dealing with various aspects of money. The Chartered Institute of Bankers publishes excellent *Updating Notes*, especially on definitional changes, and these keep candidates abreast of monetary matters.

CHAPTER 3

UK Financial Institutions

Syllabus requirements

- The nature of financial intermediation.
- The principal bank and non-bank financial institutions and their respective roles and operation.
- The relationship of banks with other financial institutions.
- The role of building societies as competitors to banks.
- The regulatory and prudential controls on bank liquidity and capital adequacy.
- The functions and the banking supervisory role of the Bank of England.

Getting started

To gain a clear insight into the mechanics of the UK financial system, you need to understand the role and functions of the financial institutions operating in the UK, the operations of the various specialised UK financial markets and the types of financial instrument bought and sold on the financial markets (see Fig. 3.1).

In this chapter, we shall look at the roles and functions of the principal banking and non-banking financial institutions in the UK, and in the next chapter, we shall study the operation of the financial markets in the UK and the financial instruments traded in these markets.

The UK *financial institutions* are an integral part of the UK financial intermediation mechanism through which the savings of households, firms, public corporations and even overseas residents are made available to borrowers at home and abroad. Financial intermediation channels the funds from the potential surplus units to potential deficit units quickly, cheaply, safely and conveniently.

The principal financial institution in the UK financial system may be classified into *bank* and *non-bank* financial intermediaries (BFIs and NBFIs). The BFIs include the Banking Department of the Bank of England, commercial banks (including overseas banks), discount houses, National Girobank, National Savings Bank and finance houses. The NBFIs include building societies, insurance companies, and unit and investment trusts. The BFIs, by and large, constitute the UK *monetary sector*.

Most countries in the world have a *central bank* as their principal banking institution to exercise monetary control, supervision of financial institutions and financial assistance to commerce, trade and industry. As the central bank of the UK, the *Bank of England* stands at the heart of the UK banking system. It supervises, monitors, guides and advises the bank financial institutions, so that the government's monetary policy objectives are fulfilled in the interest of the nation.

In the balance sheets of the financial institutions, savings received from depositors/lenders constitute the *liabilities* of these institutions, and loans and advances made to borrowers represent the *assets* of these institutions. Their liabilities, in the main, provide them with resources with which to create their assets.

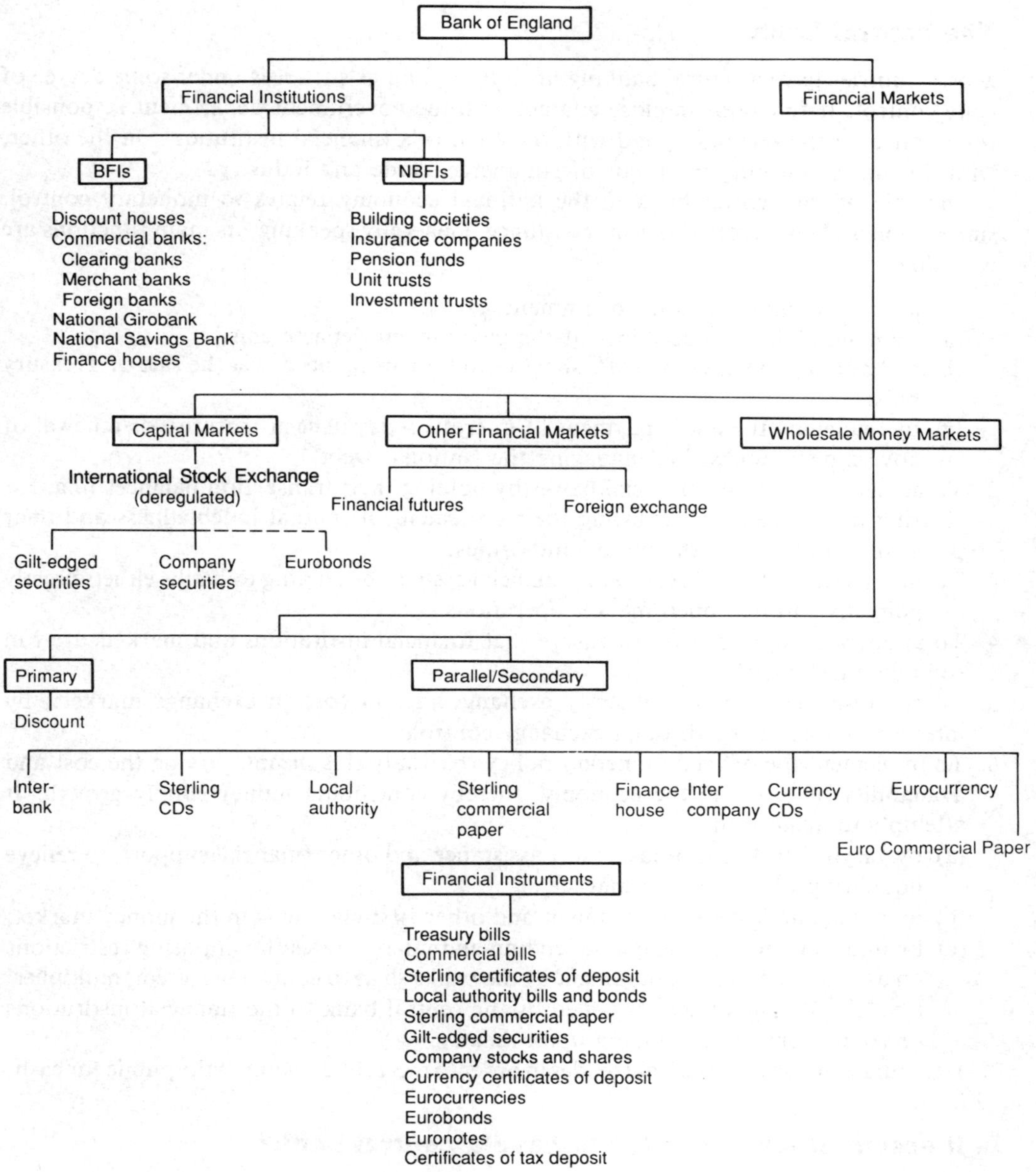

Fig. 3.1 The UK financial system

Those among the BFIs and NBFIs which are *commercial, joint stock companies* have responsibility, like other financial institutions, not only for the safety of their depositors'/investors' money, but also for the profitability of their shareholders. This dual responsibility often creates a counter-pull, i.e. safety versus profitability, and the successful institutions have to resolve this dilemma satisfactorily.

Essential principles

The central bank

Most countries have a central banking institution, and as such it is under some degree of state control. It functions in close contact with the government department responsible for finance on the one hand, and with the country's financial institutions on the other, with the aim of meeting the needs of commerce, trade and industry.

The role of the central bank in the national economy relates to monetary control, supervision and last resort financial assistance. Generally speaking, its main functions are as follows:

1. To act as the banker to the government,
   (a) by maintaining the accounts of the government departments;
   (b) by handling the government's short-term borrowing needs via the sale of Treasury bills;
   (c) by managing the issue, payment of interest, repayment at maturity or renewal of government stocks; i.e. managing the National Debt.
2. To act as banker to commercial banks by holding their transaction balances (e.g. for clearing in the UK), and assisting their settlement of mutual indebtedness and their payments to and from the public authorities.
3. To act as lender of last resort to the financial system, by lending to banks either directly or indirectly through open market operations.
4. To apply prudential control to ensure that financial institutions and markets are run soundly and honestly.
5. To stabilise the domestic currency exchange rate in foreign exchange markets, by intervening directly or through exchange controls.
6. To implement the official monetary policy: basically this means varying the cost and availability of credit in the economy, thereby controlling money supply growth. It attempts to achieve this,
   (a) by varying the terms of last resort assistance and other financial support, to relieve liquidity problems in the market;
   (b) by buying and selling government and other first-class bills in the money market;
   (c) by imposing direct controls on lending and interest rates; by imposing restrictions on asset and liability management by the banks so as to control the 'credit multiplier' (see Ch. 5). The directives issued by the central bank to the financial institutions under its control are binding upon them.
7. To regulate the issue of the legal tender in order to meet the demand of the public for cash.

Is it essential for a country to have a central bank?

Not all the central banks perform all the above functions. In many cases some of the functions are undertaken by a government department (e.g. the Treasury in the UK or the Finance Ministries elsewhere) and bank regulatory and supervisory commissions. The central banks themselves may share some of their functions with private sector institutions.

Governments need not channel their financial business, including the production and issue of the legal tender, through a central institution; instead they may seek competitive private tenders for the work involved. When a central bank intervenes in the foreign exchange markets to influence the exchange rate (see Ch. 9), it does so as the agent of the government, and uses commercial banks as agents. There is no real reason preventing the monetary authorities from using private sector banks directly in exchange rate management, which is essentially what happens in Hong Kong.

In many countries the central bank acts as a consultant to the authorities over monetary policy but the authorities make the final decision and the central bank acts as the agent of the authorities in implementing the policy, as is the case in the UK (but not in West Germany, where the Bundesbank has constitutional independence in the setting of monetary policy). Here again, there's no real reason why the implementations of the policy may not be done via private sector financial institutions.

The private sector banks may set up their own central clearing agency, empowering it to hold their settlement accounts, oversee the money transmission service, and even to act as lender of last resort, provided regulations are in place preventing banks from taking unwarranted risks and protecting the agency's resources against excessive claims.

It may, however, prove more efficient if a central bank, free from commercial pressures, performs such functions as lender of last resort with supervisory and regulatory powers; this will enhance the confidence of the public at home and abroad in the national financial system. Some central banks however, such as the Swiss National Bank, seem to be trying to divest themselves of supervisory responsibilities in order to concentrate more on monetary policy and exchange rate-related activities. The Federal Reserve of the United States of America has a very complex regulatory system, involving many agencies.

Secondly, if confidentiality were essential in the government's financial business and could not be guaranteed if the private sector institutions were involved, then a non-commercial bank might be considered a necessity.

Thirdly, a non-commercial central bank will be able to provide the government with an *independent* link with the commercial financial sector.

Central banks are *not* responsible for implementing the fiscal policy of the government (i.e. management of the economy by varying the size and composition of taxation and public expenditure). They are *not* members of the Institutional Monetary Fund; representation at the IMF is by member governments, although the central banks can act as its directors. They *are* members of the Bank for International Settlements (see Ch. 10).

Financial intermediation

Whilst the inflow and outflow of funds provide the financial institutions with the major source of their profits, the process of channelling most of the savings in the economy to borrowers is also of great benefit to both the savers and borrowers and to the national economy. This process of matching the needs of the ultimate lenders i.e. the possessors of surplus loanable funds in the personal, corporate and public sectors, with those of the ultimate borrowers i.e. those units or sectors in the economy which are in need of liquid funds, for a fee, is called *financial intermediation*, and the institutions performing the financial intermediation are known as the 'financial intermediaries' (FIs).

A financial intermediary may be a deposit taking institution, such as a bank or building society, or a non-deposit taking institution, such as an insurance company or a pension fund. Financial intermediaries are reservoirs through which the funds of surplus units flow to the deficit units in society. Financial intermediation makes lending and borrowing indirect and in doing so has a number of important advantages over direct borrowing and lending; arguably these more than justify the cost of FIs, and also make the FIs indispensable to financially developed economies.

Advantages of financial intermediation

Minimising lending risks

Default

Under direct lending, if the borrower fails to repay, then the lender may lose all or most of his capital. The risk of default is either removed or minimised if lending and borrowing take place via an FI. By interposing itself between the ultimate lender and ultimate borrower, the FI takes over from the lender the risk of loss through default by the borrower. The FI can do this for two main reasons.

1. A financial intermediary *transforms the lending risks* by spreading its risks; through making a large number of loans of varying degrees of risks, returns and maturities, the FI can reduce its risk, and therefore the risks of the ultimate lenders. Diversification spreads the lending risks, and thereby minimises them. Besides, the FI can adjust its interest charges or fees to borrowers so that in the long run the loss through bad debts is covered.
2. FIs are traditionally financially sound institutions; their capital and reserves are sufficiently large and their deposit base is sufficiently stable to meet possible loan losses, whilst still protecting the funds of their depositors.

Loss of liquidity

Other things being equal, lenders prefer to lend short-term to avoid the loss of liquidity for long periods, especially if they suspect a possible need for liquidity arising, or an increase in interest rates occurring, before the borrower repays. On the other hand, borrowers prefer to borrow long-term to take full advantage of the productivity of the capital borrowed before it is to be repaid. The FIs are, by and large, able to resolve the problem of such opposing time-preferences by *maturity transformation*, i.e. borrowing short and lending long. Three main reasons enable the FIs to do this.

1. Unlike individual lenders or borrowers, FIs, due to their large-scale operations, are able to benefit from the statistical 'laws' of large numbers; e.g. the probability of an event occurring comes closer to the probability of its not occurring, as the scale of operations gets larger. For example, the larger the number of accounts a bank holds, the greater the statistical probability that withdrawals will match, rather than exceed, deposits.
2. Their long experience enables FIs to anticipate seasonal changes in the outflow of their funds. They can therefore arrange to hold such interest-bearing assets as will mature in time to meet the seasonal pressure of outflow of funds.
3. By paying competitive deposit rates and by maintaining the confidence of depositors, FIs are able to maintain the overall level of their deposits while still providing their

depositors with the benefit of liquidity: depositors are able to convert deposits into cash quickly and without loss of capital value.

Minimising borrowing risks

Funds may not be available when required

Borrowers may be unable to obtain funds when needed, due in part to a shortage of funds from regular sources, and in part to a lack of knowledge of other sources from which funds may be available. The FIs are able to minimise this borrowing risk for two main reasons.

1. By *aggregating* the small savings of a large number of depositors and direct borrowing from the money markets, they are able to supply funds in quantity and at the required times and for appropriate maturities to the borrowers.
2. Unlike individual lenders and borrowers, FIs specialise in taking deposits from, and making loans to, many sources; hence they possess up-to-date information on the sources and terms under which funds are supplied and demanded.

Lenders may terminate lending at a time most inconvenient to borrowers

The FIs are able to minimise this borrowing risk via the fact that the economic basis of their financial intermediation lies in specialised large-scale operations. This enables them to:

1. spread default and other risks; and
2. hold a more balanced mix of asset portfolios, with regard to types and maturities, thereby reducing the risk of losses. FIs are therefore able to lend, on a contractual basis, such period loans as are most suitable to the needs of borrowers.

Borrowers wish to borrow at the lowest cost

First, due to their large-scale operations, FIs benefit from specialisation and economies of large scale; hence they are able to keep their transaction costs down. Second, because the FIs are able to reduce lending risks, lenders are prepared to accept a lower rate of return from FIs. FIs are therefore able to lend at lower interest rates to borrowers.

The nature and practice of financial intermediation shows that FIs are not just parasitic middlemen. Despite carrying liabilities (claims against them) which are more liquid than their assets (claims against borrowers), FIs are able to provide a unique financial service at minimum cost, assisting both ultimate lenders and borrowers *and*, via encouraging additional savings and investment, promoting economic growth for the nation as a whole. (See also 'A Tutor's Answer' on pp. 47–8 below.)

Reasons for the decline in financial intermediation

Despite the advantage of financial intermediation to lenders and borrowers, the practice of financial intermediation has declined in recent years.This is due to the deregulation of financial services which is making lenders and borrowers realise that the traditional advantages of financial intermediation are being overcome by the advantages of direct borrowing and lending, viz. *disintermediation*. To some investors, large companies are no more risky than a financial intermediary, hence the issue of short-term securities, such as the sterling commercial paper (see Ch.4), by the companies directly to investors. The decline in financial intermediation has increasingly caused the financial intermediaries (especially the commercial banks) merely to act as guarantors and brokers of corporate debt; this has increased their income from commissions but has decreased their traditional source of income: interest receipts. Since guaranteeing and broking are off-balance sheet transactions, they incur reduced capital/liquidity costs to financial intermediaries, which strengthens their balance sheets.

BFIs and NBFIs as financial intermediaries

Since the passing of the Building Societies Act 1986, the distinction between a bank and a building society has almost disappeared. BFIs (including building societies), and NBFIs (excluding building societies), have some common fundamental characteristics: both rely on large-scale operations in order to benefit from statistical probabilities and from the economies which result from specialisation in:

(a) matching anticipated changes in their liabilities and assets;
(b) remaining solvent despite their liabilities being more liquid than their assets.

However, there are some economists who argue that BFIs and NBFIs are very different kinds of FIs. Briefly they put their point of view as follows: when a BFI makes a loan, it creates a deposit of equal value (see Ch. 5). Therefore, the liabilities (deposits) of BFIs may be used actually to increase the volume of spending in the economy, because BFI sight deposits are generally accepted in settlements of debts. In contrast, NBFIs merely *transmit* funds created elsewhere, i.e. notes and coins by the monetary authorities and bank deposits by the banking system. Hence BFIs, because they can create credit and thereby actually increase money supply, are different in kind from NBFIs who cannot do either of the two things.

The UK monetary sector

Since 1982, the monetary authorities have established a much wider UK monetary sector. The Bank of England recognises the following institutions as the participants of the widened monetary sector: the UK offices of authorised banks, the National Girobank, the Banking Department of the Bank of England and some banks in the Channel Islands and the Isle of Man which are under the UK monetary control arrangements. By the end of February 1989, there were 295 UK incorporated banks, and 256 were incorporated outside the UK, giving a total of 551 authorised institutions under the 1987 Banking Act (see Ch.10).

It is noteworthy that not all major UK financial institutions are included even in the widened monetary sector. The notable exceptions are building societies, the National Savings Bank, insurance companies and pension funds.

The commercial banks

As commercial enterprises, these aim to make profit for their shareholders, to whom they are accountable. The main UK commercial banks are the London Clearing Banks (Barclays, Lloyds, Midland, National Westminster, TSB and Coutts), the Scottish Clearing Banks (Bank of Scotland, Royal Bank of Scotland, Clydesdale Bank), the Northern Irish Banks (Northern Bank, Ulster Bank, Allied Irish Banks, Bank of Ireland) and some other joint stock banks, who are not, like the London clearing banks, members of the Bankers' Clearing House, and whose cheques and credits are cleared via members of the Clearing House (Isle of Man Bank, C. Hoare and Co., Standard Chartered, Yorkshire Bank).

Sometimes the clearing banks, especially the London clearers, are called **retail** banks on account of their direct participation in the UK clearing system and their vast branch network serving the banking needs of hundreds of thousands of personal and corporate customers. However, the distinction between 'retail' and **wholesale** banks – e.g. the merchant banks, who provide for the specialised financial needs of large corporate customers and therefore do not require the expensive branch network – has blurred in recent years.

The wholesale banks include accepting houses (they accept bills of exchange for customers), the overseas banks and consortium banks (these are owned by other banks). The other main differences between wholesale and retail banking are that the wholesale deposits, as compared to retail deposits, might offer a higher rate to depositors, and wholesale loans, as compared to retail loans, might be at a lower rate, which is related to London Inter-Bank Offered Rate (LIBOR) and London Inter-Bank Bid Rate (LIBBR) rather than to banks' base rates. Both retail and wholesale banks raise wholesale (large) funds through the inter-bank and certificate of deposit (CDs) markets.

Most clearers are now 'banking groups', providing through their subsidiaries retail *and* wholesale banking and non-banking services 'under one roof'. They have acquired controlling interests in merchant banks and finance houses, and they have opened leasing and factoring companies and have set up unit trusts. They have established offices overseas for foreign operations and have a substantial share in the eurocurrency market, both directly and in conjunction with the London-based consortium banks. Their main role, however, is to act as financial intermediaries for the sterling and currency funds.

The clearing banks may be distinguished from other banks by the extent to which they provide current account facilities and money transmission services; because of this distinction, the volume of their demand deposits forms a major component of the total purchasing power in the UK economy. It is also for this reason that they are sometimes called **primary** banks, as distinct from **secondary** banks which (with the exception of some American and Japanese banks) take term deposits and not sight deposits. Therefore secondary banks, unlike primary banks, cannot provide money transmission services. The *secondary* banks include accepting houses, merchant banks, foreign banks, consortium banks and unit and investment trusts.

The balance sheet approach

The best way to determine the structure, functions and operations of retail banks, say clearing banks, is by analysing the items on the liabilities and assets sides of their balance sheets.

The liabilities side

Share capital and reserves

These liabilities represent amounts owed to the bank's equity (and preference) shareholders. The bank must show profit in its operations in order to pay adequate dividends to its shareholders. Profitability is therefore very important to a commercial bank.

Loan capital

These are the aggregate fixed-interest commitments of the bank; loan interest must be paid before any dividend distribution to shareholders.

Customers sterling deposits

The volume of these deposits forms the largest liability of a retail bank, but it is also the main source of its profitable operations; banks pivot the credit multiplier on the deposits they take, which generally comprise the following:

1. *Current account balances*. These are safe repositories of immediate liquidity; banks operate their money transmission services through these accounts. Either no or modest interest is paid to current account holders; but the holders of large overnight balances, usually big corporate customers, receive interest on call accounts, which are similar to current accounts.
2. *Seven-day and high interest rate deposits*. These are an excellent example of 'near' money assets, yielding a rate of return yet convertible into cash or current account on demand, with only a seven-day interest loss in lieu of notice, and no interest loss with high-rate deposits. *Savings opportunities* at competitive rates are also provided.
3. *Term deposits*. These cannot be withdrawn by depositors before the end of the term; long-term deposits are 'wholesale' deposits and tend to be larger in amount than 'retail' deposits which are generally small sight and other easily withdrawable deposits.

For their depositors, other than term depositors, retail banks provide the main payments mechanism through the Bankers' Automated Clearing System (BACS) and the Clearing House Automated Payments System (CHAPS).

Customers' currency deposits

At present there are no exchange controls in the UK and therefore UK residents, personal and corporate, can hold deposits in foreign currencies of their choice. These currency resources assist banks to participate in the eurocurrency markets. Banks pivot the *currency* credit multiplier on currency deposits as they do the ordinary credit multiplier on their sterling deposits. Note that if a bank fails, then its sterling and currency depositors are treated as a special class of creditor with increased rights and are paid before its loan stock holders or any class of shareholders. This shows that the safety of depositors' funds is of paramount concern to the banks.

Certificates of deposit

These are really large receipted term deposits with one major difference, that the receipts are bearer documents which are therefore easily marketable and negotiable items in the

CDs market. Since they are liquid-cum-safe investments, banks selling them offer a lower interest rate than on term deposits. Inter-bank and CDs markets borrowings provide banks' main funding sources.

Other liabilities

These include amounts owing at the balance sheet date, such as the proposed dividend to shareholders, amounts due to subsidiary companies in the 'group' and to the Inland Revenue towards corporation tax commitments.

The assets side

The assets of a bank result from the deployment of its loans and share capital and its deposits. The following are the main assets of a commercial bank.

Liquid assets

These are immediately available:

1. to meet cash withdrawals from demand deposits, e.g. notes and coins in the till, and
2. to effect clearing settlements and to meet unforseen contingencies.

The most liquid assets of a bank, in addition to the till money, are the first five following assets.

Operational deposits held at Bank of England

Retail banks hold non-interest bearing operational balances with the Bank of England, these balances are treated as cash. If a bank becomes overdrawn at the Bank of England, then the Bank may charge it the highest overnight interest rate of the day.

Money at call and short notice

This includes funds lent to discount houses to help them balance their books (outflow of funds on bills discounted and on purchases of Treasury bills and other short-term financial assets *minus* the inflow of funds from the maturity of discounted bills and from the sale of other short-term financial assets); also funds lent to Gilt-Edged Market Makers (GEMMs); to money and bullion brokers, to corporate customers and to other banks (the latter can be very important). Money 'at call' means that it is repayable by the borrower on demand. Money 'at short notice' implies that a notice of repayment of up to 14 days will be given by the lending bank. These monies are usually secured loans (always so in the case of discount houses) and earn interest; the rate depends upon the availability of such funds and the period of loan. After cash, these are the most liquid assets of a bank. These funds provide a suitable outlet for the surplus liquidity of the banks, and are therefore one of the principal means by which banks adjust their cash and liquidity requirements. (See also Question 4 and Answer 4 below.)

Cheques in course of collection

These represent claims of the bank for items to be collected to its credit from other banks in the payment mechanism.

Eligible bills

The Bank of England is prepared to buy these first-class, easily marketable bills, mainly from discount houses. Items qualifying as eligible bills are Treasury bills, local authority bills and first-class trade bills which have been accepted by eligible banks. Banks do not usually tender for Treasury bills directly but buy them from discount houses later on, as part of their easily realisable short-term assets. Local authorities also issue bills to raise short-term funds. The holding of eligible bills forms a significant percentage of the total assets of a bank. They are held because they provide a safe rate of return and are easily discounted by the discount houses in the bill market in the course of open market operations of the Bank of England.

Certificates of deposit and other market loans

Although a bank's holdings of CDs issued by other banks represents its short-term investments, these can easily be cashed at current rates in the CDs market. The market loans are short-term loans made to non-bank borrowers via specialised markets, to other banks via the inter-bank market and to other large customers; these loans are, of course, linked to LIBOR.

Investment other than trade investments

These are safe short-and medium-term fixed interest rate investments, mainly in gilt-edged securities of the central government. Besides being quite safe, these instruments are held both for their yield, and also for the possibility of capital gain, which occurs when interest rates fall. However, even though they are liquid, there is the danger of financial loss on realisation if the current market interest rates are higher than those operating when the financial asset was purchased.

Advance and loans to personal and corporate customers

These items form the largest proportion of a bank's assets and are traditionally seen as the most profitable. They include all types of bank lending viz. overdrafts, term loans, credit card finance, hire purchase finance (through subsidiaries) and home mortgage. In theory, overdrafts, but not fixed-term loans, are call money, but in practice, very rarely would a bank call for their immediate repayment. In fact, therefore, these balances represent a bank's illiquid assets, as they are assets which are prone to lending risks; this point is reflected in the higher interest rates banks charge on them. A bank widely diversifies its advances and loans in terms of maturity and sectors. Changes in these balances have a significant influence upon the size of the money supply. Short-term loans, e.g. an overnight loan to I.C.I., are very liquid; whereas loans that have a definite repayment period have a liquidity that is determined by the time remaining to maturity.

Investment in subsidiary and associate companies

A subsidiary is a company in which the bank has controlling power; an associate company is one in which it owns at least 20 per cent of the share capital. Most commercial banks, especially the clearers, are now fully-fledged banking groups providing banking and non-banking services 'under one roof'. Their investments in *subsidiary* companies assist them in providing services beyond the range of traditional banking services, such as factoring, leasing, insurance, estate agency. Their investments in *associated* companies often provide the commercial banks with the means through which to operate their banking services more efficiently, e.g. Bankers' Automated Clearing System.

Trade investments

Investments in a company in which the investor has less than a 20 per cent stake are called trade investments; these investments give a bank access to specialist services, as with the Agricultural Mortgage Corporation, Finance for Industry and the Bankers' Clearing House. Trade investments may also assist it in opening overseas offices, e.g. in conjunction with a consortium bank.

Non-operational deposits with the Bank of England

The Bank of England requires all institutions in the monetary sector with 'eligible liabilities' (broadly speaking, its sterling deposit liabilities) of £10 million or over to:

1. Keep 0.4 per cent of its eligible liabilities in non-interest bearing and non-operational deposits with the Bank. This cash-deposit ratio is designed to provide the Bank with a major source of its income for its open market operations. These may take place in order to relieve a shortage (or surplus) of cash in the money markets, or to influence short-term interest rates.
2. Be ready to receive 'calls' for special deposits from the Bank. As a part of the UK monetary control regulations, the Bank of England is empowered to call, from time to time, for non-operational but interest-bearing special deposits from the institutions in the 'monetary sector' (see Ch. 5). Such calls for special deposits are a means of withdrawing cash from the money market, thereby reducing the commercial banks' credit multiplier because of their 'frozen' funds in special deposits.

Premises and equipment

These are the bank's fixed assets, which are necessary for its operations. They include head office and branch bank premises, other buildings, computers, equipment and vehicles. The book value of a bank's premises and other buildings, which is much less than their market value, represents hidden reserves.

The asset structure of a bank reflects a successful compromise between its two main, but conflicting, objectives: safety of its depositors' funds and profitability for its shareholders. If the composition of a bank's liabilities changes, e.g. more current accounts and less saving deposits, then its asset structure will be adjusted accordingly, with more liquid assets and less long-term investments.

The composite rate tax deductions by banks as well as building societies from interest earned on deposits has led to much more competitive pricing of deposit rates by the banks.

Other services

More recently retail banks, in addition to their well-established services (viz. standing orders, direct debits, tax advice, ATMs and executor and trustee work) are also providing insurance broking, unit trusts, investment advice, merchant banking, factoring (buying from corporate customers their invoiced debts) and leasing (hiring to customers assets for the duration of their economic life).

Foreign banks

In 1960 there were only 77 foreign banks in London; however, in 1987, their number was around 490. They are represented in London through branches, subsidiaries, representative offices and through minority holdings in 'consortium banks', i.e. institutions which specialise in international banking activity and which are owned jointly by a group of established banks.

Foreign banks are attracted to London for several reasons:

1. To participate in the eurocurrency transactions, because London is a major eurocurrency market (see Ch.4).
2. To serve the financial needs of companies from their own countries which are operating in the UK.
3. To participate in financing trade between the UK and their own countries, and indeed between the UK and other countries.
4. To have stakes in consortium banks which specialise in international banking activity.
5. To cater for specific ethnic communities now resident in the UK.
6. To compete with the UK banks, since the 'Big Bang' in October 1986, in the investment business, mortgage finance and merchant banking, either directly or through acquired stockbroking and jobbing firms.

Therefore, the presence of foreign banks is not restricted to London; some banks are establishing networks of strategically-placed offices in major UK cities, for example, in Birmingham, Bradford and Liverpool.

Like the UK retail and merchant banks, foreign banks are 'authorised' institutions, under the 1987 Banking Act, and the regulatory changes of the past few years, viz. capital adequacy ratios and liquidity criteria, (see below), have not in fact driven off any foreign banks. They are nevertheless worried that the Bank of England's liquidity proposals will increase their costs of doing business in London. On the completion of the single European internal market by the end of 1992, overseas participation in the UK banking sector might be expected to increase, just as British banks are likely to increase their interests in Continental European markets.

Cumulatively, the foreign banks now account for over 60 per cent of total UK bank assets and 27 per cent of lending to UK customers (25 per cent of all sterling advances and 81 per cent of foreign currency advances). Among the foreign banks, the American and Japanese banks are the most prevalent. Therefore, for statistical purposes, the Bank of England classifies foreign banks as American Banks, Japanese Banks and Other Overseas Banks. In terms of balance-sheet trading, the American banks account for around 45 per cent of foreign banks' business in London and around 12.5 per cent of all lending to British corporate customers. Their prowess in oil and energy finance has enabled them to take a sizeable slice of the North Sea oil business. Probably the most aggressive banks currently operating in London are the Japanese. Their share of UK lending has more than doubled since 1977.

The American and Japanese banks, along with a few other foreign banks, are engaged in the UK domestic wholesale banking, and in particular, in providing funds to large companies. They are also competing with the UK clearing banks in retail banking in sterling, particularly that denominated in foreign currencies.

The Bank of England

The Bank of England has a history of private banking but has since become a public sector institution (1946), unlike the Bundesbank (West Germany) and Federal Reserve Board (USA), which were set up from scratch by legislation. It became the central bank because it had been adopted as government's banker. Due to its implicit government backing and its favoured position, often being designated as sole bank note issuer, it naturally evolved as agent/adviser of the government.

It is the central bank of the UK and as such its relationship with the Treasury and its functions and operations in the UK financial system are of extreme importance.

Functions of the Bank of England

(a) Adviser and agent to the UK government

One of the Bank of England's functions is to act as the adviser and agent to the UK government in formulating and implementing the official monetary policy. It is uniquely placed, on account of its specialised knowledge, contacts and experience of the UK financial market acquired over many years, to give advice to the government on the technical aspects of monetary policy as it is being formulated. Its advisory role has widened in recent years: the Bank officials serve on a wide range of official committees concerned with economic and monetary matters, bringing to these committees the Bank's economic forecasts and views on financial matters. Thus the monetary policy, when finalised, is likely both to be in line with government objectives and to meet with a large measure of agreement from within the financial community.

Since the Bank is the agent of the government for implementing monetary policy measures, its 'advice' to banks and to other financial institutions has to be obeyed. In implementing monetary policy, the Bank seeks to influence both the cost and availability of credit; this can be done by varying the terms of 'last resort' assistance to the banking system, by making calls for special deposits, by introducing direct controls on bank lending and interest rates, and by reactivating the Minimum Lending Rate, i.e. its lending rate to the money markets.

(b) Banker to the government

It is the banker to the government, and in that capacity its activities include:

1. Maintaining the Exchequer and the accounts of other government departments.
2. Arranging for the government's short-term borrowing needs by handling the weekly issue of Treasury bills.
3. Acting as registrar to the gilt-edged stock holders, thereby providing for the long-term borrowing requirements of the public sector, paying interest, arranging renewal or redemption at maturity and issuing new gilt-edged stocks. In effect, the Bank acts as the manager of the National Debt. Since 1986, it operates the new Central Gilts Office which deals in all gilts deals done by GEMMS and the commercial banks.
4. It holds and protects the UK gold reserves and manages the UK foreign currency reserves via the Exchange Equalisation Account (EEA). It often uses its management of the EEA to stabilise the foreign exchange value of the pound sterling directly against other currencies by buying and selling sterling in the foreign exchange markets.
5. As the central note-issuing authority in the UK, it is responsible for the printing, issue,

withdrawal and destruction of bank notes. The actual value of notes in circulation at the end of February 1989, was £14.1 billion, and roughly on a working day average £35.5 million worth of notes were destroyed. Whilst the note issue is free of interest, the interest-bearing securities acquired by the Bank in using some of the note issue results in profit to the Bank, which is credited to Treasury accounts.

(c) Banker to the banking system

1. A traditional role of any central bank is as lender of last resort, whereby it makes funds available when the banking system is short of liquidity. The Bank of England, in performing this traditional function, uses a unique method: it does not relieve shortages in the UK banking system (which may be due to large net payments to the Exchequer on account of tax payments or to sales of gilt-edged securities) by lending *directly* to the banks; rather it does so *indirectly*, by buying eligible bills, invariably from the discount houses, at prices acceptable to it. The discount houses can then return the call and short-notice money to the banking system, thereby removing the banks' liquidity shortage; the discount houses can then continue to cover the weekly Treasury bill issue (see below). Sometimes (e.g. during the tax-gathering season) it may lend directly to banks through repurchase agreements (REPOS), i.e. the Bank buys gilts at fixed rates and for fixed periods from the banks, which the banks agree to buy back at the end of the period.
2. As the bankers' bank, it hold their operational balances, their current accounts, which the banks use for obtaining cash and for settling clearing and other transactions among themselves and with the public sector.

(d) Supervision and prudential control of authorised banks

The Banking Act 1987 has not only made the supervision of the monetary sector a function of the Bank of England but has also given it *statutory* powers to supervise authorised banks to ensure that they are soundly run, so that any recurrence of the banking crisis can be avoided, although individual banks, e.g. Johnson Matthey Bankers, do sometimes get into trouble. More generally, the Bank has responsibility for overseeing the soundness of the UK financial system as a whole. It also applies prudential supervision and control in respect of capital adequacy, liquidity adequacy requirements and risk asset ratios (see Banking Act 1987 in Ch.10).

The discount houses

The following eight discount houses, all recognised as authorised banks, are members of the London Discount Market Association: Alexanders Discount plc; Cater Allen Ltd; Clive Discount Co. Ltd; Gerrard & National plc; King & Shaxson plc; Gerald Quin, Cope & Co. Ltd; Seccombe Marshall & Campion plc; The Union Discount Company of London plc.

Discount houses are a type of banking institution unique to the London money market. They provide a remunerative outlet for banks' liquid funds by taking secured call deposits. They provide a mechanism whereby the commercial banks adjust their liquidity positions (the advent of the inter-bank and CDs market has reduced the importance of this mechanism). When the banks call in their loans, it suggests general liquidity shortage in the system and the need for Bank of England's open market operations. These funds are then used for the purchase of Treasury bills, commercial bills and gilt-edged securities. They are the principal market-makers in bills.

Their uniqueness stems from their special relationship with the Bank of England. They are the focus of the Bank's open market operations, and act as a 'buffer' between the Bank and the rest of the banking system. They provide a mechanism whereby the Bank supplies the banking system with funds when any shortage occurs and through which it withdraws funds when there is a surplus (see Ch. 4). It is through these open market operations that the Bank influences short-term money market interest rates (see Ch. 6).

For the company sector, their primary function is the provision of borrowing facilities through discounting bills of exchange, whilst as a secondary function they offer various forms of short-term investments for the companies.

In the sphere of government finance, their major function is to cover in full the weekly Treasury bill tender, which is an essential part of the government's short-term borrowing requirements. They are active dealers in short-dated government stocks and local authority bills and bonds.

They are also active in the secondary market for negotiable dollar and sterling CDs, and by providing marketability to them, they have directly contributed to the success of this form of investment.

In the balance sheet of a discount house, the largest item, by a long margin, is its sterling and currency *liabilities* relating to funds it has borrowed from the banking sector. And the largest item on its *asset* side, again by a long margin, is 'other bills', i.e. bills other than UK and Northern Ireland Treasury bills. These statistics reflect the complementary relationship between the discount houses and the commercial banks and the importance of commercial bills in the discount market.

In 1982, new rules for the prudential supervision of discount houses by the Bank of England were introduced. Under the new system, which is designed mainly to ensure that the houses can cover any losses they may sustain if the value of their assets drops, they are allowed to carry assets up to 40 times their capital base, but the types of asset which they hold are now more tightly controlled by the Bank.

It may be that their special relationship with the Bank is being affected by the Big Bang which is reshaping other financial institutions. The eight discount houses – only four of which are independent institutions – are already looking at new business, e.g. commodities broking, leasing, money broking and gilt dealing.

Merchant banks

By *accepting* (adding their names to) bills of exchange issued by lesser-known traders to finance international trade, the merchant houses of the nineteenth century adopted banking activities in the role of accepting houses. The Accepting Houses Committee represents the 16 leading merchant banks. In addition to the finance of international trade, they are now very much involved in corporate finance, investment management, financial advisory services, foreign exchange and eurocurrency business.

On the *deposit* side – whilst a number of them operate a current account service, only a small proportion of their sterling deposits are sight deposits. Most of their sterling deposits are time deposits. Their foreign currency deposits are much larger than their sterling deposits.

On the *lending* side – they are active suppliers of corporate finance, by accepting bills of exchange issued by companies concentrating on medium-term lending in sterling and eurocurrencies. Most of their sterling and foreign currency assets are in the form of market loans. Bills accepted by the accepting houses can be discounted at fine (low cost) rates.

They are very active in the money markets and have contributed greatly towards the success of negotiable CDs. They account for a large proportion of the total bank bills (bills accepted by banks and then sold to discount houses). They help their clients in raising capital in the domestic and international capital markets.

Like the clearers, several US and other overseas banks in the UK have established their own wholly owned subsidiaries undertaking merchant and wholesale banking; it is with these subsidiaries that the merchant banks are in keen competition.

Deregulation (see Ch. 4) within the City of London has accelerated, for the clearers and merchant banks, the process of diversification of financial services. There are a number of alliances between merchant banks and the stock exchange member firms. Merchant Banks are 'authorised' institutions. Many of their specialised functions are now being performed by the clearing banks, so that a clear distinction between the clearers and merchant banks is fading fast.

National Girobank

National Girobank's money transmission service is operated through the postal system and its cash facilities are provided through post offices. It is, however, financially independent from the post office.

Despite increasing use of its payment services by local authorities, nationalised industries and government departments, and despite the introduction of a personal loan scheme and the extension of its cash and money transmission services to the business sector, its growth has been slow. To increase the public's awareness of its banking facilities it was renamed, in 1978, National Girobank (previous name was National Giro). It was incorporated in 1985, when its name was changed again, to Girobank plc. Negotiations are proceeding for its acquisition by some other financial institution, perhaps by a building society. It is a full member of the London Bankers' Clearing House.

It forms a part of the UK monetary sector and, like other constituents of the monetary sector, it is subject to the monetary control measures.

National Savings Bank (NSB)

NSB has 20 million active accounts and its banking business is handled by 20,000 post offices.

It offers two main types of account – ordinary and investment. From the *ordinary account* small withdrawals can be made on demand, but withdrawals from the *investment account* are subject to one month's notice, consequently it offers a higher rate of interest than the ordinary account. Since the NSB funds are invested in government securities – which contribute towards the government's spending requirements – certain tax benefits are offered to savers with the NSB; it pays interest 'gross', and the first £70 of interest income from an ordinary account deposit is tax free.

NSB is part of the Department of National Savings and not part of the UK monetary sector. However, its ordinary account deposits are included in the monetary aggregate, M2.

Finance houses

The provide loans to finance leasing and hire purchase transactions. At present 45 finance houses, who are members of the Finance Houses Association, control 80 per cent of the instalment credit business, which amounted to some £24 billion at the end of 1986. The majority of the finance houses are owned by the authorised banks and other financial institutions. As subsidiaries of authorised institutions, they form a part of the UK monetary sector.

Those finance houses owned by the major banks are listed below:

Finance House	*Parent Bank*
Lombard North Central plc	NatWest
Mercantile Credit Co. Ltd	Barclays
Lloyds Bowmaker Ltd	Lloyds
Forward Trust Group Ltd	Midland
United Dominions Trust Ltd	TSB
North West Securities Ltd	Bank of Scotland
RoyScot Trust Ltd	Royal Bank of Scotland

On the *deposit* side – a large proportion of their deposits comes from banks, other financial institutions and also from industrial and commercial companies. Personal sector deposits are insignificant.

On the *lending* side – most of their funds are used to finance motor trade, equipment leasing, insurance, factoring and property bonds, and the remainder for giving loans for home improvement, house purchase, leisure and holiday activities.

Their finance flows mainly to and from companies rather than individuals. Therefore, finance houses compete with banks in the company sector rather than the personal sector. However, the scale of their deposit-taking and lending activities is too small to threaten the clearing banks.

Investment trusts and unit trusts

These two financial intermediaries have several features in common, but as organisations they are not identical. Both spread investment risk on behalf of each individual investor, thus avoiding investors putting 'all eggs in one basket'. Both generally provide the investors with expert management at reasonable costs. Both mainly invest in the securities of UK and overseas companies. The types of claims that both hold (their assets) are of the same kind as the claims they create (their liabilities).

Investment trusts are public limited companies and, like any other public company, raise funds by the sale of shares and loan stock on the Stock Exchange. Nearly 90 per cent of their funds are invested in company securities and the rest in short-term assets such as sterling CDs, British government securities and local authority temporary debt. By buying shares in an investment trust the investor is, in effect, buying a 'share'; in a wide spread of assets owned by the investment trust company. Their shares can be sold on the Stock Exchange.

Unit trusts are really two companies: one acts as the trustee (a bank or an insurance company) and the other manages the trust's funds obtained by selling units to investors. The Department of Trade and Industry exercises close control over all unit trusts to protect unit holders. Units can be sold to the fund managers quite easily. When units are purchased, *new* units are *created*, and when units are sold units are *eliminated*; with investment trusts investors buy and sell *existing* shares. Hence, unlike investment trusts, there is no limit to the funds of unit trusts.

The value of the investment trust shares and the units of unit trusts depends upon the performance of the companies whose securities form their underlying assets.

In so far as most clearers have established their own unit trust schemes, the unit and investment trusts compete with the clearers for the investing public's funds.

Building societies

Traditionally, Britain's savers save with banks, building societies and national savings, although unit trusts, particularly those with life assurance links, and investment trusts are increasingly challenging the dominance of the 'big three'. Building societies are popularly regarded merely as savings and mortgage institutions. In fact they are major financial institutions: their total sterling assets were £190 billion at the end of 1988, as compared to £340 billion for the banks. They are also major deposit-taking institutions. They totally dominated the mortgage market until the banks entered the market in a significant way in 1981. Building societies are major holders and traders in short-term gilt-edged securities, substantial investors in the money markets and lately significant borrowers in wholesale markets. The similarity between bank and building society deposits has led to the inclusion of building society deposits in the official definitions of money supply (M2, M4, M4c, and M5).

As building societies are not a component of the UK monetary sector they are not subject to the Banking Act 1987. Their supervision, at present, is the responsibility of the Building Societies Commission, a government department, under the Building Societies Act 1986. Building societies are non-profit making *mutual* organisations. Mutuality means that a society cannot be purchased against the wishes of its depositors. Under the Building Societies Act 1986, which became effective on 1 January 1987, the societies are not only empowered to compete fully in the financial industry market but also can opt to become banks. The 1986 Act provides for conversion of mutual societies into corporate bodies, with effective control of the societies going 'public', and for the protection of the members' rights.

Abbey National Building Society became a public limited company in July 1989, and became an 'authorised' bank under the 1987 Banking Act.

Between 75 and 80 per cent of their assets are held as mortgage advances, over periods normally up to 25 years. Although these are long-term loans, they are secured against property which is usually an appreciating asset, and the risk of loss is low. Their remaining assets are held in liquid form to provide working capital, and to cover any short-term excess of withdrawals and lendings over deposits. Their liquid assets must equal at least 7.5 per cent of their total assets.

The type and maturity distribution of the liquid assets is regulated by the Building Societies Commission. In practice, the societies have been cautious, usually maintaining a liquidity ratio of between 15 to 20 per cent.

Competition between banks and building societies

A major feature of financial intermediation since 1980 has been the intensity of competition between banks and building societies. The distinction between the banks and the larger building societies has become progressively blurred, and will become more so as the societies exploit the freedoms given to them in the 1986 Building Societies Act. In particular, building society deposits, which are traditionally dominated by savings balances, have increasingly been used for transaction purposes in recent years. The provision by some societies of accounts with cheque book facilities, and the spread of cash dispensers has facilitated this change in usage, which may well proceed further with the introduction of cheque guarantee cards. At the moment, societies can make unsecured personal loans up to a limit of £10,000 per customer. Under the Building Societies Act there have been strict limits on services which societies can offer to companies. However in February 1989 the Treasury allowed the societies to offer companies 'temporary or occasional overdrafts'. Until this loosening of restraints, societies were forced to give up clients who wanted to borrow more than £10,000 or who decided to take on company status for their financial affairs. Another relaxation allows societies to acquire mortgage portfolios from *other* institutions.

The initial focus of competition from 1980, between banks and building societies, was *mortgage lending*. One result of the banks' successful inroads into the mortgage market was the break-up of the societies cartel arrangements for setting interest rates. Rationing of mortgage lending had helped to sustain the societies' interest rate cartel, but this became untenable after the banks' entry into the mortgage market. In consequence, building society interest rates have become more flexible and market related.

The reason why the banks have become aggressively involved in mortgage business is that they found mortgage lending to be very profitable, especially as lending on the security of a house is safer than lending on the security of a business, and mortgage loans can be used as a lead-in for the sale of their other financial services, such as insurance, tax-planning, house improvement loans. In the circumstances, it was unlikely that increased competition between the banks and building societies would be confined to mortgage lending.

Until recently, the societies were able to attack the banks where they are most vulnerable, i.e. in the personal savings sector. The societies were able to achieve this because they could offer better terms to depositors. Building societies have been able to operate on a narrower margin than banks between their rates to the depositors and borrowers (an average interest margin for a representative clearing bank is 6.2 per cent compared with a little over 1 per cent for a typical large building society) because of their (a) low management cost (due to their less complicated specialised business); (b) no requirements to pay dividends; (c) low capital requirements due to the low risk nature of their assets; and (d) because the banks have tended to subsidise their money transmission service by their deposit accounts which lessens their ability to compete in the savings market.

However the personal retail deposits of the building societies have declined during the past few years due to the government's highly successful privatisation schemes, the floatation of very popular private sector new issues, the increased importance given to national savings in the financing of the Public Sector Borrowing Requirements (PSBR) and the introduction by banks of their higher interest rate cheque accounts. The profitability of the societies' main business – mortgage lending – has been hit by the high cost in attracting retail funds. Until the societies were allowed access to wholesale funds, their rates have been as much as 2 per cent above the wholesale money market rates. Therefore the banks were able to increase returns to their new depositors towards the societies' rates in order to attract customers for mortgage loans to whom they could cross-sell their other financial services.

In order to attract more inflows of deposits, the building societies' ordinary share accounts were progressively replaced in importance first by term shares, and then by various high interest accounts. Although the new kinds of accounts were introduced in the mid 1970s, their scope was broadened during the 1980s. Whereas initially the conditions associated with these new accounts meant that they were less liquid than existing share accounts or bank deposits, these conditions were progressively relaxed through the 1980s by, for example, the introduction of term shares with withdrawal facilities and by the reductions in interest penalties for early withdrawal from term accounts.

The larger societies are able to raise wholesale funds in the form of Sterling Commercial Papers, CDs and through floating rate notes. The societies have eagerly taken the opportunity to raise money in the wholesale markets – which has frequently proved to be a cheaper source of wholesale funds – and have used these funds to even out any shortfall in the inflow of retail funds to meet the mortgage demand. (*Wholesale funds* are large deposits placed by companies and financial institutions, bearing an interest rate in line with the market rate rather than base rates.) In 1983 the societies were allowed to pay interest gross on certificates of deposit and on time deposits – and by 1986 some 40 per cent of their new funds were raised from this source. Also in 1983 they first had access to the eurobond market. (*Eurobond market* is the international market which raises long-term funds in various capital markets and in different currencies against the issue of bonds.) This has allowed the societies to borrow longer maturities more in line with the average life of mortgages. From April 1986, they have been permitted to pay interest gross on eurobonds. This enabled them to launch issues on the eurobond market. This gives the societies access to an even cheaper source of funds. The new legislation is expected to allow them to raise funds in foreign currency which they would then be able to swap into sterling at very fine terms. Inevitably all these developments have led to a change in the relationship of building society interest rates to other market interest rates.

By the end of 1984, the banks' share of deposit inflows had fallen sharply. This loss of share encouraged intensification of competition, and the extension of the composite rate arrangements provided the trigger for the introduction by the banks of high-interest retail accounts, some with chequeing facilities. These accounts substantially narrowed the gap between the interest rate offered by the building societies and those previously offered by the banks.

It seems clear that, though still constrained somewhat by the 40 per cent ceiling on wholesale borrowing, under the 1986 Act, the larger societies, at least, have shifted away from *asset management* during the period of their interest rate cartel, towards a *liability management* now – a similar shift in behaviour occurred among banks after *Competition and Credit Control* in 1971, when they abandoned their collective agreement on interest rates.

Asset liability management implies the control of a bank's deposits and lending policies to ensure safety, liquidity, capital adequacy and profitability. *Liability management* involves the adjustment by a bank of the volume of its wholesale money market deposits so that the liability of its balance sheet accommodates changes in demand for loans. *Asset management* involves the adjustment of financial assets held and loans granted to equal changes in the supply of deposits received/withdrawn.

Banks and building societies compared and contrasted

The following is the summary of the major similarities and dissimilarities of banks and building societies.

Major similarities

- Both are allowed to undertake unsecured personal lending, issue cheque books, offer money transmission services, give advice on investment, insurance and conveyancing, administer pension schemes, and provide foreign exchange to individuals.
- Both can give overdraft to corporate customers.
- Both offer home mortgage loans and a wide variety of savings accounts.

- Societies can, if they choose, like the banks, become public limited companies and be 'authorised' as banks.
- Both can raise wholesale funds.
- Both pay interest to depositors net of tax (soon both will be able to pay interest 'gross').
- Deposits of both are included in broad money aggregates.

Major dissimilarities
- Unlike banks, societies have a 40 per cent ceiling on raising wholesale funds.
- Societies can offer only temporary or occasional overdrafts to corporate customers.
- Unlike banks, the unsecured lending ceiling for the societies is £10,000.
- Banks are profit-orientated institutions, societies are mutual bodies.
- Banks are a part of the UK monetary sector, building societies are not.
- Banks are supervised by the Bank of England under the provisions of 1987 Banking Act; societies are supervised by the Building Societies Commission under the 1986 Building Societies Act, with different rules on capital adequacy, liquidity and deposit protection.
- Banks still offer a far wider range of services than the societies, particularly if their group's in-house services are taken into account.

Although the distinction between banks and building societies has been considerably blurred, and continues to be blurred further with the passage of time, it is still valid and useful to distinguish between the two sets of institutions.

Insurance companies

They provide general insurance to policy holders against particular risk, such as theft, fire, accident, and provide life assurance to those seeking life cover.

Their income comes from the deposits of premiums by policy holders and from the returns on the assets in which they invest the premium income. The claims against insurance companies (their liabilities) arising out of their general insurance business tend to be short term, and those arising out of their life business are long term. Therefore, insurance companies have to exercise financial prudence by adjusting their asset maturity structures to cope with the short term and long term nature of their liabilities and, at the same time, so to adjust their asset portfolios as to obtain maximum benefit from asset diversification. The long term investment of insurance companies is mainly in government securities, company shares, mortgage and other loans and property and their short term investment (liquid assets) is in general funds.

Although the insurance companies receive their funds from specific sources and for particular purposes, nevertheless their life-linked unit trusts and insurance business compete with the unit trust and insurance business of the banks.

Pension funds

Their 'deposits' come from the contributions paid by employers and employees and in return they undertake to provide pensions on employees' retirement. Their other source of income is the returns from the investment of accumulated and accumulating contributions. By and large, it is from the investment income that pensions are paid. Hence the paramount need in their investment policy is to maximise current and future profits from investments.

Until recently a major proportion of their funds was used in purchasing mainly the ordinary shares of domestic and overseas companies, because that was one of the ways of ensuring that the return from and the value of investment kept pace with inflationary growth of incomes. With falling inflation and interest rates, until recently, there has been a heavy switch to government securities. Even so, their funds are heavily committed to the purchase of long-term capital for the company sector. Their other investments include loans, mortgage finance and property.

The trustees of pension funds usually hand over the investment management responsibility of a significant proportion of their funds to life assurance companies, because the operation of a pension fund involves the same sort of considerations as those involved in organising life assurance business. Therefore the investment strategy is similar for both these organisations: long-term assets which continue to increase in value in order to discharge long-term liabilities which also tend to continue increasing in money terms.

Pension funds and insurance companies dominate the purchase of existing and new issues of ordinary shares as well as 'making a market' in existing securities of the Stock Exchange. It is in this field that these two types of financial intermediaries, which have grown considerably in size, will offer serious competition to banks in the deregulated capital market.

Recent examination questions

The following five recent questions have been asked in the Monetary Economics (now renamed 'Monetary and Financial System') papers of the Banking Diploma (now renamed 'Associateship') of The Chartered Institute of Bankers. These questions reflect the type and depth of knowledge required to answer questions placed in the UK Financial Institutions section of the syllabus. First try to locate, from the contents of this chapter, the main points you consider essential in answering each of these questions. Then spend ten minutes or so planning your answer to each question before turning to the section on 'Outline answers' which follows.

Question 1

What is meant by the term 'financial intermediary'? To what extent are banks the principal financial intermediaries?

Question 2

Outline the ways in which the Bank of England carries out its role as:
(a) banker to the government;
(b) banker to the banks;
(c) lender of last resort to the banking system.

Question 3

Is it essential for a country to have a central bank?

Question 4

For what reasons does a commercial bank need liquidity and how may it be provided? How has Bank of England supervision in this area evolved since 1981?

Question 5

With particular reference to the Bank of England's day-to-day operations in the money markets, discuss the Bank's present role as 'lender of last resort'. How has this role changed since 1981?

Outline answers

Answer 1

Financial intermediary – an institution which links ultimate lenders with ultimate borrowers: banks link depositing and borrowing customers; building societies link depositors and mortgagors; pension funds and insurance companies link contributors and policy holders with the companies in which they invest their capital. They are the 'go-between', linking surplus economic sectors with the deficit sectors, and deficit and surplus units within the same sector. FIs are not merely middlemen; they are principals both for lenders of funds and borrowers of funds.

Banks are arguably the principal intermediaries, because:

- other financial institutions maintain accounts;
- bank's balance sheet totals (including eurocurrency deposits) are extremely large;
- NBFIs (building societies, insurance companies, superannuation funds, unit and investment trusts) may be considered principal financial intermediaries, but at the longer end of the time scale;
- it is when ultimate borrowers and lenders by-pass banks, not other financial institutions, that disintermediation results.

Answer 2

(a) As the *banker* to the government, it:

- holds the government's main accounts: the National Loan Fund, the Consolidated Fund, the Paymaster-General, including the Exchange Equalisation Account;
- ensures that short-term (the Treasury bills) and longer-term (sale of government gilt-edged securities) finance is always available to the government;
- pays interest to government stockholders and reduces the total cost of government borrowing by purchasing securities with surplus government funds;
- issues bank notes;
- implements the official monetary policy.

(b) As the *banker* to the banks, it:

- holds banks' operational deposits and facilitates the settlement of clearing transactions between banks;
- sells bank notes to banks;
- holds the mandatory 0.4 per cent non-operational and non-interest bearing cash ratio deposit of the banks, *not* as an element of monetary control, but as a source of income for itself (a tax on banks!);
- holds the accounts of overseas central banks.

(c) As *lender of last resort* to the banking system, it:

- ensures that the banking system as a whole is not short of cash on a daily basis;
- makes good any shortages, primarily by the purchase of eligible bills from discount houses;

- mounts a lifeboat operation to save a bank in difficulties;
- ensures prudential supervision over banks.

Answer 3

- Functions which can only or best be performed by a central bank:
  (i) supervision of the banking system;
  (ii) lender of last resort;
  (iii) enhancement of confidence in the financial system by performing the above two key policy functions;
  (iv) providing the government with an independent link, free of commercial pressures, with the commercial financial sector.
- Functions which can be performed equally well either by a central bank or other commercial financial institutions:
  (i) banker to the government;
  (ii) provision of banking services to foreign institutions.
- Hong Kong with a sophisticated financial system has no central bank; the functions of the central bank are performed by a variety of public and private institutions.

Answer 4

- A bank needs liquidity:
  (i) to meet cash withdrawals from deposits;
  (ii) to effect clearing settlements via operational balances with the Bank of England;
  (iii) to meet unforeseeable problems in financing known future commitments (e.g. unused overdrafts);
  (iv) to maintain the confidence of the public.
- It provides for liquidity:
  (i) by maintaining a certain percentage of its assets in liquid assets (e.g. cash in tills, Treasury bills, call money with discount houses, short-dated gilt-edged securities);
  (ii) by the extent of diversification in its deposit base;
  (iii) by its ability to raise loans when needed from the inter-bank and the CD markets;
  (iv) by the cash flow generated from maturing assets, and the matching with maturing liabilities.
- Liquidity criteria applicable to all banks: the Bank of England ensures that individual banks are adopting prudential policies in the light of their individual circumstances, taking into account all the factors relevant to liquidity.

Answer 5

- Bank of England's traditional role as lender of last resort: it makes available funds when the banking system is short of liquid resources.
- In its day-to-day operations in the money markets, the Bank carries out this role involving eligible bill purchases only from the discount houses.
- The Bank announces a daily estimated shortage (or surplus) of 'cash'; it is prepared to buy eligible bills from discount houses which are offered at *their* own prices, but which the Bank may not accept. The Bank will, however, make good any shortage at a price acceptable to it. With the sale proceeds, discount houses discount more bills and return banks' call money.

- Sale and repurchase (REPOS) of gilts and other securities to banks at fixed rates and for fixed periods (a) to relieve cash shortage during the tax gathering season (January and February); and (b) to influence short rates and stabilisation.
- Main changes since 1981: virtually no direct lending to discount houses; abandoning the weekly announcement of the MLR, to which direct lending was generally linked; bill purchasing within four bands, depending upon maturity of the bill, is now the pivot of the 'lender of last resort' role; main change in carrying out this role is in the method of operation; discount houses remain the buffer between the Bank and the commercial banks.

A tutor's answer

The following question touches on various important aspects of the UK financial institutions. The tutor's answer is intended to help you establish the scope of the question and then to write cohesive relevant information in answering the whole question.

Question

Explain why and how the existence of financial intermediaries benefits both borrowers and lenders. Illustrate your answer by references to the main activities of commercial banks and building societies.

Answer plan:

1. State the benefits of FIs to borrowers and lenders.
2. Link the two sides of the balance sheets of banks and building societies, and illustrate the essential characteristics of financial intermediation.
3. Show how these FIs minimise lending and borrowing risks.

Specimen answer

The existence of financial intermediaries (FIs) benefits *both* the borrowers and lenders in several ways. Borrowers and lenders do not need to locate counterparties for any transaction. For borrowers, FIs provide a ready supply of credit cheaply, in large amounts and over longer term than would be possible without them. For lenders, they provide a low risk investment, convenience and ready access to funds, i.e. liquidity.

Whereas lenders prefer to lends short term to reduce the loss of liquidity, borrowers wish to borrow long term to take full advantage of the productivity of borrowed capital. The FIs resolve the opposing time preferences of lenders and borrowers by maturity transformation of funds, i.e. borrowing short and lending long; this they achieve by spreading risks, by virtue of the large number and diversity of their depositors.

Commercial banks bid for deposits from a wide variety of retail and wholesale sources. By aggregation and maturity transformation they can lend these funds in large amounts and for periods ranging from short to very long terms. Only a relatively small proportion of funds obtained is used to purchase liquid assets, partly to satisfy the known probability of withdrawals of a proportion of deposits and partly to meet any unforeseeable contingencies, e.g. unused overdrafts. The bulk of a bank's assets is therefore less liquid than its liabilities.

In the case of building societies, deposits are received in small amounts largely from the personal sector (although they are now able to obtain some wholesale funds as well) in the form of easily withdrawable shares or term shares and contractual savings schemes (e.g. SAYE). They lend their funds in much larger amounts for periods of up to 25 years, making use of maturity transformation. Some of their assets are liquid but the preponderance of their assets are less liquid than their liabilities.

Thus both categories of FIs, by interposing themselves between the ultimate lenders and ultimate borrowers, take upon themselves both lending and borrowing risks. In order to minimise their own risk in financial intermediation, these FIs, like other FIs, lend to a large number of borrowers for varying time maturities and employ suitable risk assessment and security procedures.

A step further

This section of the Monetary and Financial System syllabus requires a lot of study. What you learn in this chapter impinges on other parts of the syllabus. However, changes in the UK financial institutions do not occur too frequently. Therefore, once the characteristics and practices of the existing institutions are clearly and fully grasped, and your knowledge is kept updated, you should be able to answer regularly asked questions on this topic in the exam question paper, which invariably seek precise information.

To keep abreast with changes as they occur, you need to update your knowledge by reading *Banking world*, *Bank of England Quarterly Bulletin*, The Chartered Institute of Bankers' *Updating Notes* and *Examiners' Reports* and the financial press.

A comprehensive knowledge of the UK financial system, of which the financial institutions form a part, is essential to your understanding of other topic areas within Monetary and Financial System.

The Banking Information Service have published a very useful book, *A Guide to the British Financial System*, which covers the fundamentals of the UK financial system. Another useful publication is *The British Banking System*, published by National Westminster Bank. There is a very useful section on competition between banks and building societies in 'Measures of Broad Money' which appeared in *The Bank of England Quarterly Bulletin* May 1987. See *Bank of England Report and Accounts 1987* for a good reference to the Banking Act 1987. Very useful information is provided in *The Bank of England Banking Act Annual Reports*.

CHAPTER 4

Financial Markets in the UK

Syllabus requirements

- The nature and function of the discount market.
- The role of parallel markets.
- Financial instruments traded in the financial markets.
- The role of the capital markets in the UK economy.
- The impact of 'deregulation' on the capital market.
- The role of banks in the deregulated securities market.
- The role of the Bank of England in the money markets.
- The role of eurocurrency market in the provision of international finance.

Getting started

To complete the study of the UK financial system, we shall in this chapter look at the operation of the organised specialised financial markets and the characteristics of the financial instruments traded on these markets.

The UK **financial markets** may be divided into money markets and capital markets. The *money markets* match borrowers and lenders of large short-term (less than five years) sterling and currency funds, the discount market being of this type but having a special relationship with the Bank of England. The *capital markets* match borrowers and lenders/investors of medium- (five to 15 years) and long-term (over 15 years) sterling and currency funds.

The **financial instruments** are means of holding surplus wealth, by depositors/investors and which can be traded in the financial markets. *Treasury bills* are short-term promissory notes of HM Treasury and carry capital gains in lieu of fixed interest returns; *commercial bills* are short-term, fixed yield securities; *sterling commercial paper* represents short-term fixed interest negotiable borrowing by companies; *certificates of deposit* are bearer, short-term fixed yield securities expressed in sterling and US dollars; *gilt-edged securities* are British government short-, medium- and long-term fixed interest stocks; *stocks and bonds* are longer-term fixed interest instruments; *equities* are ordinary shares of private sector companies with no fixed rate of return; *deposits* in sterling and currency with financial institutions reflect the amounts of demand and time deposits, although interest rates vary.

There is a wide variety of financial instruments on offer in the financial markets, each with its own peculiar features, which satisfy the various objectives of numerous depositors and investors.

Since October 1986, a process of *deregulation* of the financial institutions has begun, starting with the reshaping of the Stock Exchange rules and continuing with the freeing of financial markets and the removal and modification of barriers between different classes of financial services institutions. Domestically this has led to increased competition among existing institutions and to the emergence of new sources of competition.

The *Bank of England*, as the pivot of the UK financial system, is an active participant in the financial markets (mainly through the discount market), raising short- and long-term funds for government spending, and implementing the official monetary policy as regards money supply and interest rates.

A eurocurrency deposit is in a currency other than the local currency, hence outside the control of the central bank which issued it. The eurocurrency markets have arisen and developed quickly, partly due to the inadequate availability of international liquidity from traditional sources, and partly due to eurocurrency markets being not fully regulated, and the margin between their borrowing and lending is narrow. The activity in the eurocurrency markets is different from the activity in the foreign exchange market; in the former foreign currencies are lent and borrowed, and in the latter they are bought and sold.

Essential principles

Wholesale money markets

The discount market and the Bank's role as lender of last resort

The main participants of the discount market are the eight discount houses which are members of the London Discount Market Association (LDMA). Discount houses are specialised institutions; they borrow mainly from the banking system and invest by discounting commercial bills and purchasing short-term assets, chiefly Treasury bills and gilt-edged securities. The discount houses constitute a buffer between the Bank of England and the rest of the banking system and it is through them that the Bank, as lender of last resort, regulates the availability of its funds to the commercial banks, thereby relieving shortages of liquid funds within the banking system. The discount market is used by the Bank to smooth out cash fluctuations between government and banks and to influence short-term interest rates via its *last resort* assistance.

It is very important that the mechanics of *how* the Bank of England performs its traditional role of lender of last resort are clearly understood. The present arrangement of relieving cash shortages of the banking system involves the Bank purchasing eligible bills exclusively from the discount houses; the latter maintain a portfolio of eligible bills, purchased with the funds deposited with them.

The clearing banks inform the Bank of England daily of the target level of daily balances they are aiming at. On the basis of this, and the Bank's own estimate of flows between the banks and the public sector, the Bank assesses the size of the likely shortage (or surplus) of its balances each day. The shortage (or surplus) is announced on the morning of each day to the money markets. The Bank then informs the discount houses that it is prepared to buy bills from them, or to sell bills to them. The discount houses then offer bills to the Bank at prices of their own choosing. The Bank may or may not accept the prices offered, but will always relieve the shortage, or surplus, at a price acceptable to itself.

Until 1981, the Bank of England could have lent to the discount houses directly at the *Minimum Lending Rate* (MLR). In 1981, MLR was suspended not abolished and direct lending by the Bank to the discount houses is now used only rarely. Instead, bill purchases, primarily eligible commercial bills within the four bands of various maturities (see below), have become the pivot of the system by which the Bank provides its lender of last resort assistance to the banking system.

The Bank has defined a number of 'maturity bands' which refer to the periods remaining before the bills mature. Band 1 has bills from one to 14 days to maturity; Band 2, 15 to 33 days; Band 3, 34 to 63 days; and Band 4, 64 to 91 days. While the Bank concentrates mainly on dealing in bills within Bands 1 and 2, dealings in Bands 3 and 4 are not uncommon. As well as outright purchases of bills, the Bank sometimes engages in sale and repurchase agreements with the banks, i.e. the Bank provides funds to the banks by buying bills from them with an arrangement that the banks will buy the bills back on an agreed day.

The discount market is one means by which commercial banks adjust their liquidity positions, because the discount houses mainly borrow surplus funds from the banks on a call/overnight basis. Thus the discount market provides a highly suitable and profitable place where the banks can place their surplus-to-need liquidity on a call basis. This gives the banks a means of holding near-liquid assets which can be drawn on when their operational deposits at the Bank of England get too low, due to withdrawals from operational deposits, notes and coins for more till money or settlement of debts with other banks or the government. This liquidity function is now increasingly shared with the interbank and the certificate of deposit markets (see below).

The discount market is an important provider of short-term finance to business companies; it does this by discounting commercial bills of exchange. In fact, the discount market is market-maker in Treasury bills, local authority or bank and other commercial bills, and to promote the bill market the Bank of England increased the number of eligible banks. The discount houses compete in underwriting the weekly Treasury bill tender. They maintain a secondary market in CDs and are prominent in the short-dated gilt-edged securities market. The discount market helps finance the government's short-term debt by agreeing to purchase all the Treasury bills issued by the Bank of England.

The discount market is the oldest money market for short-term funds and is often referred to as the 'traditional' money market. The newer money markets which have emerged since the 1960s, and in particular the inter-bank and certificates of deposit markets, are known as 'parallel' or 'secondary' money markets.

Secondary money markets

The certificates of deposit (CDs) market

Banks have issued CDs since 1968, and building societies since 1983. CDs are receipts issued by banks certifying that a deposit has been made of a certain sum, for a given period, and at a fixed (and also variable) rate of interest. The depositor or the holder will be paid in due course by the issuing bank at maturity of the CD. Sterling CDs are issued by London banks, in multiples of £10,000, with a minimum of £50,000 and a maximum of £500,000, for periods ranging between three months and five years. On CDs issued for a period of less than one year, interest is paid at maturity, along with the capital sum invested. For CDs issued for periods longer than one year, interest is payable annually. CDs are flexible instruments which offer advantages to both the depositor and the borrower. The depositor obtains for his minimum £50,000 investment maximum security, a good fixed rate of interest and easy marketability in the secondary CDs market, making them liquid therefore attractive to holders. Discount houses are very active in the secondary CDs market. For the original borrowing bank, a CD is a fixed period loan, and therefore not withdrawable until the expiry of that period. CDs market is an extension of, or alternative to the inter-bank market (see below). Banks hold CDs issued by other banks both as investments and as liquid assets. Societies find the wholesale funds in this market very reliable for their mortgage lendings.

The main attraction of CDs is that they can be sold before maturity in the secondary market. The certificates show the deposits as repayable to 'bearer' and thus anyone legally acquiring them is entitled to repayment. The value of CDs traded in the secondary market is calculated from a uniform agreed formula, which takes into account the interest rate at the date of issue and the original issue period, together with ruling interest rates and the period remaining to maturity.

The CDs may be purchased by banks, in preference to making interbank loans for fixed terms; by discount houses as traders in CDs; by industrial and commercial companies as safe and near-liquid investment.

The inter-bank market

This is a short-term wholesale market where banks, money brokers and other financial institutions lend to each other for periods from overnight to five years. The minimum amount of loans in sterling and currency is £250,000, normally unsecured. The rates of interest in this market for overnight money are higher than those offered in the discount market for call money. The inter-bank rates are known as LIBOR, which is important as a determinant of banks' base rates. Many loans, especially wholesale loans, are linked to LIBOR. The fundamental significance of the inter-bank market to the UK banking system is not only that it, together with the CDs market, is the largest sterling parallel market, but also that it, like the discount market, allows individual banks to adjust their day-to-day liquidity positions quickly. Banks with surpluses can lend on the inter-bank market to banks with shortages, thus reducing the need for individual banks to keep large holdings of liquid assets; this increases their profitable lending operations.

The main participants in the interbank market are merchant banks, overseas and foreign banks in London the clearing banks and large building societies. In addition, pension funds, insurance companies, commercial and industrial companies and finance companies also participate in the interbank market. A small number of money brokers synchronise the needs of the participants in the market.

The development of the market for CDs and the inter-bank market in the early 1970s has had an important effect on how the UK banking system works. Before these markets existed, whilst a bank could increase its retail deposits by offering higher interest rates, it could not be sure of doing this by a given amount quickly and with certainty. Thus, prior to the existence of these markets, a bank's lending activity, and therefore profitability, was to some extent limited by the amount of its customers' *retail* deposits. Nowadays, however, banks have much more flexibility. Banks with surpluses can lend wholesale funds in the inter-bank market to other banks with shortages, while banks with shortages can also borrow large sums by issuing CDs. Often the clearing banks have to raise large deposits from the inter-bank market. This reflects the success the building societies have had in garnering retail deposits, and then recirculating them back to the banking system, at higher rates, through the inter-bank market.

The local authority market

In 1955, the central government prevented local authorities from gaining access to central government funds. The local authorities therefore had to raise their own funds: this led to the development of the *local authority market.*

Local authority borrowing is of three kinds:

(a) *Temporary deposit receipts* – the terms of these receipts range from two days to about one year; most have a maturity of seven days or less, hence these receipts are fairly liquid instruments.

(b) *Local authority bills* – these are similar to the central government Treasury bills and first-class short-term commercial bills. Discount houses are active in making a market in these bills, thus giving them liquidity and enhancing their attraction to investors.
(c) *Local authority bonds* – these have longer maturity and are therefore not liquid assets.

Not all local authority debt is purchased by the financial institutions in the UK monetary sector (although the proportion of the local authority debt held by the monetary sector institutions is about 50 per cent); industrial and commercial companies, personal sector and overseas investors also invest in local authority debt.

The sterling commercial paper market

In response to the interest expressed by a number of companies in issuing short-term debt securities in sterling, the Bank of England notified the public in April 1986 that such securities may be issued under the title 'sterling commercial paper' (SCP). SCP represents short-term negotiable borrowing by companies that can be sold directly to investors in the money markets, thus by-passing the banking overdraft and bill acceptance facilities. SCP is equivalent to a CD issued by a company.

The framework laid down by the authorities for the issue of SCP in April 1986, was replaced by a new framework in March 1989. Under the new framework the following arrangements have been established.

1. *Issuers:* (a) UK and overseas companies with net assets of at least £25 million and whose shares are listed on the Stock Exchange or dealt in on the Unlisted Securities Market. Public sector entities cannot issue SCPs. Issuers can get a bank or a company meeting the net asset requirement to act as guarantor to their SCP. (b) Institutions authorised under the Bankers Act 1987, building societies authorised under the Building Societies Act 1986, insurance companies authorised under the Insurance Companies Act 1982. (c) International organisations which are exempted from the Banking Act 1987 and of which the UK is a member, and (d) overseas public sector bodies.
2. *Description:* an issue of SCP must carry two statements, namely: (a) that it is issued under the 1987 Banking Act or (Exemption Transactions) Regulations (this is to avoid issuers becoming deposit-takers); and (b) that the issue does, or does not, carry the guarantee of a bank.
3. *Disclosure:* if SCP is issued without a prospectus, then the issuer should make known to purchasers that the issuing company is in compliance with its obligations under the Listing Regulations of the Stock Exchange.
4. *Minimum Amount:* the issue must be transferable and should be issued in minimum amounts of £100,000. Previously it was £500,000, and its reduction to £100,000 will broaden the range of potential issues of SCP, as will the reduction of *assets* from £50 million to £25 million.
5. *Maturity:* SCP should have a maturity of less than five years but not less than seven days.
6. *Monitoring:* issuers should notify the Bank of England of the total amount of the SCP they propose to issue, details of the maturity, the name of guarantor if relevant, and full description of the intended uses of the funds raised and, within a short specified time after the issue, the amount of the issue that has been purchased.
7. *Management of issues:* issuers may issue SCP directly to investors, or they may use a bank as an intermediary.
8. *Interest payments:* interest on SCP can normally be paid without deduction of income tax, and the issue and transfer of SCP will be free of stamp duty.

The SCP market has not developed as quickly as was expected at its launch. There are two main reasons for this.

(a) Company treasurers are not as yet convinced that the cost of SCP issue and management is cheaper than, say, the UK bankers' acceptances, which can be easily discounted in the money market at fine rates.
(b) The monetary authorities originally put rather stringent eligibility conditions on issuers. The market has now found its feet and the eligibility requirements have been relaxed.

The Bank of England is in a strong position to limit the flow of SCP on to the market because of its stronghold in the competing market in bankers' acceptances. Due to the Bank's past policy of overfunding in the gilt-edged market, the Bank has built up a 'bill mountain' of eligible bills (see Ch.5). The bill mountain has depressed the yields on bankers' acceptances, making them particularly attractive borrowing instruments. Now the overfunding policy has been changed, but the speed with which the bill mountain is decreased will significantly affect the attraction to borrowers of the SCP market, which by the end of June 1989 amounted to just under £4 billion, and was issued by 145 UK and overseas companies.

The SCP market extends the range of financing options available to UK companies and provides a means of by-passing the banks and the conventional securities exchanges. The attraction of this form of finance is its cost: funds can be obtained at lower interest rates for smaller fees than either banks or the securities market can offer. This is another form of *disintermediation* with the banks losing on the loan front but earning more fee income. The SCP market also points to the potential advantages of disintermediation: both lenders and borrowers gain some benefit on interest rates. (See also page 196.)

The finance house market

The major finance houses have been 'recognised' by the Bank of England as 'banks', but there are many other finance houses which still operate to meet the needs of the consumer demand by offering hire purchase facilities for consumer durables. Due to the tight monetary policies during the past two decades, including a credit squeeze applying to instalment buying facilities, a major proportion of finance houses' funds has been channelled to meet the needs of business companies, largely through their three main services; viz. factoring, leasing and hire purchase.

As BFIs, the proportion of capital and reserves to borrowed funds differ widely in the balance sheets of individual finance houses. However, their liabilities side shows that the main sources of their funds are loans and deposits from the banking sector, discounted bills and deposits from business companies and individuals. Since finance houses are considered by the public as being less secure than banks and building societies, they have to offer higher rates to attract funds from corporate and personal sectors. The major asset item in their balance sheets is the provision of funds for hire purchase transactions, mainly for cars, to households and firms. It is a comparatively small secondary market. Most of the larger finance houses now form part of much larger banking groups.

The inter-company market

The development of the inter-company market (in 1969) was a device to get around severe credit restrictions during the 1960s. This market is another example of disintermediation.

It is a comparatively small parallel market, and its significance has been affected by the advent of SCP market.

Summary

The sterling 'parallel' or 'secondary' markets in London comprise, chronologically, local authority, finance house, inter-company, certificates of deposit, inter-bank and SCP. In connection with these markets as a whole, three points are of significance.

1. They do not work in isolation from each other; lenders and borrowers are interwoven.
2. They are largely uncontrolled markets; therefore any direct official control on lending and interest rates which is not uniformly applied to all financial institutions triggers off disintermediation and 'round tripping'. This upsets the validity of the monetary statistics and loosens the hold of any official restrictions imposed via monetary policy.
3. It is both valid and useful at least for the time being, to distinguish between the discount and parallel markets.

The currency certificate of deposit market

This is one of the two secondary money markets operating in London designated in currencies other than sterling; the other is the eurocurrency market. Like the sterling CDs, currency CDs may only be issued by institutions authorised to accept deposits under the Banking Act 1987 and the Building Societies Act 1986, or by the specifically 'exempt' institutions under the 1987 Act. At present currency CDs are denominated in US, Canadian and Australian dollars, yen, SDRs and ECUs. Like a sterling CD, a currency CD is an acknowledgement by a bank of a deposit in major currencies placed with it, for a specific period of time and at a fixed rate of interest. Like sterling CDs, currency CDs are negotiable and can be bought and sold easily on the currency CDs market. Main participants are discount houses, American banks, Canadian security companies, etc.

The eurocurrency market

Eurocurrency deposits are deposits taken by a bank in a currency other than that of the country where it is located (e.g. DM deposits with a bank outside Germany). The banks use these deposits to make loans on the international market. London is the most important centre for eurocurrency transactions. On the inter-bank eurocurrency market, banks borrow and lend wholesale funds on an unsecured basis from each other for periods as short as overnight or as long as five years, although most borrowing is for six months or less. Currency CDs have become the most important negotiable instrument in the eurocurrency deposit market.

Although the term 'euro' stems from the origins of these markets in Europe, the eurocurrency market is not restricted to Europe but encompasses transactions in eurocurrencies carried out in several non-European locations including the Caribbean (e.g. Nassau), the Middle East (Bahrain), and the Far East (Singapore and Hong Kong). The eurocurrency markets have become the largest international financial markets in the world and the major single centre of operations is London, that is why so many foreign banks have opened offices in London in the last 25 years. Any account of the British banking system must include a discussion of eurocurrency markets.

Reasons for the rapid growth of the eurocurrency markets

(a) Increase in international banking activity due to growth in world trade and to general internationalisation of the world economy.
(b) Large balance of payment imbalances; deficits for oil-using and surpluses for oil-producing countries. Surpluses were channelled to deficit countries via international banking (eurocurrency markets), in preference to the International Monetary Fund machinery, due to restrictions.
(c) Euromarkets have been unregulated and without costly restrictions (e.g. no reserve requirements), hence were able to offer favourable lending and borrowing terms – this factor has been at the heart of all other growth factors.

Prudential supervision of eurocurrency markets

The growth of these markets in the last three decades has led to concern with regard to their supervision and prudential control. Lack of regulation has led to serious problems, e.g. the collapse of several banks (Bankhaus Herstatt in 1974 and Banco Ambrosiano in 1982) which were active in these markets, the difficulties of certain heavily borrowed less-developed countries (due largely to no-questions-asked large-scale lending), the rapid growth in international liquidity, and the vast pool of 'hot' money in eurocurrency markets destabilising exchange rates and domestic monetary policies of several countries.

A committee of bank supervisors from ten major industrialised countries was set up in 1975. This committee agreed that national supervisory authorities are responsible for the supervision of foreign branches of their countries' banks. Foreign subsidiaries, which are separate legal entities registered abroad, are the joint responsibility of the authorities in the parent bank country and the host country. In 1983, the committee issued a revised agreement in Basle (Switzerland), indicating more specifically which supervisory authority should be responsible for risks on the basis of a bank's global operations. The Bank of England, for example, now scrutinises the global balance sheet of all UK banks. The capital adequacy for common international standards, announced in 1987, (and outlined in Ch.10) means that bank supervisors now have to assess the capital adequacy of 'internally-active' banks operating within their national boundaries.

Sources and uses of funds

A major attraction of the eurocurrency markets for participants is that both as depositors and borrowers they benefit from slightly more competitive interest rates than are available in corresponding domestic markets, reflecting lower transaction costs in eurocurrency markets. The main suppliers of funds to these markets are:

(a) *Commercial enterprises* seeking liquidity and security for currency holdings, thus avoiding the need to convert into local currencies.
(b) *Official institutions* including central banks, governments and international monetary organisations holding foreign currency reserves, at good returns, in these markets.
(c) *Commercial banks* are also a source of primary funds, investing surplus resources in the markets. However, much eurocurrency business is transacted by banks on-lending primary deposits to other banks.

The category of borrowers are broadly similar to the depositors: large multinational companies, government and government agencies. Companies borrow for normal trading purposes, for example to finance major projects overseas, or for direct portfolio investment, e.g. purchase of stocks and shares, Treasury bills. Central banks borrow on behalf of their national governments, to finance shortfalls on the current account of their balance of payments, and/or to offset outflows on their capital account.

Eurocurrency interest rates

Eurocurrency rates are prices of currencies outside the jurisdiction of their respective national central banks; the prices in euromarkets are, like all prices in near perfect markets, determined by the supply (eurocurrency deposits) and demand (eurocurrency loans) for eurocurrency funds.

The euromarket interest rates must be closely competitive with domestic interest rates, but they are not identical with domestic rates even where currencies and maturities are the same. Suppose the domestic interest rates in Germany rose above the eurodeutschemark rate in London, then the London eurodeutschemark rate will quickly rise to a competitive level to stop eurodeutschemark deposits flowing back to Germany to take advantage of the higher domestic deutschemark rates. Thus the relationship between the euro interest rates and domestic interest rates is such as to keep them both at the same level. Of course this relationship need not hold if there are exchange controls in operation preventing the free flow of currencies; consequently, in these circumstances, euro and domestic rates may differ substantially.

The following example shows the relationship between euro rates and exchange rates. Suppose the exchange rate of the deutschemark appreciated against sterling from, say £1 = DM3.75 to £1 = DM3.00. A customer of a UK bank holding deutschemark deposits might find it profitable to sell his deutschemarks and buy cheaper sterling, and invest the sterling proceeds into sterling deposits at sterling deposit rates. To prevent this happening, the bank will have to increase the interest paid on deutschemark deposits to reflect the appreciation in the exchange rate of the deutschemark against sterling.

The difference between the spot (current) and forward rates generally reflects the differences between the eurodeposit rates between two currencies. Euromarkets are borrowing and lending markets, and swap agreements between banks are frequent. Suppose Bank X has eurodeutschemark funds and Bank Y has eurodollar funds; the eurodollar rate is 6 per cent per annum, and the eurodeutschemark rate is 5.5 per cent per annum, and the exchange rate between these two eurocurrencies is $1 : DM3. A swap arrangement between X and Y would operate something like this: X buys, say, $100,000 from Y for DM300,000, and at the same time agrees to buy back DM300,000 for $100,000 after one year. Under this swap agreement X will gain 0.5 per cent and Y will lose 0.5 per cent on interest rate differentials between dollars and deutschemarks. Clealry Y will not agree to be a party to this swap agreement without some compensation for the loss of 0.5 per cent interest. However,the compensation comes from the difference between the spot and forward rates: the forward dollar spot rate will buy a premium margin of 0.5 per cent per annum. Due to the differential between spot and forward rates of the dollar, both X and Y would earn the same amount of interest as they would have done with their original currencies had they not swapped, because the swap agreement, seen from Y's viewpoint, will mean that a forward discount margin will apply to his deutschemarks. Forward margins of premium and discount are completely interwoven, and it is the difference between eurocurrency deposit rates that determine the forward discount and premium margins: the larger the euro rate differential, the bigger the forward margins of premium and discount, and vice versa. Therefore the forward exchange rate does not necessarily equal the market's expectation of where the exchange rate is going. (A fuller discussion of interest rates and exchange rates is given in Ch.6 and Ch.9, respectively.)

The Euro Commercial Paper (ECP) market

Trading in short-term fixed-interest securities issued by countries, companies and banks done in ECP market. As investors sought the relative safety of short-term markets after the share price collapse in October 1987, the ECP market had an extraordinary period of growth. It has the makings of a global, multicurrency pool of liquidity for better-quality borrowers to tap.

The capital market

Whereas the money markets provide very short-term loans, the capital market caters for medium- and long-term loans. It serves the needs of industry and commerce, government and local authorities. Private sector firms borrow their working capital (current assets *minus* current liabilities) from the money markets, which used to be mainly via commercial banks; the role of banks as middlemen even for the working capital requirements has now diminished. Private sector firms raise their fixed capital by the issue of shares or sterling commercial paper bonds. The shares and bonds are taken up by individuals, insurance companies, pension funds and unit and investment funds. Government and local authorities borrow medium- and long-term capital by issuing new gilt-edged stocks and bonds. The main market place for lending and borrowing medium- and long-term capital in the UK is the Stock Exchange in London.

The Stock Exchange

The Stock Exchange (SE), now known as the International Stock Exchange (ISE), is a centralised market on which longer-term securities are traded. The liquidity given to investors by this important secondary market increases the attraction of holding negotiable securities, making it easier for companies and others to raise money by issuing such securities. Since October 1986 there have been major changes which have affected ISE organisation (see below).

The company securities

There is a wide range of company securities traded on the ISE. These can be divided into two main categories – *share capital* securities and *loan capital* securities. Ordinary (equity) shares are the main share capital securities, although some companies also issue preference shares with fixed dividend rights. Ordinary shareholders' dividend receipts depend mainly on the profitability of the company.

Loan capital securities generally take the form of long-term bonds (debentures) carrying a fixed rate of interest. The market value of the company bonds, like other fixed interest securities, is inversely related to the movements in the general level of interest rates.

The gilt-edged securities

In terms of market trading the *gilt-edged* market is by far the largest on the ISE. It mainly covers British government and government-guaranteed stocks but also covers stocks issued by local authorities and by certain other borrowers. British government stocks may be 'short-dated' (with up to five years to run), 'medium-dated' (five to 15 years), 'long-dated' (over 15 years) or 'undated' (with no fixed redemption date).

New issues of the central government stock are made by the Bank of England on behalf of the government. Nearly all issues of the stock are made by way of public offers but they are not underwritten. Any unsubscribed stock is taken up by the Bank and subsequently sold in response to bids from market-makers in gilts. The time this process takes varies according, among other things, to market conditions. During this period the stock is referred to as the 'tap stock'.

Eurobonds

Eurobonds are primarily sold outside the capital market of the country in whose currency they are denominated (e.g. a sterling bond is sold mainly to overseas investors). London is the chief centre for the eurobond market. For technical reasons eurobonds are normally quoted on the ISE but are only rarely dealt in there. Most secondary market transactions are arranged over the telephone with banks and securities firms acting as market-makers.

Eurobonds are bearer securities. Governments, companies and other large-scale borrowers issue eurobonds as a way of raising medium- and longer-terms funds. Traditionally eurobonds were issued at fixed rates, though more recently floating rate bonds have become common.

Originally almost all eurobonds were denominated in dollars, but now many currencies are used, including the 'basket' currencies, i.e. Special Drawing Rights (SDRs) and the European Currency Unit (ECU) (see Ch.9).

The 'Big Bang'

The ISE already has the lion's share of international business: 25 per cent of the global banking market against New York Stock Exchange's 15 per cent and Tokyo Stock Exchange's 9 per cent. Trading turnover on the ISE in the eurobonds and euro-equities in London reached $2,250 billion in 1985. But the ISE loses out to both New York and Tokyo Stock Exchanges in the domestic securities market. Its total turnover in domestic securities in 1985 was £53 billion, compared to £272 billion and £670 billion on the Tokyo and New York Stock Exchanges respectively.

The SE members were constrained in their ability to compete in the increasingly international capital markets by three main requirements under the ISE rules: (a) the fixed minimum commission scales for the brokers restrained member firms' competition with one another, and with dealers in securities markets outside the London ISE; (b) the single capacity system prevented the development of flexible methods of doing business; and (c) the ownership rules, by preventing ISE firms from becoming part of wider grouping and limiting their access to outside capital, prevented ISE firms from developing new types of capital-intensive activities.

Technological innovation made distance unimportant and the leading financial markets became more closely integrated and competitive. Investors, particularly institutions, are beginning to look for an international spread of investments in liquid and efficient markets. The internationalisation of savings flows reflects the removal of exchange controls in the UK in 1979.

On 27 October 1986, the ISE abolished its minimum commission scales, permitted 100 per cent ownership of a member firm by a single non-member and dual capacity trading systems were introduced in the gilt-edged and equity markets.

The 'Big Bang' is a colloquial term for the lifting of many prohibitions and restraints from, and the large-scale restructuring of, the *entire* securities industry. In short, the Big

Bang is the deregulation of financial institutions connected with the UK securities industry, which acted as a trigger, not only for reshaping the structure of the SE, but also for a massive spate of takeovers and mergers, involving British clearing banks and merchant banks, stockbrokers and jobbers, foreign commercial banks and other non-bank financial companies.

This shake-up has created a new set of operators, centring on the *market-makers* who must quote, and deal in, their list of shares at all times. The lowest dealing prices are continuously quoted on the ISE wide screen through the Stock Exchange Automated Quotation system (SEAQ). It is hoped that this system will create a competitive and open market, with best terms available for all.

In the gilt-edged market there are now specialist institutions such as the Gilt-Edged Market Makers (GEMMs), who have replaced the 'old' jobbers, Inter-Dealer Brokers (IDBs), who deal only with GEMMs, acting as intermediaries assisting GEMMs to adjust their positions in gilt stocks, and Stock Exchange Money Brokers (SEMBs), who enable the various participants to balance their books by lending and borrowing stock and cash between GEMMs, major financial institutions and the discount houses. GEMMs, usually subsidiary companies of major financial groups, have various privileges: for example they enjoy the 'last resort' borrowing facilities from the Bank of England, and the deposits of commercial banks with them are considered highly liquid. GEMMs have largely eroded the 'unique' position of discount houses. GEMMs are important to the Bank in its gilt-edged stock selling activities; that is why it monitors their capital adequacy and risk positions.

The 'Big Bang' in the UK was a link in the chain of international deregulation, which was the general ending of controls over international capital flows and which has led to the globalisation of financial services which, in turn, has motivated large financial institutions to innovate and provide the new types of financial products for which demand has emerged in the international financial markets. These innovative products have introduced new concepts, such as *securitisation* (large-scale *direct* borrowing and lending by companies). Banks and other financial institutions are fast becoming brokers and guarantors of the securitised assets, and thereby in large-scale off-balance sheet business, which leaves them with surplus liquidity for traditional lending to the personal sector, say, for house loans and consumer spending.

It could be argued that the chain reaction caused by the national and international 'Big Bang', has dissolved differences between the wholesale money markets and the capital markets in the UK: many large financial groups, through subsidiaries, operate in both markets. However, the basic distinction between the two is still valid: the capital markets are for longer-term finance; and the wholesale money markets for short-term finance.

In the highly competitive and fluid environment both the risks and scope for conflict of interest will be increased, reinforcing the need to strengthen market regulation and *investor protection*. Since functions ranging from market-making to investment management and share recommendation will be under one conglomerate, conflicts of interest do exist.

To prevent such risks of insider-trading there are self-imposed 'Chinese walls', the City's five Self-Regulating Organisations (SROs), and on top of the SROs is the Securities and Investment Board (SIB). A Chinese wall is the code intended to prevent corporate finance departments in the new conglomerates passing on confidential, price-sensitive information about their client companies to market-makers in the same group who could profit from dealing in the shares. SROs are specific to functions and will provide the day-to-day supervision of the specialised financial institutions. The SIB authorises and regulates investment activities directly or through SROs. It has the power to authorise financial groups to carry out investment business, and to prosecute those who are suspected of carrying out investment business without proper authorisation.

Financial Services Act 1986

This Act is a concomitant of the deregulation of the SE. By establishing the SROs and SIB with professional members, it provides a system of regulation that is firmly based in statute, but which is essentially run by practitioners. A practitioner-run strong legal system, it is claimed, will be more flexible and will be able to identify malpractice more easily.

The Act is broad in *scope* and covers many aspects of the financial services industry. It has three basic objectives: (1) financial services should be provided in the most efficient and economic way; (2) the financial services industry must be competitive both domestically and internationally; and (3) rules and regulations must be responsive to international developments and not a cover for protectionism.

The Act *covers*: (a) all activities related to shares, debentures, options, gilts, unit trusts, long-term insurance contracts and futures; and (b) firms or sole traders who transact business in investment or who manage or give investment advice. It does *not* cover: (i) banking, which is covered under the Banking Act 1987; (ii) building societies, which have their own Act widening their powers; and (iii) insurance companies (except for selling life insurance contracts), which will continue to be supervised by the Department of Trade and Industry.

The approach to investor protection may not be effective where the parent of a conglomerate is a foreign securities firm outside UK jurisdiction. Therefore workable relationships are being established between the securities market regulations of different countries. The SE has reached an agreement in principle with the International Securities Regulatory Organisation (ISRO) representing international banks and securities houses in London, which may lead to a single regulatory organisation and single Recognised Investment Exchange (RIE) to serve both ISE members and ISRO members. (See Ch. 10.)

The response of banks in London to the challenge of 'Big Bang'

The challenge

The essence of a *global* securities and investment market is the removal of national boundaries between national markets, products, customers and delivery systems. Surplus funds of companies and wealthy individuals no longer stay in demand deposits but rather in money market funds or investment securities which can be held for short periods due to international secondary trading markets.

The stakes in the internationalised securities and investment market are high: business is likely to gravitate towards the financial centres offering the lowest transaction costs, the most liquid markets, the widest range of financial instruments and services, and the surest settlement and communication system. Over the 1990s banks will face three major challenges:

1. *The capital challenge.* Banks will need large amounts of capital to (a) finance new product development; (b) finance growth; (c) meet costs of involvement in capital market activities; and (d) strengthen capital ratios.
2. *The technology challenge.* During the 1980s the proportion of technology expense to total operating expenses has more than doubled and it is likely to account for an even higher proportion over the 1990s. Among the most profitable banks in the 1990s will be those capable of delivering products and services at the lowest effective cost.

3. *The culture challenge.* This is the toughest challenge, because it means a change in the way banks do business – banks are becoming businesses rather than institutions – which means developing a more market-driven culture without losing the reliability and meticulous attention to detail. Top bank managements are faced with the twin challenge of managing the basics of the business of banking, particularly profitability and balance sheet strength, and, at the same time, restructuring the business to manage the sea-change in the deregulated financial services market.

The response

Deregulation, which started as a trickle, has quickly turned into a flood. All kinds of new competing financial institutions have entered the market, and the lines between their activities have become increasingly blurred; so much so that it is becoming harder and harder to define a bank. Banks in the UK have responded eagerly to the challenge and opportunity to enter the new securities and investment market in London. Among the contenders there are various distinct groups: the 'Big Four' clearers, who are seeking to emulate the 'universal banks' of the continent; the London merchant banks, who are aiming to develop their capital market connections; a number of continental banks, who are building up their presence in the City; and a selected number of American commercial banks, who are building a global investment capacity.

To some extent the motivation behind the banks' response is defensive. Corporate lending is sluggish; major companies can now borrow more cheaply than the banks themselves. So it makes sense for the banks to move more deeply into the securities business. Given the riskier environment into which banks are moving, appropriately the Bank of England has begun to keep a closer eye on their activities.

(a) **The Big Four clearing banks.** Although the Big Bang is essentially about deregulating the Stock Exchange, it raises major strategic questions for the banks as they adjust to an era when financing through securities markets is becoming more popular than finance in the form of bank loans and overdrafts, and the banks' role as providers of credit has diminished.

The clearers have finalised their new investment banking operations – all of them substantial and capitalised to the tune of several hundred million pounds. In the case of Barclays, National Westminster and Midland Banks, these have been constructed round acquired stockbroking and jobbing firms. Barclays Bank have acquired de Zoete & Bevan and Wedd Durlacher Mordaunt to create *Barclays de Zoete Wedd*. Midland Bank have acquired S. Montagu, Greenwell and Smith Keen Cutler to form *Greenwell Montagu*. National Westminster Bank have acquired County Bank, Fielding Newson-Smith and Bisgood Bishop to constitute *County Securities*. Lloyds Bank have, in order to cut costs, developed such a business internally and have produced *Lloyds Bank Stockbrokers*. The two 'casualties' of the Big Bang among the clearers have been Greenwell Montagu; they have withdrawn, due to unacceptable losses, as market-makers in equities and Lloyds Bank have ceased to be market-makers in gilts.

The investment banking operations of all four clearers are broadly similar: they combine securities issuing and trading with corporate finance, asset management and stockbroking services. Three clearers are primary dealers in the gilt-edged market.

The clearers are well equipped to become the major suppliers of investment services in Britain's high streets. But the move into the securities market poses several managerial and cultural problems for them. The clearing banks are unionised, bureaucratic and slow-moving, very different from the hire-and-fire, payments-by-results attitude of the ISE firms.

(b) **The merchant banks.** Although the new investment banking operations of the clearers are *really* new to them and will test their mettle, the merchant banks, on the other hand, are probably mentally better equipped to cope with the ISE changes. For the UK merchant banks, the move into the securities markets will pose a much less extreme culture clash. But they lack the great capital resources of the clearers. To go seriously into the securities market, they have had to raise large new sums in capital and to increase their managerial staff considerably. Several of the merchant banking groups may feel that they need to tie up with clearing banks in order to gain the financial and personnel resources to compete in the global securities markets.

(c) **The foreign banks.** With the deregulated ISE, the City is destined to play a leading role in the world-wide market in serucities and other financial investments, as it already does in the field of international banking. And this can only enhance further its attraction to foreign banks as a base for their international activities. At present the City has a bigger representation of foreign banks than any other international centre. And, in spite of the cost of running a London operation and efforts by other centres to pull in international banking, London is likely to remain a dominant force. The *attractiveness* of London for foreign banks, in *this* context, is for three main reasons: (i) London is in a time zone conveniently overlapping New York and the Far East; (ii) English is the language of international banking; (iii) London has a pool of experienced talent, both in dealing in financial instruments and in producing new ideas in financing techniques.

The Bank of England has, however, made it clear to foreign banks operating in London that they will be expected to adhere to UK standards, whatever the situation may be on their own domestic markets.

(d) **The discount houses.** It is possible that their privileged position as the buffer between the Bank of England and the rest of the banking system may be affected by the Big Bang, which is reshaping other financial institutions.

The eight discount houses – only four of which are independent institutions – have been looking at new businesses themselves, e.g. commodities broking, leasing, insurance, money broking and gilt dealing.

The other four discount houses which have been taken over by larger institutions (three of them foreign), are all being used by their parents as the short-term money market dealing arms of much larger capital market operations.

Summary

1. *Deregulation* of the UK financial services industry has removed the barriers to foreign competition in domestic markets and to the ability of borrowers and investors to participate in foreign markets. In other words it has led to the 'globalisation' of financial services markets.
2. The *Big Bang* has allowed the formation of commercial banking groups which, through their major investment subsidiaries, have entered into non-traditional areas such as mortgage finance, estate agency, insurance broking, unit trusts, and so on. On the other hand, building societies are now themselves allowed into banking operations, such as unsecured consumer credit and other financial services. Thus the roles of BFIs and NBFIs are being further blurred. However, although individual FIs do now have a wider range of financial services, it is still important to maintain a reasonably clear conceptual difference between the various activities.
3. At the company level, the trend towards '*securitisation*' – replacement of bank loans

by marketable securities – is on the increase. The sterling commercial paper provides a recent domestic example of securitisation. Soon mortgage-backed securities will be on offer in the UK.

4. *Disintermediation* is replacing intermediation (typically by a bank), as borrowers and lenders find that the traditional advantages of intermediation are being overcome by the greater availability of information and increased liquidity; some investors see large companies as being no more risky than a bank. The banks are now increasingly acting as guarantors of debts, and since such transactions are off-balance-sheet they incur reduced capital/liquidity costs. Their fee income is ''increasing but interest earnings are declining.
5. The *jurisdiction* of commercial banking remains the province of the Bank of England. The overriding aim of banking supervision, under the 1987 Banking Act, is the protection of bank depositors. Building societies will continue to have their own regulatory framework under the Building Societies Act 1986, which has widened their powers. Investment business will be subject to the Financial Services Act 1986 and its SROs will be overseen by the SIB whose powers will derive from the Secretary of State for Trade and Industry. However, the trend towards financial service conglomerates means that supervision will overlap: banks and building societies wishing to do investment business will have to register with one or more of the SROs.

Insurance and commodities markets

A variety of other financial markets are to be found in the City. The **Lloyd's insurance market** and the **commodity markets** are very important organised financial markets. Members of Lloyd's are individuals who group together into syndicates to underwrite (insure) various risks. Each syndicate is managed by an underwriting agent who deals with brokers wishing to place business on the Lloyd's market. On commodity markets a large number of commodities are traded for spot (immediate) or future delivery. These markets assist businessmen to make sure of future supplies of raw materials they require.

The financial futures

A *financial futures contract* is an agreement to buy or sell a standard quantity of a specific financial instrument (e.g. a bond or a currency) at a future date, at a price agreed between the parties. The London International Financial Futures Exchange (LIFFE) operates the financial futures market in London.

There are seven contracts traded on LIFFE. Three of them are related to movements in interest rates, the other four cover specific currency movements against the dollar, namely sterling, deutschemarks, yen and Swiss francs.

The main role of LIFFE is to allow people to *hedge* against movements in interest and exchange rates. It enables people to look into known exchange rates or interest rates for transactions which they know they have to undertake later. The delivery period to which contracts relate can be up to 15 months. Members of LIFFE include banks, stockbroker-dealers, and money brokers. Apart from hedging, LIFFE can be used for *speculative* purposes.

The foreign exchange

London is an important foreign exchange market. In a foreign exchange market one currency can be bought and sold in terms of another currency. The organised foreign exchange market in London is almost exclusively a market between banks. The foreign exchange markets in other major centres throughout the world are in close contact with each other through very fast means of communications, which means that the *arbitrage* operations (profiting from the inconsistencies between exchange rates) are quite common (see Ch.9).

Instruments used in the money markets

The instruments used in the bill market include 'bills', which are short-term securities issued by borrowers (government – Treasury bills, companies – commercial bills, local authorities – local authority bills) to obtain short-term finance. The lenders (bill holders) keep the bills as 'near' money assets.

Treasury bills are issued by the Bank of England on behalf of the government in *amounts* ranging from £5,000 to £1 million (the minimum *tender* is £50,000), usually for a period of 91 days. There is no interest on Treasury bills and therefore these are issued below par and repaid at par; the capital gain is in lieu of interest rate. The discount houses agree to cover the entire weekly issue; the sale proceeds provide the short-term funds needed by the central government.

Commercial bills become eligible bills for discount in the bill market and for re-discount at the Bank of England when accepted by an eligible bank – mainly the UK commercial banks and the larger overseas banks. 'Accepting' literally means guaranteeing for a fee that the bill will be paid at maturity. Bills of exchange accepted by banks are called 'bank bills' and are easily marketable before maturity at the 'finest' rates, i.e. the person selling or discounting a bank bill receives a higher price for it.

Local authority bills are 'receipts' issued by the borrowing local authority needing funds in advance of its yearly community charge inflow. To obtain large sums quickly, from seven days to a year, the local authorities operate through bill brokers and merchant banks. These bills are quickly marketable. Discount houses play an important part in making local authority bills liquid. (The above three instruments are used in the Bank of England's open market operations: OMOs.)

Sterling Commercial Paper (SCP) is a short-term fixed interest security, issued by the UK and overseas commercial companies. It can be resold on the SCP market. The term of the SCP is between seven days and five years.

Certificates of Deposit (CDs) are bearer certificates stating that a certain amount in sterling (or certain other currencies) has been placed with a particular bank for a given period and at a particular rate of interest. The CD is a negotiable instrument and can be resold in the secondary CDs market. The term of the deposit is between three months and five years.

Certificates of Tax Deposit (CTDs). A CTD is issued by the Inland Revenue acknowledging that money has been placed with it as an advance payment of a tax liability. The minimum purchase is £5,000 and it cannot be redeemed against PAYE liabilities. Therefore CTDs are most commonly used by companies with corporation tax liabilities. CTDs earn interest until applied to tax payments. Their issue smooths out the inflows of corporation tax receipts. In recent years they became significant instruments of financing the Public Sector Borrowing Requirement (PSBR).

Gilt-edged Securities are British government fixed-interest securities of varying periods of maturity. Like all fixed-interest securities, their market value is inversely related to the movements in the general level of interest rates. They are easily negotiable on the gilt-edged market.

Stocks and Bonds are longer-term fixed-interest securities issued by local authorities and private sector companies. Company bonds can be bought and sold on the International Stock Exchange.

Equities are ordinary shares which give the holders the residual ownership of the assets and earnings of a company. They have no fixed rate of return, and can be bought and sold on the International Stock Exchange.

Eurobonds are issued in various capital markets and in different currencies to raise long-term funds.

Euro Commercial Paper (ECP) is a short-term fixed-interest security.

Euronotes shorter-term finance is raised through the issue of these notes which are underwritten by banks.

Eurocurrencies are held in deposit by banks outside the countries from which the currencies originate.

The role of the Bank of England in the financial markets

The role of the Bank is three-fold and ensures that:

(a) the liquidity of the banking system is in balance;
(b) the short-term interest rates are in line with the monetary policy stance; and
(c) the National Debt is so managed as to achieve certain specific monetary objectives.

Government transactions with the rest of the economy usually total several hundred million pounds in each direction each day. A net flow of funds *from* the government to the banks is reflected in the accumulation of operational deposits of the clearing banks at the Bank; a net flow from the banks *to* the government results in a drain on them. Through its open market operations (OMOs) in the money markets (buying and selling eligible commercial and Treasury bills) conducted mainly through the discount houses as intermediaries, the Bank offsets shortage or surplus of liquidity caused by these flows.

The Bank can use its OMO not only to relieve the liquidity shortage or surplus in the markets, but also to influence the levels of short-term interest rates.

If the amount of eligible bills the Bank sells exceeds the amount required to offset the liquidity surplus, money supply will decrease. If the amount of bills it buys exceeds the amount required to offset the liquidity shortage, money supply will increase.

If the Bank offsets the liquidity shortage (or surplus) at its bill dealing rates which are higher or lower than the current level of short-term market interest rates, it will result in raising or lowering the marginal cost of funds to the banking system which, in turn, will raise or lower the level of short-term money market rates.

The National Debt is the total of outstanding debt of the central government. It can be divided into marketable debt (e.g. gilt-edged securities) and non-marketing debt (e.g. National Savings Certificates). The Bank, as the manager of the National Debt, aims in its debt management to achieve three main objectives:

(a) to influence the level of money supply and the structure of interest rates in line with the current monetary policy;
(b) to ensure a stable market for government debt; and
(c) to minimise the interest costs of the debt.

1. The marketable debt is of great importance to almost all financial institutions: it provides an excellent balance between safety, liquidity and yield (rate of return). If the non-bank public purchase it by drawing on their bank and building society deposits, then there will be no increase in money supply (see Ch.5). But it is not always possible to sell the entire marketable stock to the non-bank public when the existing debt matures and/or the government needs additional borrowing. When the demand is weak, the Issue Department of the Bank can take up the unsold stock and, at a later date, when demand is strong, offer it to the market at acceptable prices.
2. If demand for government securities is to remain stable, fluctuations in the gilt market need to be moderated. In the past, the Bank used to enter the market directly to buy large quantities of gilt stock to keep the market prices and the yields on government stocks fairly steady. However, the purchase of large amounts of government bonds, although it stabilised the yields, increased money supply; thus the control of money supply was sacrificed to stabilise interest rates. This debt management technique as a normal practice was given up in the early 1970s. The authorities are now willing to accept more fluctuations in interest rates – though reserving the right to intervene in the market if the market falls too much – to emphasise that the control of money supply has been the prime target of monetary policy. However, more recently the control of the money supply as a prime target of monetary policy seems to have lost its emphasis.
3. In refinancing the maturing debt, the Bank does not wait until the stocks reach final maturity date; instead it buys stocks when they come on the market any time within the year to final redemption – this avoids large refinancing problems and the consequent disturbance in the gilt market. The new stock is taken up by the Issue Department of the Bank and then fed to the market as conditions permit. This technique is known as the 'tap' issue of the stocks, and avoids depressing the gilt market by the sale of large amounts of gilts immediately. As a rule, the Bank attempts to refinance the maturing stocks and Treasury bills by long-term debt (the process is known as 'funding') to reduce the frequency of debt refinancing.

Variations in government revenue and expenditure directly determine the size of the *budget deficit*. The budget deficit determines the level of the government's borrowing requirements. If the Bank directly sold *more* gilt-edged stocks than warranted by the budget deficit (along with deliberate increased sales of National Savings securities) to the non-bank, non-building society public, then bank and building society lending would be depressed – and so would the money supply – for longer periods.

The Bank can order commercial banks to place with it non-operational, but interest-bearing, *special deposits*, with a view to mop up surplus liquidity in the market. It can release the accumulated special deposits to the banks to offset an expected shortage of liquidity in the banking system.

In order to depress consumer spending and to improve the balance of payments, the Bank can impose *qualitative lending controls* on the banks, which would restrict lending to personal customers and property companies but would encourage lending to manufacturing and exporting businesses.

Recent examination questions

The following questions have been asked in the recent exam question papers. After you have read and *understood* this chapter, you should be able to answer them. Try first to answer these questions in point form, before checking your points with the outline answers given below.

Question 1

To what extent is it now valid or useful to distinguish between the discount and parallel markets in London?

Question 2

Assess the role of the so-called 'parallel' sterling London money markets in the present-day UK financial system.

Question 3

Discuss the significance of the following in the UK financial system:

(a) the inter-bank market;
(b) commercial (eligible) bank bills;
(c) the Stock Exchange, including reference to the changes introduced by 'Big Bang'.

Question 4

(a) Describe in detail the way in which the Bank of England currently seeks to influence rates in the money markets.
(b) To what extent do the Bank's operations influence changes in commercial banks' base rates?

Question 5

What factors have contributed to the rapid growth of the eurocurrency markets in recent years? To what extent has this growth been a cause of concern to the world's monetary authorities?

Question 6

What is a eurodollar? Why are changes in eurodollar interest rates of importance to the foreign exchange markets?

Question 7

For what reasons are rates of interest paid on deposits in the euromarkets usually higher than comparable rates paid on domestic deposits? How far does this factor explain the rapid growth in the euromarkets?

Outline answers

Answer 1

- Briefly describe the role of the two markets, highlighting the essential differences (lending in the discount market is secured) and similarities (both deal in wholesale short-term funds) in their present-day function.
- Show that it is both valid and useful, *at least for the time being*, to distinguish between them by explaining the following exclusive aspects of the discount market:
  (i) Through it the Bank provides its 'lender of last resort' facility.
  (ii) The Bank's daily operations through it influence the short-term interest rates and offset the net financial flows between the government and the banking system.
  (iii) It provides the vital buffer between the Bank and the commercial banks.
  (iv) It underwrites the weekly Treasury bill tender.
  (v) It maintains the secondary market in bank CDs, and is prominent in the short-dated gilt-edged market.
- Point to changes in recent years affecting the special position of the discount market:
  (i) Blurring of traditional boundaries between it and the parallel markets.
  (ii) Its significance as a market where banks adjusted their liquidity, which to a large extent is now replaced by the inter-bank and CDs markets.
  (iii) The deregulation of financial institutions could soon remove its exclusive position as the buffer between the Bank and the banking system.

Answer 2

- Parallel sterling London money markets are specialised short-term money markets. Discount market and eurocurrency market are *not* included.
- Chronological order: local authority, finance house, inter-company deposits, inter-bank and CDs, sterling commercial paper.
- In order of size: inter-bank first.
- These markets provide:
  (i) liquid assets for participants – banks (including clearers and accepting houses), local authorities, building societies and companies (companies are able to buy and sell CD);
  (ii) profitable lending opportunities for participants;
  (iii) LIBOR (London Inter-Bank Offered Rate) plays a significant role in the inter-bank market in:
    (a) determining the cost of market-related borrowing by the banks' customers,
    (b) calculating the internal cost of funds charged to banks' branches by their head office, and
    (c) determining the level of base rates.
- Parallel money markets play no direct role in the Bank of England's implementation of monetary policy.

Answer 3

(a) *The inter-bank market*

- It provides commercial banks with the opportunity to lend and borrow *wholesale* funds, short-term and unsecured.

- It's significant as a market which allows *day-to-day liquidity positions to be adjusted* – enabling banks' surplus funds to be employed profitably, and marginal funds to support additional business to be raised.
- The interest rate in this market is LIBOR, which is important as a determinant of base rates. Many commercial loans are directly linked to LIBOR.

(b) *Eligible bank bills market*

- EBBs are commercial bills which have been accepted by eligible banks.
- Bank of England deals mainly in EBBs in its OMOs to influence short-term interest rates. Such dealings are normally in Bands 1 and 2 of the form band structure.
- If there is a cash shortage in the market, the Bank will provide relief by purchasing EBBs from the discount houses at rates which are consistent with interest rate policy.

(c) *The International Stock Exchange*

- It constitutes the capital market where long-term securities can be traded.
- It enhances the attraction of the primary market, enabling companies to raise equity and long-term loan funds.
- 'Big Bang' deregulated the securities industry – it abolished minimum commissions, replaced jobbers and brokers by dual capacity, removed barriers to the entry of banks and overseas investment houses.

Answer 4

(a)
- The Bank of England, dealing *predominantly* through eligible *commercial bills*, influences the short-term interest rates (basically seven-day rates), leaving longer-term rates to be determined by the market forces.
- The Bank also deals in Treasury bills and local authority bills.
- If a net shortage of cash seems likely, due to the net flow *from* the banks to the government, the Bank will undertake to offset the shortage by buying eligible commercial bills from the discount houses.
- Discount houses offer bills to the Bank at their own prices; if the short-term interest rates implied by these prices are compatible with the Bank's interest rate objective, it will accept the discount houses' offer prices. If not, the discount houses are forced to make new offers which are consistent with the monetary policy on interest rates.
- The bill market operations of the Bank (OMOs) are conducted in maturity Band 1 (up to 14 days to maturity) and Band 2 (15–33 days to maturity). If there is a scarcity of short-dated bills, the Bank may provide funds to the banks by the sale and repurchase of longer-term bills.

(b)
- Commercial banks' base rates follow the trend of *all* money market rates (particularly the LIBOR) because they determine the marginal cost of a large proportion of their funds.
- But the base rates do not automatically respond to sharp day-to-day movements in the money market rates.
- If the market rates are higher than the banks' base rates, 'roundtripping' or arbitrage could occur and harm banks' profitability.
- Roundtripping is a process whereby large bank customers borrow from their banks at base rate plus one, and on-lend the borrowed funds at higher rates in the money markets.
- The Bank also undertakes *direct intervention* in the market, to relieve the liquidity shortage and also to influence short-term rates by lending directly to the discount houses (no buying and selling of eligible bills is involved) and to banks via sale and repurchase of gilts at fixed rates and for fixed periods.

Answer 5

Reasons for the rapid expansion of international banking in euromarkets are: increase in international banking activity due to growth in world trade and to general internationalisation of the world economy; large balance of payments imbalances – surpluses channelled to deficit countries via international banking (in preference to IMF machinery, due to restrictions); euromarkets are unregulated and without costly restrictions (no reserve requirements, etc.), hence can offer favourable lending and borrowing terms. Growth in euromarkets has slowed dramatically due to world recession and heavy indebtedness of Less Developed Countries. Lack of regulation of euromarkets has led to problems, e.g. the extent of mismatching of lending and borrowing, capital inadequacy, etc.

Rapid growth in euromarkets leads to rapid growth in international liquidity, hence the concern about the possible inflationary effects.

A vast pool of 'hot' money in euromarkets potentially destabilises both exchange rates and domestic monetary policies.

Note: The main point is the lack of restriction, which has been at the heart of all these other growth factors. This is now changing.

Answer 6

A eurodollar is a dollar deposit held by a US or a non-US resident with a bank outside the USA, so long as the deposit escapes the 'jurisdiction' of the Federal Reserve Bank of New York.

Importance of changes in eurodollar interest rates: *ceteris paribus.*

(i) An increase in rates will put upward pressure on the spot dollar exchange rate (because relative international interest rates are a key determinant of exchange rate movements).

(ii) An increase will widen the forward discount, or narrow the premium, on the dollar exchange rate, and a decrease the reverse.

Answer 7

The technical reasons for higher intrest rates paid:

(i) the eurocurrency market is unregulated;

(ii) the absence of reserve and liquidity requirements lowers the effective costs of these deposits and enables the international banking system to offer higher returns;

(iii) the existence of exchange controls or regulated domestic banking systems often prevents the free flow of deposits from the domestic market to the euromarket.

Higher deposit rates and lower lending rates (because of the absence of the cost of reserve and liquidity requirements) are the two major determinants of the level of the eurocurrency rates, and therefore the major explanation of the rapid growth of euromarkets.

A tutor's answer

An essential element of the MFS syllabus is the relationship between domestic interest rates, eurocurrency market interest rates and the exchange rate. The following question seeks to test your understanding of this relationship. Prepare a brief outline plan for your answer, and then write according to the plan so that you answer the question, the whole question and nothing but the question.

Question

Examine the relationship between rates of interest for a currency in the domestic money markets and the euromarkets. Other things being equal, what effect would a change in domestic interest rates have on:
(a) the spot foreign exchange rate, and
(b) the forward exchange rate?

Answer plan:
1. The close link between the two markets.
2. Euromarkets enjoy a marginal cost advantage.
3. Relative interest rate levels determine exchange rate movements.
4. Interest rate differentials and the forward premiums/discount on currencies.
5. Forward cover cost equalises the interest rate differentials.

Specimen answer

If there are no exchange controls, then there is no fundamental difference – apart from location – between currencies in domestic money markets and the euromarkets. The two markets are closely linked, and interest rates in the eurocurrency markets will closely follow the trends in national rates.

However, euromarkets possess a marginal cost advantage over the domestic markets. The absence of compliance costs of reserve asset and liquidity requirements, plus the economies of large scale associated with purely wholesale transactions, mean that for any given loan maturity, prevailing eurocurrency rates will be slightly lower for borrower and slightly higher for depositors than will be the case in domestic markets.

(a) Changes in domestic rates will influence the exchange rate, because relative interest rate levels are a major determinant of exchange rate movements. Therefore, other things being equal, an increase in domestic rates would exert an upward pressure on the country's current, or spot, exchange rate.
(b) The spot rate is the basis of all forward exchange rates. To ascertain the foreign forward exchange rate of a currency, the 'discount' is added to, or the 'premium' is subtracted from, its spot rate.

The forward premium or discount generally reflects the difference in the interest rates ruling in the inter-bank market for the currencies being exchanged. Currencies with lower interest rates (the stronger currencies), say DM, normally stand at a premium against currencies with higher interest rates (the weaker currencies), say sterling. Therefore a buyer of DM, to be delivered a few months hence, will find that his sterling will buy less of DM in a few months' time than it buys today. Similarly, if his stronger sterling (lower interest rate) will buy more of the weaker drachma (higher interest rate) in the future than it buys today, the drachma will be quoted at a discount in the foreign exchange markets.

Forward exchange rates generally reflect interest rate *differentials*; and the cost of covering forward the risk of exchange rate movement equalises the interest rate differentials, because the differentials directly determine the cost of covering forward. If this were not so, arbitrage would be triggered. Therefore if any part of the relationship between domestic interest rates and the exchange rate changes, the forward margin is automatically adjusted. Thus if a country's domestic interest rates rise, other things being equal, the forward premium on it narrows or the forward discount widens, depressing its forward exchange rate. (See Ch.6 and page 158 for fuller discussion of interest rates and exchange rates.)

A step further

Due to the deregulation of the financial institutions and markets connected with the UK securities industry, the UK financial system is in a state of flux. It is vital that you understand the reasons behind the changes and that you keep abreast of the changing scene as it develops.

In this connection, you will find the articles listed below (to which I am indebted) of especial relevance: 'Change in the Stock Exchange and regulation of the City', Bank of England *Quarterly Bulletin*, December 1985; 'Changes in the structure of financial markets: a view from London', Bank of England *Quarterly Bulletin*, March 1985; 'The City after the Big Bang' and 'The global financial village', *Banking World*, October 1986; and 'UK banking' (A *Financial Times* survey, 2 October 1986).

With regard to the euromarkets: they are the products of their time; they evolved because there was need for them and because conditions favoured their development; but their unregulated nature is cause for concern. It has led to international debt and banking problems, in which there are several distressed, overborrowed countries and distressed, overlent banks: if these problems are not resolved, either by the international banks on their own, or in partnership with the IMF – which has assumed an important intermediary role – the consequences of failure could be catastrophic.

To keep abreast of changes in this area of the MFS, you should regularly study: the Bank of England *Quarterly Bulletins*, *The Economist*, *Finance and Development*, a quarterly publication of the IMF and the World Bank, *Banking World*, The Chartered Institute of Bankers *Examiners' Reports* and *Updating Notes*. The excellent BIS publication, *A Guide to the International Monetary Systems*, will give a good understanding of the fundamentals of international liquidity and eurocurrency markets. The *Signpost* article in *Banking World* (March 1986, pp. 55–57) is worthy of careful study.

CHAPTER 5

The Money Supply

Syllabus requirements

- Money supply as an important indicator.
- Credit-creation multiplier.
- Constraints on the growth of bank deposits.
- Causes of changes in money supply, in particular:
  - (i) the Public Spending Borrowing Requirements;
  - (ii) public sector debt sales;
  - (iii) overfunding;
  - (iv) bank and building society lending to private, public and overseas sectors;
  - (v) external transactions.
- Causes of distortion in money supply.
- Interrelationship between changes in money supply and bank balance sheets.

Getting started

In Chapter 2 we saw how difficult it was to give one all-embracing definition of money, and we considered the reasons for such difficulty. We also noted that in most money-using economies, money supply, or money stock, has two types of definition: the narrow and the broad definitions.

Under the *narrow* definition, the money supply of a country is comprised solely of the means of payment, i.e. the total money available to the public for immediate spending. This money is made up of the notes and coins (the cash) in *circulation* and the sight deposits held by the public in financial institutions: it is often referred to as 'spending' money. The distribution between cash and sight deposits depends entirely on public preference and the degree to which the financial system has developed. When a sight deposit holder cashes a cheque at his bank, the amount of deposits held by the bank is reduced and the amount of cash in circulation with the public is increased. The cash in *tills of the banks* is excluded from spending money because it is not directly available to the non-bank public for spending.

The *broad* definition of money supply comprises not only the spending money at the disposal of the non-bank public, but also 'near' money assets, because these can be converted with no or little difficulty and financial penalty into spending money. For money supply control purposes, monetary authorities may use either narrow or broad money definitions or some combination of both.

The quantity of money in a country is determined both by the actions of the non-bank public (consumers and businesses), and by the decisions and actions of the commercial banks and other financial institutions, central bank and the government.

The growth rate of the money supply is an *important indicator* to the authorities of its likely impact on the monetary policies, as expressed by Fisher's Equation ($MV = PT$).

If the money supply rises too fast in relation to the volume of goods and services, inflationary pressures begin to build up in the economy. Inflation has serious consequences for the level of interest rates, savings, profits, wages and employment. On the other hand, insufficient money supply growth will adversely affect economic growth, commercial activity and employment. Thus the rate of growth of the money supply must be such as will encourage 'real' economic growth. It is for these reasons that the authorities place much emphasis on controlling the rate of growth of money supply in pursuit of their broader economic objectives (see Ch. 7) – notably economic growth and inflation.

Essential principles

Money-creation by commercial banks

Sight deposits with commercial banks (and building societies, in the UK) form a major part of the real or spending money in a country with a developed banking system. Cash, which forms a very small part of the total spending money, is provided by the central bank. If the banks and building societies could increase the volume of sight deposits, without causing a reduction in the amount of cash in circulation, they would therefore increase the quantity of spending money in the UK.

The banks and building societies are in fact able to do this, for two main reasons.

1. Sight deposit holders have full confidence in the ability of banks and societies to pay cash on demand. Therefore the public accepts payments by cheques, and other means provided by banks and societies, because it is both more convenient and safer than receiving payments in cash.
2. Whenever a bank or a society makes a loan to a customer, somewhere in the banking and building society system a deposit of equal value is created. When the banks and societies are increasing the supply of loans (their assets), their deposits (their liabilities) are also increasing by an equal amount. Not only do these loans increase the purchasing power in their own right but also, in turn, provide a base for further loans, i.e. for credit creation.

Suppose there is only one bank in a community, and the public, with absolute confidence, deposit their surplus cash in that bank. Customer A deposits £100 cash, which is surplus to his immediate spending needs, with the bank, which credits A's account. The bank's liabilities (A's deposit) and assets (£100 in the till) have increased by the same amount. Let us assume that the bank, as a matter of policy, keeps 10 per cent of all deposits in cash or near cash assets to meet customers' withdrawals of cash. The bank can on-lend £90 from A's £100 deposit to, say, customer B. The bank then credits B's current account and debits B's loan account with £90; once again the bank's liabilities and assets have increased by the same amount. Most probably, B has borrowed £90 to repay a debt for purchasing goods or services, say, from C. C accepts B's cheque for £90 with confidence, and deposits it in his account at the bank. The bank's liabilities and assets are not affected by this transaction, because the credit of £90 is now in C's account and the debt of £90 is still in B's loan account. The bank is now able to advance £81 (£90 less 10 per cent liquidity cushion) to, say customer D.

The process of receiving deposits, on-lending them (less 10 per cent) and creating more deposits can continue until the total amount of deposits, or spending money (low-powered money), created by the bank on the basis of A's £100 cash deposit (high-powered money) reaches £1,000; i.e. the bank has increased the narrow money supply by a multiplier of 10.

The *credit-creation multiplier* measures the amount of new deposits created from the original deposit. It can be measured by the following formula:

$$\frac{\text{Total value of new deposits created (say, £1,000)}}{\text{Total value of original deposit (say, £100)}}$$

The fact that in real life there are several banks (and building societies) does not invalidate the credit-creation principle. Although the assets and liabilities of the *individual banks* connected with the process of the above £1,000 credit-creation may increase by larger or smaller amounts, the liabilities and assets of the *banking system as a whole* will increase by £1,000.

When in response to a greater demand for cash by the public the central bank issues, via commercial banks, an additional supply of cash (high-powered money), most of the additional cash will 'seep' back into bank and building society deposits, enabling them to start the credit-creation process. For example, a bank may increase its deposits by buying securities from an individual or firm or by buying government securities; in each case the bank increases the deposits of the vendors *and* its own liabilities by the same amount. Note that the banks and building societies' liabilities, in the shape of deposits, constitute money.

Can banks create money indefinitely?

The credit-creation process is triggered when there is an injection of 'high-powered' funds from the monetary authorities into banks and building societies. The banks and building societies receive high-powered money deposits when the authorities borrow from them to finance the government's borrowing requirements, the redemption of maturing government stock held by the non-bank and non-building society sector, and the return of special deposits held by the Bank of England, to the banks.

Assuming that an injection of high-powered money has increased the deposits of banks and building societies, their power to create credit in terms of low-powered funds is limited due to the following considerations.

Cash leakages

Internal

Suppose, in the above example, B needs some cash, and therefore deposits, not £90, but £80. This will reduce the bank's ability to create credit, as will a purchase of government securities by B.

External

If there are no foreign exchange restrictions, then bank customers can transfer funds overseas, perhaps to earn a higher rate of return. Such transfers of funds overseas reduce the credit-creation multiplier.

Customer demand for loans

If the economy has been suffering a long period of recession, then the level of business profits will be low and the level of unemployment high. Consequently, the demand for loans by the corporate and personal sectors would be low. Banks and building societies are seriously hampered in credit-creation if the non-bank non-building society public *do not want to borrow*. They could lower interest rates charged to borrowers and attempt to attract demand for loans. Other things being equal, a decrease in interest rates extends the demand for loans by the non-bank non-building society public, especially by business firms, because lower borrowing costs increase their profitability. Conversely, an increase in interest rates contracts demand for loans by firms and households; they will defer such purchases as can be deferred until borrowing costs come down.

Self-imposed constraints

Banks and building societies will not knowingly risk their depositors' funds or their own surplus resources if there is a likelihood that the loan they give may become a bad debt. They may not lend, especially in times of economic recession, to firms which are on the verge of bankruptcy. Therefore credit-creation may not take place to the extent that the demand for loans at the prevailing interest-rate would allow.

Liquidity cushion

To maintain the confidence of the non-bank non-building society public in their ability to pay on demand, and to avoid a 'run' on themselves, prudent banks and building societies keep a cash-reserve-to-deposit ratio in cash and near-cash assets. They must keep a proportion of their assets in liquid (cash in tills) and near liquid (CDs, short-dated gilts, Treasury bills) form. The higher this liquidity ratio, the smaller the credit-creation multiplier. In addition to a self-applied prudential liquidity ratio, the central bank may impose on the commercial banks' liquidity its own prudential requirements, e.g. they may be obliged to maintain a *specific* reserve-to-deposit ratio in liquid or near-liquid form. Such official constraints on the banks' liquidity would curb their ability to create credit. Banks in the UK are required to maintain 0.45 per cent of their deposit liabilities with the Bank of England.

Government policy

Money supply in developed economies is ultimately under the control of the monetary authorities. If the authorities fear that the credit-creation is exceeding the desirable level, they may restrict the ability of the banks and building societies to lend. This may be done by asking banks and building societies for some form of deposit at the central bank that will reduce their ability, and indeed desire, to lend, or it may be done by direct instruction.

Profitability versus safety

Commercial banks are business organisations. They market financial services to make a profit, from which to meet their running and capital costs and to distribute dividends to their shareholders. Like most other commercial enterprises, they usually aim to maximise profits. In theory, maximising profits requires that they should on-lend all the deposits they take at the highest rate possible; this might mean lending to the riskiest borrower for the longest period of time! However, in practice, banks cannot neglect the safety of their deposits. Sound banking demands a fine balance, which *both* maximises safety for their depositors' funds and maximises dividends for their shareholders. Banks solve the dilemma of safety versus profitability by maintaining a prudent liquidity cushion in the form of cash in tills, operational deposits with the central bank, loans to money markets on a call or short notice basis, first-class commercial bills, government short-dated bills and CDs issued by other banks and building societies. After the liquidity cushion portfolio is satisfactorily constructed, banks make advances. Making advances is traditionally a bank's major activity and the interest on them is its traditional source of profit. Banks may also buy long-term, fixed-interest government securities, partly for security and partly because they produce a higher income than near-money assets.

Useful applied material

The broad money aggregates have been reclassified and redefined since May 1987. Therefore, the monetary authorities' attention will probably focus increasingly on the behaviour of M4. When considering the factors underlying the growth rate of broad money supply through the counterpart analysis (see below), emphasis in the examination will be on M4.

Counterparts of M4

A *change* in M4 equals:

1. sterling lending by banks and building societies to the UK non-bank non-building society private sector;
2. *plus* the PSBR;
3. *minus* public sector debt sales to the non-bank non-building society private sector;
4. *plus/minus* external flows (i.e. external finance of public sector debt and external transactions of banks and building societies);
5. *minus* the change in sterling net non-deposit liabilities of banks and building societies.

Factors which cause changes in the broad money supply (M4)

A very large proportion of the money supply in the UK is made up of bank and building society deposits. Therefore *anything* which affects these deposits affects the level of broad money supply. The following are the major influences which affect bank and building society deposits.

1. Lending by banks and building societies to the UK non-bank and non-building society private sector (M4 private sector)

Since every loan creates a deposit, therefore all sterling lending by banks and building societies to *this* sector increases money supply in its own right; at the same time, it enables especially banks to operate the credit-creation multiplier, thereby increasing the money supply still further.

2. The Public Sector Borrowing Requirement (PSBR)

The UK public sector comprises the central and local governments and the public corporations (mainly nationalised industries). The total public sector expenditure includes spending on goods and services, interest payment on National Debt, grants to industry and financing of losses of nationalised industries. The total public sector receipts include tax revenue, repayment of grants, interest received, profits of nationalised industries and, more recently, the sale proceeds of the public sector assets, i.e. privatisation proceeds.

The levels of public sector expenditure and revenue, and any excess of expenditure over revenue are normally announced in the annual budget. The budget deficit, i.e. the excess of public sector expenditure over public sector revenue, is called the PSBR, and, as committed expenditure, it has to be financed almost at once by borrowing by the central government.

The PSBR can be financed from the following *four* main sources, and it makes a great deal of difference to the growth of the money supply by which source the PSBR is substantially financed.

(a) Borrowing from the UK non-bank non-building society private sector

This sector does not hold operational balances with the Bank of England, it holds sight deposits with banks and building societies. The government borrows from this sector by the sale of its securities: gilts, National Savings products, etc. The large institutions in this sector (e.g. pension funds, insurance companies) and individuals purchase government securities by sending their cheques, drawn on their deposits with banks and building societies, to the Bank of England. The payments by this sector for its purchases of public sector debt will reduce the deposits of banks and building societies; i.e. the money supply will be decreased by the same amount that the public sector spending will increase it. Hence the level of money supply will change little.

(b) Borrowing from the UK bank and building society sector

When this sector lends to the public sector, either directly or by the purchase of government securities, then its operational deposits with the Bank of England decrease by the same amount as its holdings of claims against the government increase. Hence, at this point, no change occurs in the money supply. However, as the borrowed sum is spent by the public sector, it creates new bank and building society deposits, *without* any offsetting leakage; therefore the money supply *increases*; and it will increase further as this sector pivots the credit-creation multiplier on its new deposits.

(c) Borrowing from the Bank of England

This is an orthodox way of financing the PSBR. Sales of government debt to the Bank will *increase* the money supply, because when the sums borrowed are spent by the government the high-powered money deposits of banks and building societies will increase and that will, of course, enable the credit-creation multiplier to be operated and for the money supply to *increase*.

(d) Sales of government securities to overseas residents

If overseas residents already hold sterling deposits with banks and building societies in the UK, then the money supply will *increase* directly. If sterling was held overseas then there would be a *secondary expansion* as the credit-creation base of banks and building societies is increased.

3. The stance of the UK monetary policy

The stance of the monetary policy (see Ch. 7) has a bearing on the banks' and building societies' ability to lend and create deposits. If the monetary policy is *contractionary* (i.e. aims at making money more expensive and difficult to obtain), it may require banks and building societies to keep a cash-to-deposit ratio, and may also place qualitative (lending priorities) and quantitative (lending and interest rate ceilings) restraints on the banks' and building societies' lending activities, which will *reduce* the money supply, unless the banks and building societies are able to obtain reserve funds from uncontrolled sources and can find ways of lending without transgressing the official requirements. An *expansionary* policy, on the other hand, by making money cheaper (lower interest rates) and easier to obtain (no constraints on bank and building society lending), *increases* money supply.

4. Financing the external trade balance

The official financing of the balance of payments *deficit* or surplus (see Ch. 8) affects the money supply figures. Financing a deficit broadly means that money is leaving the country; hence causing a *reduction* in the money supply. Conversely, financing a balance of payments *surplus* broadly implies that money is coming in which, when spent, will increase the bank and building society deposits and therefore will *increase* the money supply.

5. Increase in banks' and building societies' non-deposit liabilities

These liabilities include their share capital and reserves. The net non-deposit liabilities of a bank or building society equal the total of its capital and reserves *minus* its land, buildings, capital equipment and the like. Since in any balance sheet, liabilities and assets must always equal, an increase in the net non-deposit liabilities of banks and building societies reduces their deposit liabilities, and that *reduces* money supply.

6. Investment returns overseas

If the branches of *foreign banks in the UK* offer better terms to small depositors than those offered by the UK banks and building societies and thereby attract deposits then this will, in the first instance, reduce the deposits of the UK banks and building societies. Since there are no exchange controls in the UK, some of the deposits *lost* by the UK banks and building societies may be invested overseas in search of better returns. This may cause a semi-permanent *reduction* in money supply until the interest rates offered in the UK become competitive with overseas rates. UK institutional investors may invest in overseas financial assets directly to earn higher yield.

7. Bank and building society lending to overseas sector

If money lent overseas finds its way into the UK private sector's sterling deposits, the money supply will *increase*. If it stays overseas the money supply will *decrease*.

8. Overfunding

Sales of government debt to the non-bank and non-building society sector, in *excess* of the PSBR, will reduce the deposits of banks and building societies, and that will *decrease* the money supply.

9. Privatisation

The net revenue from the sales of public sector assets *reduces* the PSBR, and consequently the money supply may be reduced. Privatisation proceeds have, however, distorted the value of the PSBR as a statistic.

Changes in money supply and banks' balance sheets

The connection between changes in money supply and banks' liabilities and assets is of considerable significance and must be clearly understood.

A large proportion of increases in sterling bank lending (banks' assets) ends, in due course, in the sterling deposits with the banks (banks' liabilities). This provides the banking system with a larger deposit base upon which to pivot the banking multiplier which increases bank deposits even further. Since the sterling bank deposits of the UK non-bank private sector are included in the broad monetary aggregates, increases in sterling bank deposits increase the broad money supply.

As the bank lending increases, banks hold larger amounts in their tills and in operational balances with the Bank of England. Since both these banks' assets are included in the narrow money aggregate MO, an increase in bank lending increases the narrow money supply too.

Thus the policy implications of the above analysis are that if the authorities wish to control the narrow and broad money aggregates, they must find effective means to control the growth of sterling deposits held with the UK banks by the UK non-bank private sector.

Recent examination questions

The following six questions should give you an idea of the types of questions that may be set on the 'Money Supply' section of the MFS syllabus. First try to identify from the text the main points you would use to answer these questions. Then spend ten minutes or so planning your answer to each question before turning to the section on 'outline answers' below.

Question 1

Outline the main ways in which a government can finance a budget deficit. How might the need to finance a rising deficit affect commercial banks?

Question 2

Discuss in detail the main factors which cause changes in the money stock.

Question 3

Explain in detail how an increase in government borrowing influences:
(a) the money supply;
(b) conditions in the money markets.

Question 4

What effects do changes in a country's money stock have on its commercial banks?

Question 5

(a) What is meant by the term 'Public Sector Borrowing Requirement' (PSBR)?
(b) Assuming the PSBR is zero, discuss the factors which could generate an increase in a country's money supply.
(c) Can the credit-creation process be carried on indefinitely?

Question 6

(a) Define the measure of money supply known in the UK as M4.
(b) Discuss in detail the main factors which cause M4 to grow.

Outline answers

Answer 1

- Budget deficit may be financed by borrowing from:
  (a) the M4 private sector: issue of notes and coins, marketable debt, non-marketable debt;
  (b) the banking and building society sector: sale of short-dated marketable debt;
  (c) the central bank: against the issue of new gilt-edged securities;
  (d) the overseas sector: direct currency borrowing, sale of government debt.
- Effects on commercial banks of:
  (a) borrowing from the M4 private sector and/or overseas residents with bank deposits in the UK: deposits of the banking system will fall first (temporary reduction in liquidity), then restored after the government spends the borrowed money;
  (b) sales of additional debt to the banking and building society system together with the government spending the borrowed funds: banks' liquidity increases and so does their potential for lending;
  (c) rising budget deficit creates competition for the available funds, which raises interest rates, affecting the banks' lending and profits.

Answer 2

(i) *Increase in PSBR* increases money supply, unless funded by the sales of government securities to the M4 private sector.
(ii) *Increase in bank and building society lending to the private sector* will increase money supply.
(iii) *A deficit in the balance of payments* broadly reduces money supply (money flowing out) and a *surplus* increases money supply (money flowing in).
(iv) *Overfunding* will decrease the money supply.

Changes in interest rates, quantitative and qualitative controls and reserve ratios will influence bank lending, which will affect money supply.

Answer 3

(a) If the government borrows from the:
  (i) banking and building society system – money supply will increase;
  (ii) M4 private sector and overseas in foreign currency – money supply will change very little.

(b) If borrowing is from:
  (i) bank and building society sector – liquidity will increase and put a downward pressure on very short-term interest rates;
  (ii) M4 private sector – the liquidity effect is neutralised, and the operational balances of banks with the Bank of England are first reduced, and then increased by the same amount.

Beware the common fault: government borrowing does not *automatically* mean higher interest rates. An increase in PSBR means that money supply goes up and, in the first instance at least, interest rates will fall.

Answer 4

Bank deposits are a major part of the money stock.

- Increase in the money stock will increase bank deposits.
- Increased deposits enables increased lending; increase in profitability of retail banks (no change in interest rate is assumed).
- Profitability of wholesale banks will fall, as margins of bid and offered interest rates narrow.
- Increase in the money stock may lead to economic growth (if there is spare capacity) and a consequent increase in consumer spending.
- Increase in consumer spending and imports provides an opportunity for increased bank lending and services.
- If the increase in the money stock is excessive, then interest rates may fall and diminish retail banks' profits.
- If the money stock decreases, the above effects will be reversed.

Answer 5

(a) • PSBR = total public sector expenditure *minus* total public sector receipts. PSBR must be financed by borrowing.

(b) • If PSBR is zero, money supply will still grow as a result of:
  – bank and building society lending to the M4 private sector;
  – net external flows;
  – underfunding;
  – decrease in non-deposit liability of banks and building societies.
- Extra lending by banks and building societies is the most important contribution to money supply growth.
- The ability of bank and building societies to create money means that the authorities often take steps to restrain bank lending.
- External flows: bank and building society lending in sterling to the overseas sector
  – money supply will increase if the money lent is spent in the UK; current account position: surplus increase money supply, deficit decreases it.

(c) • Factors which restrict the credit-creation process by banks and building societies:
  – a proportion of their assets must be kept liquid or near liquid;
  – there may be leakages from the system (e.g. internal, into gilts; external, overseas);
  – insufficient demand for loans by M4 private sector (e.g. due to recession);
  – restriction on lending may be imposed by the authorities.

Answer 6

(a) • M4 essentially consists of:
  – notes and coins in circulation with the public;
  – private non-bank non-building society sector } sterling sight and time deposits with banks; sterling CDs issued by banks and building societies; building society shares and deposits.

(b) The counterparts analysis shows that:
a *rise* in M4 equals:
PSBR
less
Public debt sales to non-bank non-building society sector
plus bank and building society lending to the rest of private sector
plus/minus
External flows
minus
Increase in sterling non-deposit liabilities of banks and building societies.

From the above analysis it follows:
– that M4 will grow to the extent the PSBR is financed by public debt sales to banks, building societies and the Bank of England.
– that the creation of deposits via the credit-multiplier through bank and building society lending is an important potential contribution to M4 growth, which is significantly influenced by the interest-rate policy; lower interest rates tend to generate a larger growth in M4.
– that M4 can grow as a result of external flows, e.g. government borrowing in sterling held overseas by overseas residents; current account surplus. Again, the interest policy will bear on the extent of M4 growth.
– that a decrease in sterling non-deposit liabilities of banks and building societies will cause M4 to grow.

A tutor's answer

The following question deals with various aspects of money supply. It has been updated. The specimen answer is intended to help you establish the scope of the question, so that you write relevant information when faced with similar questions in an examination.

Question

Define the measure of money supply in the UK known as M4. Explain how M4 would be directly affected by each of the following:
1. increased sales of gilt-edged securities by the Bank of England;
2. the payment by companies of value-added tax;
3. an increase in sterling bank lending to the overseas sector.

Answer plan:
- Briefly define M4 and state its components.
  (a) Who purchases? Only the direct effects of purchases asked.
  (b) Are current accounts of companies reduced?
  (c) Are there matched increases in lending and deposits?
- Explain only the direct effects; avoid second-round effects.
- Keep asking: does a direct effect cause changes in the *components* of M4?
- Once the effects are technically and correctly explained, *stop*.

Specimen answer

M4 is an official monetary aggregate in the UK which measures the 'broad' money in the country. It comprises 'real' money (immediate purchasing power) *plus* 'near' money (real money, once removed).

The Bank of England definition of the M4 aggregate includes the following components:

(a) notes and coins in circulation with the public,
(b) *plus* private sector interest-bearing and non-interest bearing (sight) sterling bank and building society deposits,
(c) *plus* private sector sterling time bank and building society deposits,
(d) *plus* private sector holdings of bank certificates of deposit,
(e) *plus* private sector holdings of building society shares and deposits and sterling certificates of deposit,
(f) *less* building society holdings of bank deposits and bank certificates of deposit, and notes and coins.

Public sector sterling bank and building society deposits are excluded from M4's composition because such deposits are both small and unlikely to influence economic behaviour.

1. The *direct* effect on M4 of an increase in sales of gilt-edged securities by the Bank of England will depend upon who purchases them. If the purchasers are the UK *M4 private sector*, then M4 will be reduced. This will happen because when the M4 private sector make payment to the Bank of England for their security purchases, they will draw cheques on their sight deposits with banks and building societies. This will reduce the private sector's non-interest bearing sterling sight deposits with banks and building societies. This, in turn, will reduce M4 because these deposits are a component of M4. If the *banking and building society sector* purchases the

gilt-edged securities, then there will be no change in M4. The reason for this is two-fold:

(a) Banking and building society sector purchases of securities reduce the operational deposits of the banking and building society sector with the Bank of England; but the banking and building society sector's operational deposits **are not** a component of M4.

(b) Banking and building society sector purchases of securities do not affect the bank and building society deposits of the UK *M4* private sector, which **are** a component of M4. The purchases of gilt-edged securities by *overseas residents* will reduce their sterling sight deposits with banks and building societies, but these deposits are not included in the components of M4. Hence M4 will not be affected.

2. If the companies pay VAT by drawing cheques on the credit balances in their sterling sight deposits with banks and building societies, then M4 will be reduced: 'companies' are a part of the UK private sector, and UK private sector sterling sight deposits with banks and building societies are a component of M4. However, if the companies paid their VAT bill by increasing bank and building society borrowing, say, by overdrawing their sterling sight deposits with banks and building societies, then M4 will remain unaffected; the increase in bank and building society lending is offset by a reduction in bank and building society operational deposits, so that sterling deposits remain the same.
3. An increase in sterling lending to the overseas sector has the same effect as any bank and building society lending, i.e. a rise in bank and building society deposits. If a rise in bank and building society deposits is 'matched' by an increase in the sterling deposits of overseas residents, then M4 will be unaffected; simply because overseas residents' deposits are not a part of M4. If, however, the overseas residents have increased sterling borrowing in order to meet their commitments to the UK non-bank and non-building society public, say, in respect of export credits, or the purchase of a business, then the UK private sector sterling deposits with the banks and building societies will increase, and so will M4.

A step further

Once again, as with 'Money', your best source for money supply figures and definitional changes is the *Quarterly Bulletin* of the Bank of England. Articles on money supply matters appear often in the quality newspapers, *Signpost* articles in *Banking World* and in the *Updating Notes* and *Examiners' Reports* (published by The Chartered Institute of Bankers); these are of extreme importance not only to keep abreast of the latest changes in the topic of money supply, but also to see an analysis of the reasons for, and the expected effects of, such changes. More important than the statistics of money supply are the *principles* underlying the concept of money supply.

The recent change in broad money definitions was discussed in a *Signpost* article in the Jan/Feb 1990 issue of *Banking World*.

CHAPTER 6

Interest Rates

Syllabus requirements

- The determinants of:
  (i) the general level, and
  (ii) the pattern of the interest rates.
- The role of interest rates.
- The significance of LIBOR, overnight rates, base rates.
- The term structure of interest rates.
- The distinction between 'real' and 'nominal' interest rates.
- The relationship between domestic and international interest rates and exchange rate.

Getting started

In money-using economies, money creates claims because it is an asset, a store of value, as well as a means of exchange. Therefore those who lend money expect to be recompensed for handing over their claims for the period of the loan to those who borrow money. The recompense is the interest rate. It is expressed as a rate per cent per annum because it is a convenient way of calculating and comparing the cost of borrowing money. Thus one commonly used definition of the interest rate is that it is a 'price' at which money is lent and borrowed.

Borrowers borrow money because they are short of funds to meet their current needs for goods and services, whereas lenders lend funds which are surplus to their current needs for goods and services. Therefore the interest rate can also be defined as the 'price' the lenders expect (and the borrowers pay) for exchanging current claims for greater future claims to goods and services.

In modern economies the principal lenders are often those at one stage removed, since most of their funds are obtained from others. Individual lend to banks and other financial institutions by depositing their savings with them, or lend to businesses and the government by directly purchasing their securities and bonds. Banks on-lend much of their deposits to individuals, firms and countries as overdrafts and term loans. Building societies lend most of their accumulated deposits from the public to house buyers. Finance houses lend funds out of their accumulated borrowings to finance the hire-purchase transactions of the public. Insurance companies collect premiums for various kinds of insurance policies they sell to the public, and then lend or invest significant proportions of their receipts in government and company securities. Firms use their surplus funds to make deposits with banks or to lend to the government by purchasing government debt or lend to other firms against their promises to repay. Governments borrow huge sums of money from anyone who is willing to purchase their securities, and in turn lend a portion of their borrowed funds to nationalised and other industries, to foreign governments and other borrowers. Virtually all of this lending and borrowing activity is linked by the receipt and payment of interest rates.

High interest rates encourage savings but may discourage investment. The cost of credit, which is dependent on the level of interest rates, significantly affects spending, exchange rates and economic activity of a country. The Bank of England uses its control over short-term interest rates to achieve monetary policy objectives.

Essential principles and useful applied material

Determination of the level of interest rates

Although no single theory of interest provides a complete explanation of the determination of the *level of interest rates*, yet the following points can be identified as influencing that level.

(i) *Real and nominal rates of interest*. The real rate can simply be defined as the nominal rate (the rate actually paid) *if* there is no inflation over the term of a loan. In the *long term* the real rate will be determined by the 'fundamental factors', such as: (a) the rate of return which the private sector borrowers hope to achieve when undertaking capital investment; and (b) the attitude of lenders to forgoing spending today in favour of higher spending tomorrow. However, once inflation is introduced then other factors will also affect the long-term rate of interest, at least as regards the nominal rate: it must be high enough to yield an amount: (a) which would compensate lenders for the *expected* fall in the value of money; and (b) which would compensate lenders for the uncertainty over the course of future inflation, i.e. a risk premium.

The major problem with this approach is that it is not possible exactly to allocate the split between nominal rate, real rate and the *expected* change in inflation rate.

To overcome this problem, the general practice is to deduct the *current* inflation rate, as measured by, say, the RPI over a given period from the *nominal* interest rate to arrive at the *real* rate. The real rate would be *positive* where the nominal rate exceeds inflation rate, and *negative* when reverse is the case. This practice is fair enough for short-term rates but is misleading for long-term rates because it makes no allowance for the risk and uncertainty concerning the *expected* rate of inflation.

In the UK, with the introduction of index-linked gilt-edged securities, it is possible to measure the real rate with some precision on securities of different maturities. For instance, if the rate of return on long-term index-linked gilts is, say, 3.25 per cent, and the rate of return on similar non-index-linked securities is, say, 9 per cent, then after allowing for a premium for uncertainty (say 1.75 per cent) it could be estimated that over a period of 20 years the inflation rate would average around 4 per cent per annum. A fall in inflation, nominal rates unchanged, raises the real rates.

(ii) *Government borrowing requirements*. A large increase in government borrowing to finance current spending will push up interest rates if there is no parallel increase in private sector savings. This will occur even with an inflation rate that is stationary.

This point has been well illustrated by the huge US budget deficit, which has attracted much of the private savings of the free world and has pushed up real rates of interest around the world.

(iii) *Term structure of interest rates*. When lenders/investors are uncertain about future interest rates they may wish to hedge their bets; this introduces a new dimension into interest rate calculations and gives rise to the *term structure* of interest rates. It makes sense for investors to attempt to arrange their portfolio of investments so that the *expected* return on a series of short-term investments during a certain period *equals* the return on long-term investment over that period. If short-term rates are *below* long-term rates, this broadly implies that short-term rates are expected to rise; and of course vice versa. However, since future rates cannot be predicted with absolute certainty, allowance has also to be made for a risk premium. Therefore both *inherent uncertainty* of future interest rates, and the investors' *own perception* of the risk involved in that uncertainty, will be important in determination of the level of interest rates.

(iv) *Defence of exchange rate.* The authorities may counter any excessive downward pressure on the exchange rate, caused by a perceived weakness of the national currency, by deliberately raising the level of short-term rates. This will help attract large amounts of interest-sensitive, overseas short-term capital into the country, thereby helping ease the downward pressure by increasing the demand for the national currency.

(v) *Market expectations.* If the market believes that the authorities are succeeding in their counter-inflationary policies, and that a relaxed monetary policy is in the offing, then these expectations will help bring about a fall in the level of interest rates. For instance, lenders/investors will no longer seek such a high nominal interest rate to cushion them against future inflation. Of course, interest rates will tend to rise if market expectations are for a 'tighter' credit policy.

(vi) *Supply and demand of loanable funds.* The level of interest rates will rise when the demand for loanable funds increases *relative to* the supply of loanable funds, and of course vice versa.

(vii) *The level of interest rates overseas.* Provided there are no exchange controls, the level of other countries' interest rates, other things being equal, will affect the level of domestic interest rates (see (ii) above).

Interest rates in the UK

In most countries the monetary authorities determine the level of short-term interest rates; in the UK the unique position of the Bank of England as lender of last resort to the banking system, almost exclusively through the discount houses, ensures its dominating influence on the determination of the level of short-term interest rates. It can raise or lower the marginal cost of funds to the banking system by raising or lowering its dealing rates in its OMOs relative to the prevailing money market rates. The Bank uses its dominance over short-term rates of interest: (i) to control changes in bank lending and therefore changes in money supply; (ii) to curb inflationary pressures; and (iii) to influence exchange rate movements. If the Bank chooses to raise the level of short-term rates, its activities will *override* any free market forces in the supply and demand of loanable funds, i.e. the short-term rates will be determined *administratively* and not by the market forces.

If the *short-term* rates are totally determined by the *monetary authorities*, and the *long-term* rates primarily by the *fundamental factors* relating to the real rate of interest and the expectations regarding future inflation, then there may still be a problem of reconciling the levels of short with long rates. For example, if the authorities *pushed up* the short rates, this could lead to less bank lending and a higher exchange rate, both of which could in turn lead to lower future inflation, and therefore *lower* long rates; but the theory of the *term structure* of interest rates suggests that a rise in short rates directly points to a rise in long rates in order to compensate long term investors for the higher short rates currently available (see below).

Broadly speaking, it is true that any uncertainty surrounding future inflation and future interest rates will be *outweighed* by the movement of short rates; i.e. a rise in short rates will usually lead to a rise in long rates, though perhaps not to the same extent. Nevertheless, there are times when short rates rise and long rates fall. This happened, for example, in the UK during the first three months of 1986; short rates rose from 11.5 per cent to 12.5 per cent, but the long rates actually fell. The rise in short rates was administratively engineered in order to shore up the sharply falling exchange rate of the pound caused by the slump in oil prices. The fall in long rates was due to an improved inflation outlook (due to the fall in oil prices!) and to the market expectation that the rise in short rates would be temporary. Indeed, the short rate fell back to 11.5 per cent by mid-March 1986, and fell again later in 1986 and 1987. During 1989, long rates were generally lower than short rates (14 per cent), largely because the money markets accepted that the high short rates, after causing the inflation rate (over 8 per cent) to come down, would fall, i.e. the high short rates were temporary.

The level of *short rates* is therefore the *pivot* of the interest rate system. Other rates do not in general move too far from the level of short rates. Since the monetary authorities can totally control the level of short rates, it might appear that it is the monetary authorities who, directly or indirectly, determine the *general* level of interest rates; both short and long-term rates. This is not entirely so. For instance, the sudden reduction in the Bank of England's money market dealing rates in April 1986, should have led to a reduction in long rates. However, due to the strong market expectation that long rates would not fall and might even rise, the long rates did not fall. The reason for this anomaly was the market expectation that the UK inflation rate would probably rise and a belief that UK interest rates would not remain out of line with overseas interest rates, which were themselves expected to rise. This anomaly illustrates the point that the monetary authorities' ability to engineer drastic changes in interest rates is largely limited to short-term rates.

The determinants of the *general level* of interest rates may be summarised as follows.

(a) The short-term interest rates are influenced by:
- (i) the stance of the short-term monetary policy objectives;
- (ii) the extent of credit-creation by the financial institutions;
- (iii) the defence of the exchange rate by the authorities;
- (iv) the level of interest rates in other countries, provided there are no exchange controls and other things being equal.

(b) The longer-term interest rates are influenced by:
- (i) the longer-term stance of the monetary policy;
- (ii) the expected rate of domestic inflation;
- (iii) the market belief in the efficiency of the official anti-inflationary policy;
- (iv) the expected rate of return on investment at home and overseas.

Significance of the 'real' interest rate

Their importance relates to the following considerations:

(a) *The cost to corporate borrowers*. Positive real rates increase companies' costs by being higher than RPI. Negative real rates decrease their costs and encourage borrowing.
(b) *The attitude of lenders*. When the real rates are negative (i.e. when the nominal interest rate is lower than the current rate of inflation), lending is discouraged; it is encouraged when the real rates are positive.
(c) *The international comparisons*. Other things being equal, and assuming no exchange controls are in operation between countries, comparatively higher domestic real rates

will encourage the inflow of overseas funds, which, in turn, will influence the domestic exchange rate and balance of payments position (see Ch.8 and Ch.9).

The way the Bank of England fixes short-term rates

You studied earlier how the Bank of England, while performing its lender of last resort-role, ensured that the level of short-term rates was in line with the stance of monetary policy. Now you'll see once again in some detail how the mechanism functions, and this will strengthen your comprehension of this very important part of the syllabus.

The Bank of England as the central bank of the U.K. has aimed to keep the *short-term* (up to one month) interest rates within a narrow unpublished band, but to allow market forces in the money markets a greater role in determining the *longer-term* rates. This policy helps shape the structure of money market rates.

The control of the Bank over the very short-term rates is assured, for three main reasons.

1. It offsets, at its own terms, shortages (or surpluses) of liquidity in the money markets via the discount houses; in this way, it can control the marginal cost of funds to the banking system. In theory, the Bank is not expected to act as the lender of last resort to the banking system, yet in practice it does; it has to, for it cannot abdicate its responsibilities as the central bank!
2. In its money market operations, the Bank buys and sells eligible commercial bills and Treasury bills in the discount market in four bands, according to the maturity of the bills. The bands where the Bank's control is the strongest are Bands 1 and 2, i.e. bands in which bills have maturities of up to 14 days and 33 days respectively. Bands 3 and 4 include bills with longer maturities; in these bands the Bank's direct influence is less strong. Changes in the Bank's dealing rate in Bands 1 and 2 are taken by the money markets to mean that the Bank intends to bring about a change in the marginal cost of funds and therefore in the general level of short-term money market rates. Clearly if the Bank makes short-term funds more expensive to the banking system, the banks in turn will charge more for overdrafts and short-term loans. Thus despite the suspension (not abolition) of the Minimum Lending Rate in August 1981, the Bank exerts the key influence on the level of short-term rates in the money markets. The interaction between the bill operations of the Bank and market expectations is the main determinant of the level and structure of short-term rates in the UK, and it plays an important part in determining long-term rates in the money markets.
3. Occasionally cash shortages can be relieved by direct lending to discount houses at the Bank's own lending rates. Also the Bank may enter into agreements of sale and repurchase of gilts (REPOS) at fixed rates and for fixed periods with the commercial banks to relieve liquidity shortage (usually during January to April, the tax gathering season) and to influence the level of short rates and stabilisation.

With the more aggressive deposit-gathering stance of the building societies, the clearers have come to rely increasingly on funds from the money markets e.g. wholesale deposits – in recent years. Still more recently, clearers have themselves been collecting higher interest-bearing retail deposits. Therefore, bank base rates will have broadly to move in line with the money market rates. In fact, after December 1973, the clearers even geared the advances made to certain corporate customers to market rates rather than to base rates. Using market rates such as the sterling London Inter-Bank Offered Rate (LIBOR) as the basis for setting interest rates on term lending is of benefit to the banks; it gives them the opportunity to match their lending rates and conditions with those for the wholesale deposits they obtain through the inter-bank market. Non-bank financial institutions who, like banks, obtain wholesale funds, apply a similar criterion in on-lending for longer-terms. Thus, although the Bank openly fixes the short-term rates, yet the direction given by it to short-term rates permeates right through the whole spectrum of interest rates in the monetary system.

The effects of changes in the general level of interest rates on banks

1. The effects of a FALL in interest rates

(a) It will reduce both the cost of funds acquired by banks and the interest received by them from advances. However, if the demand for advances is interest-elastic, the total advances might rise substantially; increased advances will create increased deposits in the banking system as a whole and may improve the banks' profitability.
(b) It will squeeze the net return or the 'endowment' effect of the non-interest bearing deposits of the retail banks considerably, thus reducing their profitability. On the other hand, their profit margins on fixed-rate lending would be increased. Now that the banks, under competition from the building societies, have begun to offer some interest on current accounts, the endowment effect of the 'free money' has declined considerably.
(c) Building societies have been slow to reduce their interest rates on deposits; *banks* have been relatively quicker to reduce their deposit rates as the level of interest rates falls, and have therefore tended to lose retail deposits to building societies as interest rates fall.
(d) Banks, in order to maintain acceptable profitability levels, as their interest receipts fall, might widen the margin between interest paid and interest received, and might also increase service and commission charges.
(e) A fall in interest rates would increase the capital value of the banks' fixed interest investments; banks might realise the capital gains by selling some of these investments.
(f) The loan repayment burden of banks' customers is reduced when interest rates fall; therefore there will be fewer bad debts and the banks will probably reduce their bad debt provisions and thus release additional resources for lending.
(g) To ward off the adverse effect of falls in interest rates, banking groups may actively encourage lending at fixed rates via their subsidiaries, e.g. hire purchase companies.

2. The effects of a RISE in interest rates

By and large, the effects on banks of a rise in interest rates would be exactly opposite to those of a fall in interest rates.
(a) Higher loan and deposit rates of the banks might suggest that their profit margins would remain unchanged, but for retail banks margins improve because of the endowment effect of non-interest bearing deposits (now reduced). On the other hand, their profit margins are reduced on fixed-rate lending.
(b) Higher price of loans may reduce loan demand of the banks' business customers; although in practice necessity overcomes price, at least in the short term. The demand for loans for capital goods, and more particularly working capital, tends to be interest-inelastic, and therefore, provided that profit margins are maintained, the loan demand for capital goods by the banks' private sector business customers is unlikely to change. The same is true of public sector investment expenditure.

(c) Banks are in competition with non-bank financial institutions, chiefly building societies, National Savings and the government, for the savings and deposits of the public. Whether the banks' deposit inflow would increase or decrease would largely depend upon how well the banks' interest rate structure compared with that of the other financial institutions and with that offered on government securities. Apart from the banks' large and sophisticated corporate depositors, most of the other depositors tend to be sluggish in switching their deposits between financial institutions.
(d) High interest rates tend to depress the economy by depressing demand in certain sectors of the economy, e.g. in the consumer goods industry. The more the economy becomes depressed, the lower are profits and the greater becomes the significance of the interest rate bills for business firms; this may lead to more bad debts for the banks (as has been the case during 1989 and 1990), who would probably have to increase their bad debt provisions, which will reduce their profitability.
(e) Relatively higher rates in the UK would tend to act as a magnet for large short-term capital flows from abroad and this would raise the exchange rate of the pound. It would benefit the UK's capital account under floating exchange rates provided overseas rates remained unchanged. However interest payable on foreign capital would eventually produce an increase in net outflows on invisible account (see Ch. 8). The rise in the exchange rate under a fixed exchange rate system would reduce the value, in sterling, of overseas residents' deposits and of the earnings of the overseas subsidiaries of the UK parent banks, thus reducing their profitability. A higher exchange rate would also reduce the competitiveness of UK exports and import substitutes, tending further to depress the economy as in (d) above.

Banks' base rates

The clearing and other deposit-taking commercial banks cater for the major proportion of the borrowing needs of the public, other than house purchase. Although the rates payable by customers are a matter for negotiation, most lending banks quote a 'base rate' and grant overdrafts at a fixed margin over this rate.

There are three main determinants of the banks' base rates:

(a) Marginal cost of raising funds in the inter-bank and CDs markets (the wholesale markets). The shorter-term market rates (overnight or seven-day rates) are more volatile and fluctuate daily and sometimes several times during a day. The three-month money market rates are more stable, and banks pitch their base rates between 0.25 per cent and 0.5 per cent above this rate. This margin is expected to cover the cost of holding required liquid assets, loan operating costs, and profits. Banks usually charge their blue chip customers base rate *plus* 1 per cent for loans and overdrafts, but from personal customers the rates charged can range from 3 per cent to 8 per cent over the base rate, depending upon the credit rating of the borrowers.
(b) When the more volatile shorter-term market rates and the banks' base rate move sufficiently apart, banks' corporate customers can take the 'arbitrage' profits, i.e. they borrow cheaply from their banks and on-lend at a higher rate in the wholesale markets, or make 'round-tripping' gains by borrowing to their overdraft limits and then on-lending the borrowed funds back to the banks at higher market rates. Arbitrage has led to the growth in LIBOR-linked lending by the banks, which causes the base rates to change much more quickly. LIBOR-linked lending enables banks to match their lending rates and conditions with those under which they themselves borrow wholesale funds.

(c) The Bank of England can, through its OMOs, influence the level of short-term rates in the money markets. If it raises or lowers the market rates, it will also raise or lower the marginal cost of wholesale funds to the banks, who, in turn, will adjust their base rates accordingly.

The pattern of interest rates

Although many of the interest theories assume that there is **one** rate of interest, which moves up or down, this is, in reality, both incorrect and misleading. You have only to look at the daily, and especially the weekend, newspapers to notice the wide pattern of interest rates. For example, the sterling money rates prevailing in London are shown in Table 6.1. The three most important sets of rates are those under 'Interbank', 'Bank Bills' and 'Sterling CDs'. The double-barrelled quotation of rates displays the spread between the bid (deposit) and offered (lending) rates. Where there is a single rate, it is the offered rate.

The existence of so many interest rates broadly reflects variations in the risk, supply and demand considerations and period of loans, expectations of future rates, needs of investors and borrowers, credit rating of borrowers, and maturity of loans. Lenders are willing to accept lower interest rates from those borrowers who minimise lending risks.

The lending risks

The *lending risks* may take the following forms:

1. The risk of default

The borrower may become unable to repay the loan. For this reason, for three-month money, Treasury bills (government IOUs) are considered safer by lenders than, say, bank deposits; therefore Treasury bills offer a slightly lower rate of return than do bank deposits. Similarly, banks offer a slightly lower interest on savings deposits than do finance houses.

2. The loss of liquidity

That is, how quickly, conveniently, and without significant loss in income and/or capital value the lender can convert his lending (e.g. bond, bank and building society deposits, share certificates) into cash. The longer the loss of liquidity, the higher normally will be the rate of return. For example, banks offer a higher rate on *term deposits* than on *seven-day deposits*, and building societies offer higher returns on *deposits* which have a *penalty clause* for immediate withdrawals, than for *normal share deposits*. The concern with the liquidity aspect of lending is reflected in the preference of lenders for relatively short-term lending. However, money is borrowed, especially by business firms, for relatively long periods of time. Consequently there is a greater supply of short-term funds, but a greater demand for long-term borrowing; hence, short-term lending usually earns a lower rate of interest, and borrowers wanting longer-term loans have to offer higher rates to overcome the lenders' reluctance to part with liquidity for longer periods.

3. Fall in market value

The market value of the asset held by the lender may fall. A major reason for this lending risk, especially for fixed-interest lending, is rapidly rising inflation. In times of a rising inflation rate, the longer the maturity period of a loan, the greater the lending risk. Therefore in such times lenders expect to receive a rate of interest which is higher than the *expected*

Table 6.1 Sterling money rates

	Overnight	7 Days Notice	One Month	Three Months	Six Months	One Year
Interbank offer/bid	$15\frac{1}{2}/14\frac{7}{8}$	$15/14\frac{7}{8}$	$15/14\frac{7}{8}$	$15/14\frac{7}{8}$	$14\frac{15}{16}/14\frac{3}{4}$	$14\frac{5}{8}/14\frac{1}{2}$
Sterling CDs	–	–	$14\frac{15}{16}$	$14\frac{13}{16}$	$14\frac{25}{32}$	$14\frac{13}{32}$
Local Auth. Deposits	$14\frac{7}{8}$	$14\frac{7}{8}$	$14\frac{7}{8}$	$14\frac{7}{8}$	$14\frac{13}{16}$	$14\frac{9}{16}$
Local Auth. Bonds	–	–	–	–	–	–
Discount Mkt Deposits	15	$14\frac{7}{8}$	$14\frac{3}{4}$	$14\frac{1}{2}$	–	–
Company Deposits	–	–	$14\frac{29}{32}$	$14\frac{7}{8}$	$14\frac{23}{32}$	$14\frac{7}{16}$
Finance House Deposits	–	–	$14\frac{29}{32}$	$14\frac{29}{32}$	$14\frac{25}{32}$	$14\frac{5}{8}$
Treasury Bills (Buy)	–	–	$14\frac{19}{32}$	$14\frac{5}{16}$	–	–
Bank Bills (Buy)	–	–	$14\frac{5}{8}$	$14\frac{11}{32}$	$13\frac{13}{16}$	–
Fine Trade Bills (Buy)	–	–	$15\frac{1}{4}$	$14\frac{31}{32}$	$14\frac{7}{16}$	–
Dollar CDs	–	–	8.10	8.10	8.15	8.25

London Clearing Banks Base Rate: 11.5 per cent from April 1991
Note how rates vary, both between markets and over different periods.
Source: *Financial Times*, 20 July 1990.

rate of inflation; or alternatively that their lending should be index-linked; index-linked securities yield positive, real rates.

4. Capital loss considerations

Suppose that the general level of interest rates is 10 per cent per annum, but that it is expected to rise. An investor buying a £100 bond with a 10 per cent per annum yield will expect to receive £10 every year until the bond matures for repayment. Suppose, later on, that the general level of interest rates rises to 20 per cent per annum; this will cause the *market price* of the 10 per cent per annum bond to fall to £50: because an investor investing £100 in 20 per cent per annum bond will earn £20 per year. An expected (or actual) rise in interest rates means a fall in the market price of fixed-interest lending, i.e. a capital loss or depreciation; conversely, an expected (or actual) fall in interest rates will cause the market price of fixed-interest lending to rise, that is it will benefit from a capital gain or appreciation. Therefore if investors expect interest rates to rise in the future, they will require higher rates than currently available to compensate for the probable capital loss.

Lenders may, however, be willing to accept a lower rate of interest for longer-term lending if they strongly expect a substantial **fall** in the general level of interest rates, in the hope of making a gain on the capital value of their lending.

The current and future tax positions, therefore investment needs, of lenders/investors also influence acceptable interest rates.

The term structure of interest rates

This means the level of short-and long-term rates and the relationship between them. This relationship can be seen in the movements of the normal money market curve, viz. the *yield curve* (Fig.6.1). A yield curve is the relationship between yields on similar financial assets with different terms to maturity. Its steepness shows that generally the **longer** the term to maturity, the **higher the yield, because lenders require a larger compensation for a more sustained loss of liquidity, a higher lending risk and greater uncertainty.**

Curve 1 is the normal money market yield curve which slopes upwards signifying that, other things being equal, lenders lending for longer terms require larger compensation for longer loss of liquidity, higher lending risks and greater uncertainty. They are not expecting any future interest rate changes.

The 'other things being equal' assumption is upset, chiefly, by the role of *expectations*. If the expectation of the majority of lenders is that the future rates will *fall*, then long rates will be below short rates, as shown by the yield *curve 2*; here the long rates will tend to approximate to the *average* of expected future rates.

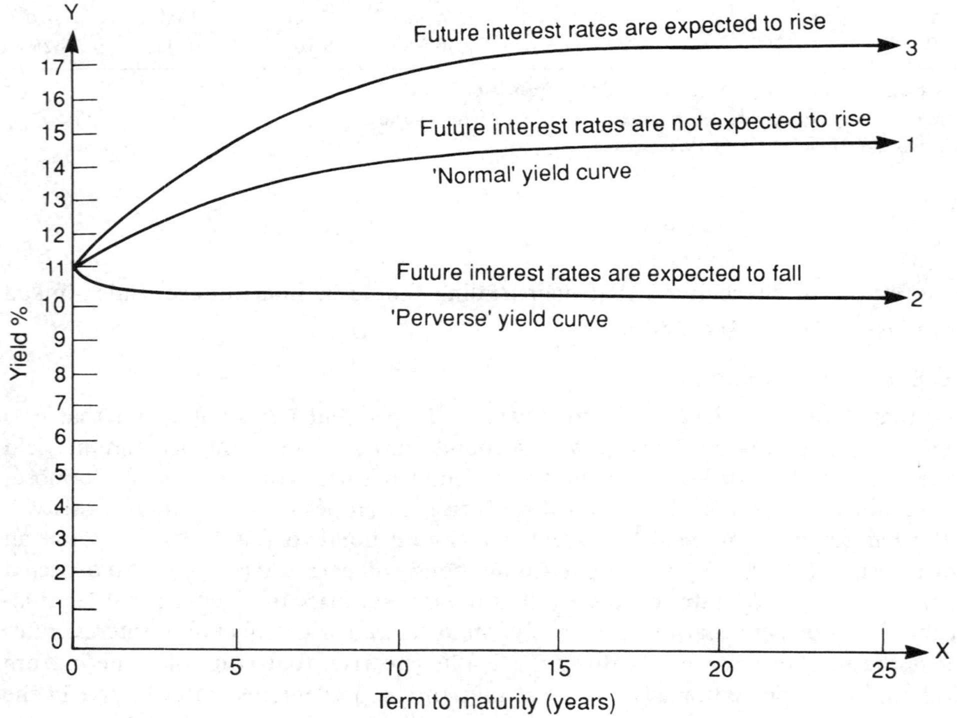

Fig. 6.1 Yield curves

Suppose the current market rate is 11 per cent per annum, but is expected to fall over the year as follows: after three months to 10.5 per cent p.a., after six months to 10 per cent p.a. and after nine months to 9.5 per cent p.a. A bank makes a loan of £500,000 to a business customer for one year. What rate per annum should the bank charge to the customer, taking into account the expected fall in rates over the year? The following schedule shows the bank's interest earnings for each quarter, during the year (compound interest considerations which would be relevant in an actual case of this kind, are ignored, to keep the calculations straightforward).

Interest earned for the first three months

$$= \frac{£500{,}000 \times 0.25 \times 11}{100} = £13{,}750$$

Interest earned for the second three months

$$= \frac{£500,000 \times 0.25 \times 10.5}{100} = £13,125$$

Interest earned for the third three months

$$= \frac{£500,000 \times 0.25 \times 10}{100} = £12,500$$

Interest earned for the fourth three months

$$= \frac{£500,000 \times 0.25 \times 9.5}{100} = £11,875$$

Total interest earned for the whole year = £51,250

The average of the four short-term rates

$$= \frac{11 + 10.5 + 10 + 9.5}{4} = 10.25 \text{ per cent}$$

The bank will charge a rate of 10.25 per cent per annum to the customer. Thus, although the current short rate (three months) is 11 per cent per annum, the longer rate (one year) is lower at 10.25 per cent per annum; this is because future interest rates are expected to fall over the year. If, after one year, future interest rates are expected to stabilise at 10.25 per cent, then the yield curve will become horizontal at 10.25 per cent, as in yield curve 2.

If current short rates are higher than long rates, this could be due to several reasons:

1. Future interest rates are expected to fall.
2. The high short rates are expected to be temporary; perhaps the need of banks and other financial institutions for funds to balance their books at the end of each financial year and half-year has pushed short rates up temporarily.
3. The monetary authorities have raised short-term rates in response to general economic developments; for example, to control inflation, or to deal with a downward pressure on the exchange rate, the authorities may deliberately raise short-term rates temporarily, in order to encourage the inflow of short-term capital flows and to discourage the outflow of funds.
4. The belief that the authorities will succeed in curbing inflation soon, hence the expectation that a relaxed monetary policy, with lower interest rates, will follow.

Yield *Curve 3* reflects a situation in which the expectation of the majority of lenders is that interest rates will rise, and therefore that the capital value of lending will fall; hence long rates will be much higher than short rates to compensate both for the lengthier loss of liquidity as well as the possible capital loss.

In Fig 6.1, the gradients of the three yield curves flatten out and become parallel to X axis. The reason for this is that the uncertainty element in the minds of lenders/investors becomes the same for a loan maturity of 20 years as for a loan maturity of say, 25 years. Therefore the interest rate for the two maturities will probably be the same. After very long periods the length of the term loses its effect on interest rates.

To maximise the returns from lending, lenders will, other things being equal, switch between longer and shorter loans/ bonds according to their expected yields over the period for which they wish to lend. There is no further gain to be made by such switching when the yield on long loans is equal to the average of the expected yields on short loans during the period in question (as shown by the above calculations). If lenders then begin to expect a rise in future rates, they would prefer to lend short-term so that on maturity they may lend the repayments at higher rates. Conversely, if they begin to expect future rates to fall, they would prefer to lend long at fixed rates in order to make capital gains as the level of interest rates falls.

While the short-term interest rates in the UK rose sharply during 1989 (to 14 per cent), longer term rates increased much less. As a result the yield curve had been downward sloping for most of 1989, reflecting the expectation that short-term rates would not stay high for too long.

The patterns of interest rates in the UK

The following factors can be identified as affecting the various individual interest rates which together constitute the general pattern of interest rates *in the UK*:

1. In the case of long-term gilt-edged securities, it is their respective supply and demand which strongly influence the interest rates offered by the authorities. The supply of these securities is linked to the government's borrowing requirements and to the nature of the monetary policy in terms of 'funding', i.e. the extent to which a given PSBR is being supported by long-term borrowing as opposed to short-term borrowing. A large increase in the issue of long gilts tends to raise the level of long rates to induce investors to take up the extra stock. Conversely, if the monetary policy is to bring down the long rates, the government will refrain from issuing long-term gilts.
2. Lending to the government can be regarded as being free of the risk of default as compared with long-term lending to private sector companies. Therefore private sector companies must offer a higher rate than that available from gilt stocks to compensate lenders for the higher default risk.
3. When there is a cash shortage in the money market, the discount houses offer eligible bills for sale to the Bank of England. The rate at which the Bank purchases them sets the pattern of short-term rates in the UK. Sometimes, when the cash shortages are very large (e.g. during January and February, the tax-gathering season), the quantity of eligible bills the discount houses can offer for sale may be insufficient fully to relieve the shortages. This may require the Bank to enter into purchase and resale (REPOS) agreements of certain financial assets of the commercial banks directly. The cost of the purchase and resale agreements will affect the level and pattern of the UK interest rates.

   The authorities do not, as a rule, intervene directly in the money markets, and the money market rates, especially the *inter-bank* rates, can sometimes depart from the Bank's dealing rates. The main driving force for the level of inter-bank rates tends to be expectations over the future course of interest rates. Thus if the three-months inter-bank rates rise above the Bank's dealing rates, it will be expected that the Bank will sooner or later have to raise its own dealing rates. Nevertheless, it is the Bank of England which retains the predominant influence over the level of short-term rates, for reasons discussed earlier.
4. The bank base rates are pitched at a level broadly equal to the imagined cost of funds (as determined by the Bank's dealing rates); this cost generally corresponds to the rate prevailing in the inter-bank market *plus* the cost to banks of holding low-yielding liquid assets (to satisfy the 'safety' criterion) against their deposits.

   The level of the banks' retail deposit rates offered to depositors is traditionally set below the money market rates. This allows a margin for covering the cost of running large branch networks and for covering the higher administrative cost of raising relatively small retail deposits compared with raising large wholesale deposits in the money markets.

The level of banks' retail borrowing rates charged to customers are linked to the banks' base rates or directly to LIBOR, and make an allowance for banks' profit margins or for the riskiness of the borrowers.

5. The main competitors of the banks for retail deposits are the building societies. The behaviour of building society interest rates is broadly determined by the demand for mortgages and the supply of retail deposits. Unlike banks, building societies were, until recently, unable to raise cheaper wholesale funds in the money markets. Therefore the building societies have tended to pay rather more for retail deposits than the banks, causing the banks' share of retail deposits to decline steadily over the years. The banks have therefore had to depend increasingly on wholesale deposits in the money markets, especially in the inter-bank and CDs markets.

   Since 1985, however, the competitive situation between the banks and the building societies has changed dramatically, in at least two respects:

   (a) Firstly, *both* the banks and the building societies now pay interest to depositors net of the basic rate of income tax (from 1991 both will pay interest 'gross'); this exposed further the banks' relatively poor retail rates of interest compared with building society rates. To redress the balance the banks responded aggressively by introducing very competitive 'high interest rate' deposit accounts.

   (b) Secondly, the building societies, like the banks, are now able to borrow cheaper wholesale funds, subject to a ceiling of 40 per cent on the money markets. Also they can provide, in competition with the banks, up to £10,000 of consumer finance. Therefore it is the level of *money market rates* which should now impose the limits on the rates of interest that both the banks and the building societies will pay for retail deposits – with two *qualifications*. First, the retail deposit-taking institutions, e.g. banks, building societies, finance houses, unit and investment trusts, might be willing to pay more to ensure a stable retail deposit base, in preference to being too dependent on the more volatile money market wholesale funds. Second, these institutions might accept the payment of high retail deposit interest rates in the hope of a profitable trade-off in terms of selling other financial services. This element of cross-subsidy is especially significant in the context of those current accounts on which interest is not paid, but where free banking can be enjoyed in lieu of interest.

The trend of the pattern of interest rates, due to increasing innovation and competition in the financial system, is towards a narrowing of interest rate differentials among the various financial institutions; retail deposit rates are now moving up towards wholesale rates; even the growth of free banking is a move towards narrower interest rate differentials as the current account holder is getting the equivalent of a higher rate of interest.

Retail borrowing rates are subject to similar competitive forces; these rates generally reflect three *additions*, over and above the cost of funds: (i) a margin which covers the administrative costs, *plus*; (ii) a margin which allows for risk, *plus*; (iii) a profit margin. The banks have reduced the rates they charge on endowment mortgages, thus bringing these rates closer to the rates charged by building societies.

Recent examination questions

The following six questions give an indiction of the types of questions you will need to answer on interest rates. You could usefully spend ten minutes or so on each question, trying to identify the main points you would use in your answer, before turning to the outline answers below.

Question 1

(a) What is meant by the term 'yield curve'?
(b) Examine:
   (i) the factors which, in normal conditions, produce higher rates of long-term rather than short-term maturities;
   (ii) the relationship between short-term interbank rates and commercial bank lending rates.

Question 2

(a) Why and how does the Bank of England intervene in the money markets?
(b) Discuss the view that the level of mortgage rates is primarily determined by the rates at which the Bank of England deals in 14-day bills of exchange in the money market.

Question 3

Discuss the factors which affect the level and pattern of money market interest rates in the UK. To what extent do changes in money market rates lead to changes in commercial banks' base rates?

Question 4

Analyse the effects of a rise in a country's interest rates on:
(a) the personal sector;
(b) the corporate sector;
(c) the commercial bank;
(d) the capital account of the balance of payments.

Question 5

(a) What is meant by 'real' rates of interest and how are they calculated?
(b) Why have real rates remained high in most major economies for the greater part of this decade?

Question 6

Why, in practice, are there so many different rates of interest in a country such as the UK?

Outline answers

Answer 1

(a) A yield curve shows in its slope the relationship between yields on *similar* assets with *different* terms to maturity.

(b) (i)

- *Liquidity preference* – longer-term rates will be higher than short rates because lenders/investors require greater compensation for longer loss of liquidity.
- *Risks involved* – greater risks of default, and capital erosion by inflation are involved in lending long term.
- *Expectations of an increase in interest rates* – these expectations will intensify, the longer the gap between short-term and long-term maturity. Lenders will therefore prefer to lend short (increasing supply and depressing rates) while borrowers will prefer to be locked in for long periods at the prevailing low rate (increasing demand and rates at the long end).

(ii)

- Short rates in the inter-bank and CDs markets represent the banks' marginal cost of funds.
  This affects:
  – the rate charged to market-rate related loans;
  – the level of rates on lending linked to base rates.

Answer 2

(a) *Why*

- To influence very short-term interest rates.
- To smooth flows between the government and monetary sector.

How

- If a shortage is likely to develop, the Bank will indicate to the discount house its willingness to buy (mainly) eligible commercial bills.
- The houses offer bills at prices of their own choosing.
- If the interest rates implied in these prices are in line with the monetary policy (i.e. within the undisclosed band), the Bank will accept the prices offered, otherwise the houses are forced to make offers of higher rates.
- These OMOs of the Bank are usually conducted in Bands 1 and 2 (14 days and 33 days bill maturity).

(b)

- The factors affecting the *general level* of interest rates (inflation expectations *plus* a margin to give lenders normally a positive return) are also the most important determinants of *mortgage rates*.
- *Long rates* are also influenced by the demand/supply of long-term funds (market forces) and changes in short rates (a change in short rates engineered by the authorities gets translated into movements along the entire interest-rate spectrum).
- Since the Bank can influence short rates by its OMOs, there is close relationship between this rate and the level of mortgage rate.
- In practice, a significant change in Bank's dealing rate will be quickly reflected in the same directions of mortgage rates.

Answer 3

Two-part question; make sure you answer both parts.

1. (a) Determination of short rates:
   Bank of England exerts the major influence:
   - Controls marginal cost of funds to the banking system through its operations in the bill market, via discount houses.
   - Interaction between the Bank's bill operations and money market expectations is the chief determinant.

   (b) Long rates greatly influenced by the above two points.
2. Bank base rates depend upon:
   - Wholesale rates in the inter-bank market (LIBOR), because of less dependence on traditional retail deposits and more on wholesale funds. Base rates move in line with short-term (up to three months) money market rates,
   - The extent of competition for deposits,
   - The monetary policy directives,
   - The rate of inflation – positive returns, and
   - The rates in overseas financial centres.

Answer 4

(a) Effects on the *personal sector*:
- Mortgage payments will be increased.
- Customer spending may be discouraged (borrowers are not normally concerned with the interest element in total repayment costs).
- Savings may be encouraged, by those who can afford to save, i.e. those with high incomes.
- Distress borrowing tends to be interest-inelastic.

(b) Effects on the *corporate sector*:
- Capital investment by companies would be discouraged, particularly if higher rates were seen as a part of the package to deflate the economy, adversely affecting business prospects.
- Corporate costs will increase, but not significantly as interest costs are only a small part of total costs.

(c) Effects on the *commercial banks*:
- Profitability of retail banks is enhanced because of the 'endowment' effect; but this may be offset by a reduction in loan demand, increased provisions for bad debts, reduced profits on fixed rate lending.

(d) Effects on the *capital account of the balance of payments*:
- Capital inflows may increase, provided overseas interest rates remain unchanged.
- Capital inflows would be mainly through portfolio investment (e.g. to purchase Treasury bills).
- Such inflows are largely short term and are often called 'hot money'.

Answer 5

(a)
- The real rate of interest is the rate actually paid (nominal rate), adjusted for inflation.
- The real rate is positive where the nominal rate exceeds inflation rate; negative if the reverse is the case.

- The real rate may increase either due to increase in the nominal rate or a decrease in the rate of inflation.
- It can be calculated by deducting the rate of inflation as measured by the RPI over a given period from the nominal rate of interest.
- Since investors and borrowers are influenced by the future, rather than the historical, rate of inflation, the *expected* rate of inflation should be used in calculating the real rate of interest.

(b)
- The need to curb inflation has meant restrictive monetary stances.
- Lax fiscal policies in many economies, e.g. the US economy, have meant large budget deficits, which have had to be controlled by tight monetary policies for much of the period.
- The strength of the dollar, coupled with high interest rates (to finance the budget deficit), have necessitated high real rates of interest in other major economies to prevent serious falls in their exchange rates.

Answer 6

Reasons for so many interest rates:

- Risk element: e.g. Treasury bills considered safer than bank deposits, therefore offer lower rate of return; the rate may become even lower if Treasury bills are in short supply.
- Time element – yield curve explanation.
- Size of loan: larger loans may attract higher rates.
- Cost of funds in the wholesale money markets.
- Type of currency involved, e.g. eurocurrency rates generally lower than sterling rates.
- Consumer Credit Act requires the publication of the true rate as well as the flat rate for personal loans.
- Floating base rates: to estimate the future course of interest rates, for term loans, to crystallise customer's repayments.
- Bank of England's bill dealing rate: determined administratively, not by the market.
- Status of the borrower, e.g. blue chip rate (base rate + 1) for blue chip customers only.

A tutor's answer

A specimen answer is given below to a question on an aspect of interest rates which is of increasing importance. The answer plan is intended to help you assess the scope of the question. Try to plan an answer to the question yourself before turning to the answer plan, and the full specimen answer given below.

Question

Assess the likely effects of an increase in the general level of interest rates on:
(a) a country's economy;
(b) the commercial banks.

Answer plan:
Effects of an *increase* only to be discussed.
(a) (i) deflationary effects;
(ii) inflationary effects; and
(iii) balance of payments effects.

(b) (i) effects on profit margins;
(ii) endowment effect;
(iii) fixed interest lending effects;
(iv) changes in banks' balance sheets;
(v) competitive advantage and disadvantage; and
(vi) effects of a higher exchange rate.

Specimen answer

(a) Higher interest rates will tend to depress demand, output and employment levels because all these are to some degree sensitive to changes in interest rates.

Consumer spending is likely to be reduced for three main reasons: higher cost of consumer credit, higher mortgage payments and higher prices of consumer goods (assuming the consumer goods industry passes its own higher interest costs on to the consumers). The demand for consumer goods, due to more expensive loans and higher prices, will tend to decrease, which in turn will cause contraction of output and employment within the consumer goods industry. The increase in unemployment will reduce tax revenue and increase government spending, particularly on unemployment benefits.

The effect on the capital goods industry will be different, largely because the demand for capital goods tends to be interest-inelastic. Since a large part of capital expenditure comes from the public sector, and public sector expenditure of this type is highly insensitive to interest rate changes, capital expenditure will therefore be little affected by higher interest rates. Output and employment within the capital goods industry will, provided profit margins are maintained, remain largely unchanged by higher interest rates.

Higher interest rates will tend to attract short-term investment and speculative balances from overseas to take advantage of any interest rate differential. Assuming that the conversion of 'hot money' balances into the national currency is on a large scale, it will increase the exchange rate of the national currency. The higher exchange rate will raise export prices, making exports less competitive, and reduce import prices, making imports more attractive. If the elasticities of demand for exports abroad and for imports internally are sufficiently elastic, then not only will the balance of trade go into deficit, but domestic output and employment will also be reduced by the production of fewer exports and by the increased penetration of imports.

Higher interest rates will also increase the cost of export finance which, in turn, will increase export costs and, possibly, export prices. However, this *direct* effect of higher interest rates on exports is likely to be less significant – interest costs are a small part of the selling price of exports – than the *indirect* effect of the higher exchange rate.

Higher interest rates, if persistent, will tend to increase the level of inflation, because of higher industrial costs of production and higher mortgage costs. On the other hand, higher interest rates will have a deflationary effect on aggregate demand, cutting consumption, investment and exports. This will 'weaken' both goods and labour markets, which would mean reduced profit margins and lower pay settlements, i.e. lower inflation. Cheaper imports, because of the high exchange rate, and a reduced money supply, because of high interest rates, may again lead to lower inflation.

(b) A general statement that higher interest rates increase bank profits is incorrect. The banking system may be divided into wholesale banking and retail banking. *Wholesale banking* (e.g. merchant banking) will not be much influenced by an increase in interest rates, because it relies to a much greater extent on the *margins* between lending and borrowing rates for its profits, rather than on actual rates. Higher loan *and* deposit rates for the wholesale banks would mean that their profit margins would largely remain unchanged.

For *retail banks* (e.g. clearing banks), higher loan rates also mean higher deposit rates, and therefore the increase in the profitability due to higher lending rates is largely offset by higher deposit rates. However, the profit margins of retail banks increase from the 'endowment effect' of their non-interest bearing deposits, i.e. the increase in net returns or non-interest bearing current accounts, which are now rather rare. On the other hand, their profit margins would be reduced on fixed-rate lending. Also, due to a fall in the value of assets charged as security for bank advances, their capital value may fall as interest rates rise. Furthermore, the authorities may claw back a portion of the extra profit from the endowment effect by imposing a windfall tax. This may explain, in part, why some banks traditionally choose to reduce the margins between deposit and lending rates when interest rates are rising, and to increase them when interest rates are falling.

There will be several likely changes on a bank's balance sheet from an increase in interest rates. The higher price of loans may reduce loan demand to buy consumer goods, if not capital goods. However, 'distress borrowing', especially by businessmen, is interest-inelastic and will still take place, increasing the retail banks' profitability. An increase in interest rates results in higher interest rate bills for bank customers, especially large borrowers; this may cause an increase in the bad debt rate and the banks would have to increase their bad debt provisions, which will reduce profitability. The effect on banks' deposit-taking vis-à-vis their competitors, especially building societies, would largely depend upon how well the interest rate structure of banks compares with that of their competitors. Building societies, unlike banks, have been slow to change their rates in response to changes in market rates, and it is likely that the banks' inflow of deposits may increase temporarily at the expense of building societies. Against this, an increase in interest rates slows down the growth of current accounts, since the opportunity cost of holding such accounts is more interest foregone. In fact, there may be a considerable switch from interest-free current accounts to interest-bearing accounts. If interest rates are expected to fall in the future, fixed-interest government securities become more attractive, which may further curtail the banks' current accounts.

A step further

Interest rates are an item of vital concern to banks. The *Financial Times* is an invaluable source of up-to-date data and information on the level, structure and pattern of interest rates. There are also many useful articles on interest rates and interest rate-related issues in the past editions of the *Financial Times*, which can be located via the *Financial Times Monthly Index*. The *Examiners' Reports* and *Updating Notes* published by The Chartered Institute of Bankers highlight those areas of interest rates which are most important to bankers. Articles in the quality financial press and in banking magazines will keep you abreast of major changes in this topic of the syllabus. The two-part *Signpost* article, 'Interest rates – theory and practice', in the May and June (1986) issues of *Banking World* is of particular importance. Be sure to read both parts of that article. Bank of England *Quarterly Bulletin* (BEQB) provides an authentic guide to the movements in the yield curve, and the reasons for movements.

CHAPTER 7

Economic Policy

Syllabus requirements

- Aims of economic policy, problems in achieving them, and the extent to which they have been achieved.
- The intermediate targets of monetary policy and the techniques of achieving them.
- The relationship of monetary policy with fiscal policy.
- General techniques of monetary control (portfolio constraints, interest rates, size of PSBR).
- The influence of monetary policy on the banking system.
- Principles of demand management through physical controls (prices and incomes policy) and fiscal policy techniques.
- The effectiveness of monetary and fiscal policies.

Getting started

Monetary economics is one aspect of a much broader area of economic study, called 'macro-economics', and monetary policy, fiscal policy, and prices and incomes policy (when in operation) fit into the broader economic policy.

Monetary policy is a set of measures by which the authorities attempt to regulate the aggregate expenditure in the economy by influencing liquidity and the terms and availability of credit in the country.

There are of course other policies which the authorities may use, either singly or in combination, to regulate aggregate demand in the economy. They attempt to regulate the level of economic activity by influencing public receipts (i.e. taxes) and public expenditure, (e.g. by using *fiscal policy*). Alternatively, the authorities may attempt to control the spending ability of the private sector directly, e.g. by pursuing a prices and incomes policy.

The objectives of monetary policy are set within the broad framework of national *economic policy*, so that the techniques of monetary policy may influence aggregate purchasing power in a manner which is consistent with the broader economic objectives. Such broader economic objectives may be divided into internal and external objectives. Internal objectives might include stable prices, a high employment level, rising economic growth and living standards, and a fair distribution of wealth among individuals, industries and regions of the country. External objectives might include a stable exchange rate for the national currency, a satisfactory balance of payments and level of foreign currency reserves, and the provision of aid to developing countries.

The dilemma that confronts the authorities is that achievement of some of these objectives may clash with the achievement of others. For example, the pursuit of high economic growth and employment may lead to inflationary pressures which may destabilise prices internally. Again, the maintenance of a stable exchange rate externally, may become difficult if inflation internally is making exports less attractive overseas and imports more attractive than domestically produced import substitutes. It is doubtful whether *all* the economic policy objectives can be achieved simultaneously. Hence it is a question, for the authorities, of assigning priorities amongst the objectives: which of the objectives should be given highest priority will depend upon the needs of the economy at any given period of time.

In recent years, most governments in the free world have faced varying degrees of rising inflation rates, which have undermined the value of people's incomes, savings and profits. Hence the main objective for most governments has been, for several years, 'stable prices', to help money regain and retain its legitimate value, both internally and externally. The belief has been that stable prices will in themselves lead to a higher rate of economic growth and a higher level of employment.

Essential principles

Economic Policy

The scope of macro (meaning 'large') economics concerns questions such as the following: What determines the general level of prices (i.e. the rate of inflation)? What determines the percentage of the overall labour force that is unemployed? What determines the total quantity of goods and services (national output) produced in a year? What determines the level of interest rates? What determines the rate at which the national currency exchanges for other currencies? What determines the country's balance of payments with other countries?

Macro-economics is concerned not only with the *level* of, say, unemployment and prices, but also with the *rate* at which they change.

Since the Second World War, British governments have formally committed themselves to achieve the following *major* economic policy objectives: (a) substantially full employment; (b) a stable level of prices; (c) annual growth in the level of national output; and (d) a balance over time on the balance of payments. Other objectives of the economic policy are concerned with the redistribution of income through the taxation system, and with the structure of industry – for example, should there be more or less public ownership?

The dilemma that confronts the authorities is that achievement of one objective may clash with the achievement of another. For instance, the pursuit of a high level of economic growth and employment may lead, via increased expenditure and rising wages, to inflationary pressures which, in turn, may destabilise prices internally. Or the maintenance of a stable exchange rate externally might become difficult, since the raising or lowering of interest rates internally could adversely affect domestic economic growth and employment. It is doubtful whether *all* the economic policy objectives can be achieved simultaneously. Therefore, it is a question of assigning priorities among the objectives by the authorities, depending upon the perceived needs of the economy at any given period. For instance, in the early 1960s it was full employment; in the late 1960s and 1970s, it was the eradication of balance of payments deficit; in the 1980s it has been the control of inflation, reduction in taxation, and privatisation.

There are two major economic policy disagreements among economists: (a) Should economic policy be *specific* or *detailed*? With specific policies the authorities select a very few highly-aggregated economic variables – such as the exchange rates, money supply, government expenditure – and try to control them, intervening very little in other areas. Detailed policies imply a plethora of devices aimed largely at achieving broad economic objectives. Such a policy may include a prices and incomes policy, minimum-wage legislation, interest rate manipulation, regulation of private industry and trade, exchange rates, and controls and subsidies. Under a detailed approach to economic policy, the government will involve itself in all aspects of the economy; (b) Should there be *rules* or *discretion* in the implementation of economic policy? The government announces a set of rules and targets publicly and commits itself to them, never deviating (the 'U' turn) from them. On the other hand, with discretion the government's intervention is responsive to current developments in the economy, and the policies are adjusted in the light of current economic events at the authorities' discretion, with no stigma attached to the policy alterations.

Very generally, those economists who favour specific policies also favour rigid rules, and those who favour detailed policies also favour discretionary intervention.

Economic policy instruments

Governments have at their disposal a number of instruments of economic management to aid them in pursuit of their policy objectives. The set of measures are: Monetary Policy; Fiscal Policy; Prices and Incomes Policy; and Exchange-rate Policy.

Since 1985, the stability of the exchange rate of the pound sterling, especially against the US dollar and the German mark, has been assigned an elevated position among the economic policy objectors. However, the flare-up in the inflation rate since 1988 has led to the unique prominence to the interest-rate policy, or rather, a high-interest-rate policy, to depress domestic spending and demand for credit, and thereby to reduce inflation, balance of payments deficit and bring the economy down to a 'soft landing', i.e. bringing the level of spending down without severe recession. However, the prolonged high interest rates are beginning to hurt the UK commerce and industry, and the adverse balance of payments is showing no signs of improving. The high interest rates are causing the mortgage rates to stay at high levels and that, in turn, *causes* the inflation rate to remain high.

Conduct of Monetary Policy

Let us assume that the authorities in a 'free' economy decide that the control of inflation is the *broad economic objective* that has highest priority, and that to achieve it, the major *monetary policy objective* is to be the control of expenditure. In the achievement of particular monetary policy objectives, central banks play a pivotal role.

In a free economy, the central bank cannot use monetary policy to control expenditure directly: there is no physical rationing under 'free' economies in normal times. Instead it tries to control expenditure by using indirect methods, such as setting intermediate monetary targets, e.g. controlling the rate of increase in money supply. To control the increase in money supply it sets operating targets on the banking and financial institutions, e.g. reserve asset requirements to reduce the credit multiplier. To accomplish its various operating targets the central bank employs a range of monetary instruments, e.g. open market operations or imposing its own interest rates.

There are therefore various stages in the conduct of monetary policy, which are invariably interlinked:

Instruments → Operating targets → Intermediate targets → Monetary policy objective; and of course vice versa

While the central bank has complete control over its own instruments, which in turn exert control over *operating targets*, yet from then onwards its control becomes gradually weaker. It cannot, for instance, fully control the *intermediate targets*, e.g. the growth of money supply, because the growth of money supply in a free economy depends on the behaviour of banks and their customers. For instance, the central bank has no control over how much credit bank customers demand or banks provide at a given level of interest rate. The link between the *intermediate target* and the *monetary policy objective*, e.g. the control of expenditure, also depends upon the behaviour of the general public: it is the general public which decides how much will be spent from a given amount of money supply available within the economy.

Thus the main issue in monetary policy is how far the things that the central bank *can* control enable it effectively to influence the things it *cannot* control wholly. The more reliable the links between the various stages of the monetary policy, the more successful will the central bank be in achieving the various objectives of monetary policy. We have assumed, for the purposes of analysis, that the *monetary policy objective* is to *control expenditure* (in order to control inflation). The central bank should then choose as the *intermediate target* that monetary variable which is most reliably linked to expenditure and upon which the central bank can exert most influence.

Monetary policy targets

There are five main variables from which the central bank, observing the above criteria, may choose intermediate targets in order to control expenditure: (1) The Money Supply; (2) Credit; (3) Interest Rates; (4) Exchange Rates; (5) Expenditure.

The money supply

The monetarists think that money supply is a good intermediate target. They believe that increases in money supply will, via the 'transmission mechanism', increase expenditure, some of the new money being used to buy goods and services, which increases expenditure directly, and some being invested in safe securities, such as first-class fixed-interest bonds, which increases expenditure indirectly. Buying bonds increases the market prices of such bonds but lowers interest rates: lower interest rates increase investment and consumption expenditure. Hence, the monetarists argue, the central bank should choose the growth in money supply as the intermediate target when it seeks to control expenditure.

There are some problems in making money supply growth the intermediate target for controlling expenditure.

A problem arises with regard to how interest-elastic is the demand for money. Suppose firms decide to increase investment, while money stock is stationary; this will raise interest rates which, in turn, will lower the demand to hold money and increase its velocity of circulation. Therefore higher levels of both income and expenditure will be possible with no increase in money stock.

The extent to which the change in velocity upsets the relationship between money, income and expenditure will depend upon how interest-elastic is the demand for money. If the demand for money is, as monetarists believe, interest-inelastic, then any change in interest rates will cause a small change in velocity, so that money, income and expenditure may still have quite a close relationship.

In any case, the central bank could reduce the *rate* of monetary growth to compensate for any increase in velocity. This, however, would involve the central bank in doing two very difficult things: first, *estimating* fairly closely the extent of the reduction in the demand for money (increase in velocity), and second, judging whether this reduction is temporary or likely to continue – if it misjudges, it could make things worse rather than better by reducing the rate of money supply growth. Besides, cutting the rate of monetary growth will not have its full effect on expenditure until the private sector has had time to adjust its expenditure pattern to it. The danger then is that, if the level of private sector expenditure does not decrease to the expected level, an impatient central bank may *further* reduce money so that, in due course, the twin action of a double reduction of money supply growth may create undesirable fluctuations in expenditure.

Thus for money supply to be a useful intermediate target, it is essential that the velocity of circulation of money is reasonably stable. This in turn, will depend upon whether the demand for money is interest-elastic or inelastic. The velocity of circulation of money will be more stable the more interest-inelastic is the demand for money.

Assuming that the monetary authorities do decide to make money supply an intermediate target, they then will need to make further decisions in respect to the following:

(a) Which monetary aggregate should they choose as a target? Most central banks monitor a range of narrow and broad monetary targets, which include a widening range of financial assets on the liquidity spectrum. Each central bank would choose that monetary aggregate as a target which is most closely related to expenditure and over which it has the most control.

(b) Having chosen the monetary aggregate, should the authorities publicly announce it? If the public believed that the central bank would be able to achieve the target, and that this achievement would cut inflation, then the public, including trade unions, might accept lower future money incomes, without anticipating a fall in their 'real' incomes and therefore in their standards of living. Business firms would then require lower price increases to achieve a particular level of 'real' profitability. These are some of the advantages of publicly announcing the targets and their growth rates. However, a disadvantage of such announcement would be to curtail the authorities' flexibility of action. The authorities would not be able to change the targets for the monetary aggregate without being accused of making a 'U'-turn, even though changes in economic conditions might require such changes in targets.

(c) Should there be *point* targets or target *ranges*? While precise point targets reduce uncertainty in the minds of the public, they are also very difficult to achieve, especially during a fluctuating economic climate. Therefore, it would probably be more realistic to set a target range, e.g. 7–10 per cent per annum growth rate in the targeted monetary aggregate; this would also allow some flexibility of action to the authorities.

Credit

In modern economies, credit (bank and building society lending, in the UK) and money are closely linked. An increase in bank and building society lending usually leads to an increase in bank and building society deposits and therefore an increase in the money supply. As modern economies become more and more 'cashless', the role of bank (and building society) lending (including credit cards) becomes crucial to aggregate expenditure in the economy.

The volume of bank and building society lending is, however, determined not only by the banks and building societies but also by the overall demand for credit in the economy. The immediate effect of a rise in total credit will be to increase bank and building society deposits, but some of the increase in deposits may disappear if the borrowers substitute, say, government bonds for their bank and building society deposits; in this case, government accounts with the central bank will increase and the banking sector's balances with the central bank and their share of total deposits will fall by the same amount. It is when the public buy more of other financial assets, using their bank and building society deposits, that the total stock of bank and building society deposits will be reduced. The volume of bank lending will also be determined by the amount of competition from *non-bank and non-building society lenders*.

Is credit (bank and building society lending) a good intermediate target? Although money supply and credit are closely linked, and a rise in credit is one of the ways in which money supply and therefore expenditure may increase, yet there is no reason why money supply and credit should grow at the same time or at the same rate: if banks and building societies increase lending to the public, but at the same time the central bank sells securities to the public, then there is no increase in money supply, even though credit has increased.

Some economists argue that credit is a better intermediate target than money supply in controlling expenditure, because households and firms rarely borrow unless they wish to spend. Therefore, an increase in credit should have a predictable effect on expenditure, and the control of credit should, more predictably, control expenditure. However, *if* credit is taken as an intermediate target of monetary policy, then *all* credit should be the basis for the control of expenditure by the authorities – bank and building society credit (including debit and credit cards and unused overdraft) *plus* funds borrowed by the public from other non-bank financial institutions in order to avoid disintermediation.

Interest rates

If the authorities knew reasonably well what level of expenditure would result from a given level of interest rates, then interest rates would be a possible candidate for the intermediate target. However the problem with interest rates as a target is that it is the *expectations* of businessmen, and not interest rates, which determine expenditure by firms. If business expectations of future demand and profitability rise considerably, then firms will increase their borrowing of investment funds, no matter what the level of interest rates. Even if the authorities do stabilise interest rates, at any given level of interest rates, the level of expenditure may fluctuate widely, due to sudden changes in business expectations. Furthermore, 'distress borrowing' of the non-bank public, and the government's borrowing to fund the PSBR are interest-inelastic. Rising inflation encourages borrowing, irrespective of interest rates, since the 'real' value of debt becomes gradually less, especially if the loans are used to buy goods which rise in price rapidly, e.g. houses. Therefore interest rates may have a poor correlation with credit and/or money supply, and therefore an unreliable link with expenditure. A prolonged period of high interest rates would probably reduce expenditure, and therefore inflation, but would seriously harm economic growth, employment and exports, and would cause recession in the economy.

Exchange rates

The exchange rate is the price of domestic currency in terms of foreign currencies. In those economies in which international trade accounts for a relatively high proportion of economic activity, changes in exchange rates can cause considerable disturbance in the domestic economy. For example, a fall in exchange rates will make exports more, and imports less, competitive, which will stimulate domestic economic activity; if the exchange rate rises, the reverse will happen, and domestic economic activity will be depressed.

If the country has a fixed exchange rate as its intermediate target, but has a higher domestic inflation rate than that of its trading partners, then the competitiveness of its exports will suffer, leading to pressure for a devaluation of its exchange rate to such an extent as would neutralise the inflation rate differentials.

While the authorities, by intervening directly (through buying and selling domestic currency) or by manipulating domestic interest rates, can influence the exchange rate of the domestic currency, a country's foreign currency reserves, or its ability to borrow currency overseas, or the advantages of interest-rate manipulation, are not limitless. Hence direct official intervention can only be to a limited extent; and manipulation of interest rates beyond certain levels may have dangerous effects for the economy. This could happen if external pressures lead to higher domestic interest rates than domestic economic conditions might warrant.

Expenditure

The authorities could choose expenditure itself as an intermediate target to control inflation; however, if they did so, two major problems would confront them. First, there is a time lag, often of up to two years, before expenditure by households and firms responds fully to changes in monetary policy; impatient monetary authorities might change the monetary policy *before* the full effects of the current monetary policy measures on expenditure levels had become apparent. Second, since current information on the growth of expenditure is not readily available, the authorities could be seriously handicapped in their monetary policy decisions for lack of up-to-date information on expenditure growth.

Instruments and methods (techniques) of monetary control

The two main components of money supply are cash (notes and coins) and deposits with banks and non-bank financial institutions. Central banks do not normally control the supply of cash in circulation; this is determined by the preference of the public for cash or deposits; there can, for instance, be large seasonal variations in the public preference for cash or deposits. Central banks, however, attempt to regulate, in several ways, the growth of total deposits, but especially the growth of bank deposits, because these deposits constitute a significant proportion of the total money supply.

The following methods or techniques (instruments) are commonly used by the central bank to control the level of deposits with financial institutions.

1. Direct controls

This technique places direct restrictions on bank lending or deposit growth. There are two instruments of direct control: lending ceilings and direct interest rate control.

Lending ceilings

The central bank instructs the commercial banks (and any other financial institutions under its jurisdiction) not to lend above a prescribed ceiling, say 6 per cent per annum. Since the commercial banks have to abide by the direct instructions of the central bank, the main advantage of this instrument is that bank lending, and therefore bank deposits, will not increase beyond 6 per cent per annum. This is called 'quantitative' ceilings. As against this advantage, there are two serious disadvantages:

(a) Unless the lending ceilings are applied uniformly to *all* lending institutions, the borrowing public could quite easily switch that part of its borrowing requirements which are *in excess* of the bank lending ceilings to uncontrolled non-bank lending institutions; then disintermediation, with all its distorting effects on money supply measurement, would occur.
(b) Competition and innovation among banks would be inhibited to the detriment of bank customers.

Qualitative guidance

Priority lending to certain sectors of the economy (e.g. manufacturers and exporters), and restraints on lending to other sectors (e.g. property companies, households).

Direct interest rate control

On the assumption that the public's demand for funds is interest-elastic the central bank imposes differentials and ceilings on interest rates paid on deposits and charged on lending to influence public borrowing and saving according to money supply growth targets; setting a higher rate to decrease bank lending and to increase deposits, and a lower rate to achieve the reverse. Direct interest controls can, however, cause several complications:

(a) Unless interest rate control is uniformly applied to all lending institutions, 'round tripping' or arbitrage could be triggered: if controlled rates are below uncontrolled rates, then non-bank public could borrow cheaply at controlled rates and lend the borrowed sum, at a quick profit, at uncontrolled rates. Round tripping leads to a misallocation of funds.
(b) The size of the PSBR is determined by the government's tax revenue and spending policy; *public sector borrowing* is largely interest-inelastic, therefore insensitive to interest rate controls.
(c) *Private sector borrowing* is not always interest-elastic. The possibility of profitable investment may be related more to business expectation than to the level of interest rate. 'Distress' borrowing (e.g. the need for working capital) are also largely unrelated to interest rates. Also note that people often prefer to use the much more expensive credit card rather than bank borrowing because of convenience and 'no-questions asked' spending.
(d) Direct interest rate control has a delayed, or lagged, effect on bank lending: this is because the expenditure commitments of firms and households take time to adjust to changed interest rates. It may therefore be just when the non-bank public has begun to adjust its borrowing requirements in line with the objective of controlled interest rates that the central bank may decide to alter the level of the controlled rates again.
(e) Rigid interest rate control may clash with other economic policy objectives, e.g. a rigidly applied high interest rate policy may militate against the need to increase investment in order to counteract rising unemployment and to avert recession.

Borrowing ceilings

Restrictions may be placed on the quantity of deposit liability which the controlled institutions may raise from a particular source (e.g. no more than 40 per cent from the wholesale markets).

2. Indirect controls

Open market operations of the central bank

Open market operations are a two-way weapon in the armoury of the central bank. On a day-to-day basis the technique is used to smooth out fluctuations in liquidity in the money market. This means the central bank selling high quality, money market instruments to mop up excess liquidity, and buying these instruments to relieve any liquidity shortage in the market. This type of open market operation will be applied at the existing interest rate level. However, if the authorities wish interest rates to change, then the central bank will do so by altering the *cost of 'last resort'* assistance to relieve the liquidity shortage of controlled institutions by buying and selling money market instruments at a rate higher or lower than is consistent with the existing interest rate level. Sometimes the central bank may deliberately create a shortage of liquidity in the money market by selling excessively attractive government and money market instruments, and then relieve the shortage at its own terms; this will raise the level of money market interest rates.

Cash-to-deposit ratio and reserve asset ratio requirements

Both these requirements place constrains on the controlled institutions' asset structures. If the central bank requires them to maintain, say, a 20 per cent cash-to-deposit ratio, it will clearly reduce their ability to lend by 20 per cent. If the central bank now requires that a portion of their cash-to-deposit ratio should be kept in specified reserve assets, so that if the reserve asset ratio falls below the required level, the banks will either have to curtail lending by raising lending rates, or have to bid for more deposits (by raising deposit rates or converting their non-reserve assets into reserve assets). The effect of imposing these requirements is to reduce the credit multiplier.

Call for special deposits

The central bank may instruct controlled institutions to deposit a specified percentage of deposits as 'frozen' funds, i.e. these interest-bearing deposits cease to be a part of their liquid funds, and are therefore not available for lending and credit-creation.

Supplementary Special Deposits ('Corset')

In addition to operating on commercial banks' reserve assets, the central bank can control the money supply by acting on *banks' liabilities*, via Supplementary Special Deposits. If a bank's, say, quarterly average of interest-bearing liabilities exceed a specified percentage, a *non-interest-bearing* Special Deposit becomes payable to the central bank (central bank's corset). Corset technique makes it less profitable for the banks to bid for deposits beyond a certain level.

Fiscal and monetary policies

The word 'fiscal' comes from the Latin 'fiscus', meaning pertaining to the public treasury, i.e. the income or revenue of a state. Thus fiscal policy implies management of aggregate demand in the economy by varying the size and the content of public revenue (i.e. taxes) and government expenditure, and making good any deficit by borrowing. Fiscal policy establishes the size of the PSBR or PSDR (Public Sector Debt Repayment) by determining the level of 'government' revenue in relation to its expenditure. 'Government' includes central and local governments, *plus* nationalised industries. A deficit annual budget implies a PSBR, and a surplus annual budget may imply a PSDR.

The objectives of fiscal policy, within the wider framework of economic policy, are:

1. Internal – to achieve a high level of employment; to promote economic growth and increase national income; to bring about a fair distribution of wealth and resources among individuals, industries and regions; to protect vital and infant industries against foreign competition, and to raise the living standards of the population as a whole.
2. External – to achieve a satisfactory balance of payments, to defend the foreign exchange value of the national currency, and to give aid to less developed countries.

In order to achieve these objectives, the authorities act by varying the size and direction of government spending, the size and composition of public revenue – mainly by alterations in direct and indirect taxes – and the size and sources of government borrowing.

The Public Sector Borrowing Requirement (PSBR) is the excess of government or public sector spending over government or public sector revenue. Monetary policy is responsible for financing PSBR or neutralising a PSDR, either by transactions with non-bank and non-building society sector, or by transactions with the central banks and the commercial banks, or by transactions with overseas residents. If it is financed mainly by *banks* and *building societies*, in the UK in exchange for government securities, then they will be able to use these securities to increase their deposits, and the money supply will increase. On the other hand, if the PSBR is to be financed by the *non-bank non-building society* public, then there will be no net impact on the money supply growth, but the yields (interest rate returns) on the government bonds (securities) will have to be raised sufficiently high to attract the public to buy the government bonds. High interest rates will tend to curb investment and consumption expenditure. Thus, fiscal policy measures cannot be implemented independently of monetary policy measures. However, monetary policy can be implemented by the authorities independently of fiscal policy: the central bank can alter its lending rate and/or issue instructions to commercial banks on their lending activities, thereby putting into motion the desired changes in the growth of the money supply and in the general level of interest rates.

Useful applied material

Monetary policy in Britain

By 1973, control over the growth of money supply became the main objective of the monetary authorities. In 1976, the official practice of announcing targets for money supply growth was started, and since then the authorities have tried gradually to reduce the rate of growth of money supply. Successive governments attached greater importance to the intermediate target of controlling the growth of money supply, believing this to be vital in containing inflation. This gave monetary policy the prominence previously accorded to fiscal policy. The policy of monetary control was designed to limit private sector demand in the economy, particularly by influencing private sector expectations as to future inflation; hence the monetary targets have been publicly announced in advance.

However, the target ranges have frequently been exceeded. The reason for this lies in the difficulty confronted by the monetary authorities in controlling money supply. If the Bank of England were to use changes in interest rates to control money supply, then it had to estimate fairly precisely the total demand for credit by the private sector at various levels of interest rate. Again, if the exchange rate is too high and attracts short-term capital flows, then domestic interest rates will need to be lowered; but lowering interest rates will increase money supply! Yet again, the level of interest rates required to keep the exchange rate at a particular level may well be different from the level of interest rates required to meet the money supply growth target. Since changes in the exchange rate have significant effects on the rate of domestic inflation and on economic activity, the authorities gave priority to the control of the exchange rate during the 1980s, at the expense of monetary targets. There was no official exchange rate target in the UK monetary policy; however, since the January 1985 sterling crisis, when sterling fell sharply the exchange rate has been apparently assigned an elevated role in the UK monetary policy, and since March 1986 has become an instrument of monetary policy.

In the Budget for 1987/88, the Chancellor stated that *no* target range would be set for the growth of the broad money aggregate.

These two important changes in the monetary authorities' approach to broad money marked the end of an era which began in 1976 when sterling M3 (the then broad money aggregate) was first targeted and which, during the early years of the Medium Term Financial Strategy (MTFS) (see below), was assigned a central role in the anti-inflationary battle. The authorities believed that there was a reasonably *close* relationship between the behaviour of sterling M3 and the inflation rate. In the event, the inflation rate was progressively reduced to around 4 per cent but the inflation success seemingly owed little to the behaviour of sterling M3. In every one of the past years, until it ceases to be targeted, the growth of sterling M3 exceeded the inflation rate and the increase in money incomes. The formal abandonment of sterling M3 targeting was, therefore, an official recognition of the fact that the path of broad money targeting had not been a good guide to the course of inflation in recent years.

The absence of a target range for broad money growth, however, should not detract from the way in which broad money and credit behaviour are strong influences on both the authorities' and the financial markets' assessment of overall monetary conditions.

The conduct of monetary policy has become increasingly complex in recent years, which has unavoidably led to a pragmatic approach. The appropriateness of the policy stance therefore takes several indicators such as exchange rate, M0 (which is still formally targeted, its 1990/91 target range is 1–5 per cent), growth of demand in the economy, wage and inflation prospects as well as broad money and credit behaviour into consideration.

Funding policy

Funding policy relates to the role played in controlling the money supply by the authorities' transactions in government debt instruments such as gilt-edged securities. In recent years the authorities have pursued a *full* funding policy, ensuring that the impact of government financial activities on the money supply is neutralised, i.e. the public sector as a whole does not inject liquidity into the economy, nor does it extract liquidity from it. In the early 1980s funding policy was deliberately used to reduce money supply growth – by *overfunding* the PSBR. Since then the PSBR has been replaced by a budget surplus and an accompanying public sector debt repayment (PSDR) programme. The intention has been to off-set the contractionary impact on the money supply of a budget surplus by repurchasing gilts from the private sector.

The authorities' objectives when conducting a gilt sales or repurchases with the non-bank and non-building society private sector (or the M4 private sector) are not confined simply to neutralising the impact on the money supply of a budget surplus or deficit, and the authorities also consider the effect on the domestic money supply of the direct intervention on the foreign exchanges. In 1989, for example, the UK's official reserves of gold and foreign currencies fell by over $14 billion, reflecting considerable Bank of England action to support sterling. The effect of such intervention is to drain liquidity from the system, and in order to neutralise this, additional repurchases of gilts from the M4 private sector were necessary. The reverse is of course also true. When the Bank of England intervened to prevent sterling from appreciating in 1988, the authorities neutralised the accompanying monetary increase by gilt sales.

The authorities are committed to their full funding policy, but with two exceptions: (a) neutralising intervention on the foreign exchanges would not necessarily be undertaken in the course of one year, but over a period; and (b) Treasury bill operations would, for technical reasons, be excluded from the funding equation. This move has assumed additional significance since the Treasury bill issue was raised significantly in 1989 to absorb liquidity from the system. This keeps conditions in the money market tight so that, in subsequent operations to relieve shortages of cash, the authorities can purchase eligible gilts at rates of interest of their own choosing and consistent with the monetary policy.

Targeting of MO

A 'target' is an economic variable which, unlike an economic policy 'instrument' (e.g. interest rates), is beyond the direct control of the authorities. A target is significant because it shows how the changes in instrument setting are affecting the ultimate policy objectives, and whether the policy is on course.

Suppose the authorities, in order to slow down the growth of total spending in the economy (i.e. Money Gross Domestic Product), raise the interest rates. It will take months before the government's statisticians confirm the decline in money GDP. Therefore any monetary aggregate whose growth relates closely to the level of money GDP, and for which weekly and monthly figures are available, provides the authorities with an invaluable guide to setting interest rates in the short and medium term.

The authorities have found the broad money aggregates, especially M3, in this respect unreliable, in that although M3, in recent years, rose rapidly, the rate of inflation actually fell quite considerably. Hence the authorities have suspended, at least until the pace of financial innovation in the UK (which largely caused the erratic behaviour of M3) has subsided, the targeting of broad money, leaving M0 (narrow money) the only targeted monetary aggregate.

M0 was introduced as a target in 1984, initially alongside M3, and since 1987 has been the only targeted monetary aggregate. M0 is basically notes and coins in circulation with the public. If the public's demand for notes and coins for spending increases they draw upon their sight deposits with banks and building societies. The Bank of England refills banks' tills with newly-issued notes and coins, and debits the banks' operational deposits with it by an equivalent amount. Thus the relationship between aggregate spending (money GDP) and notes and coins in circulation is simple and straightforward; as the money GDP increases, so does the M0, and M0 will only remain within its target range so long as money GDP is on course. When the money GDP goes off course, M0 statistics provide the authorities with early warning, thereby telling them to raise or lower interest rates.

Raising the interest rates would encourage the public to economise on spending by transferring funds from non-interest-bearing sight deposits to interest-bearing savings deposits, and thus the M0 will get back within its target range. M0 is like a 'thermometer' which gives accurate, early warning to the authorities of the 'temperature' money GDP has reached, so enabling them to change instrument settings so that the policy remains on course. In February 1990, M0 rose by 6.5 per cent; 1.5 per cent above its 1989/90 target range, thus signalling the authorities not to relax on the high interest policy.

Medium term financial strategy (MTFS)

Broadly speaking, the government employs fiscal policy in support of its monetary policy objectives, e.g. reducing public sector borrowing and spending in order to reduce money supply and thereby interest rates. The government has sought to restrain the public sector's demand for funds in order to achieve its monetary targets at lower interest rates, and thus to encourage more domestic investment and output in the private sector. The combined objectives for money supply **and** public sector borrowing were first established in 1980, and are known collectively as the Medium Term Financial Strategy.

The basic aims of MTFS are to reduce inflation by reducing the growth of total spending power in the economy, as measured by the cash value of UK national output, to transfer more resources to the private sector via a balanced budget, to keep the growth of M0 (narrow money) within the range of 0–4 per cent in 1991/92, and to base decisions about interest rates on a continuous assessment of all monetary conditions. The reasoning underlying the MTFS objectives is that a higher PSBR requires higher interest rates to finance it and that public sector borrowing tends to be interest-inelastic, whereas private sector borrowing trends to be more sensitive to higher interest rates. Therefore the higher interest rates required to meet the increased needs of the public sector borrowing requirement 'crowds out' private sector expenditure; this arrests economic growth and employment.

In the early 1980s, the authorities emphasised control of the money supply through the MTFS. Targets for narrow and broad money aggregates were set each year and publicly announced with the objective of reducing public expectations of future inflation. More recently, partly due to the changes in the financial markets, only M0 has been targeted. The broad measures have been allowed to grow strongly: M4 rose by 17 per cent in 1988.

The MTFS also set a target for reducing the PSBR over a number of years, starting from its 4 per cent of Gross National Product level in 1980. The fiscal years since 1987/88 have in fact seen the replacement of a PSBR by a PSDR, indicating the success of the government's aims in this area, albeit assisted by large privatisation receipts.

However, upward pressure on prices has not been relieved by the reduction in public sector spending; by the middle of 1990, the inflation rate had climbed up to very nearly 10 per cent. The authorities maintain that a huge increase in the private sector consumption, due to high wage settlements and large increases in borrowings from banks and building societies, has fuelled inflation to nearly double figures. Hence the authorities' determination to keep the interest rates as high and for as long as is necessary to bring down the private sector spending, which will bring down inflation to zero. The authorities have been criticised for using a one-club approach in tackling the problem, and that they should affect bank lending, in addition to raising the interest rates, by imposing credit 'ceilings' and calls for special deposits, and even applying the 'corset' (supplementary special deposits) on the banking system. The authorities claim that under the present liberalised financial markets, with no exchange controls, the UK households and companies could easily borrow from overseas lending institutions; and over those institutions the UK authorities have no control.

Current monetary control techniques in the UK

The monetary policy in the UK is designed, in the main, to control money supply, interest rates and the exchange rate of the pound sterling. Until 1980, the authorities used several control techniques, such as reserve asset ratio requirements, quantitative and qualitative controls on bank lending, Minimum Lending Rate (MLR) changes, open market operations, calls for special deposits and supplementary special deposits. Of these control techniques, only open market operations, the possibility of resurrecting the MLR, calls for special deposits and 'qualitative guidance' (requests by the Bank of England to banks that they give priority in lending to certain sectors of the economy, and restrain lending to other sectors) have survived the 1981 changes. (See p.124.)

1. *Open market operations* (OMOs) involve the buying and selling by the Bank of England of eligible commercial and Treasury bills to influence:

(a) the cash and liquidity base of the banking system and therefore the capacity of banks to lend; and
(b) directly the level of short-term interest rates and indirectly the structure of longer-term interest rates. Short-term interest rates are an essential instrument of UK monetary policy. Changes in interest rates have a reasonably quick and direct effect on narrow money, as they do on the exchange rate. Their effect on broad money, however, is more complex and much more delayed.

If the objective of OMOs is to *affect the growth of bank advances* in order to control the growth in money supply, then the Bank relieves the liquidity shortage in the market at a bill dealing rate which is higher than the current money market rate. In this way the Bank is able to control the marginal cost of funds to the banking system. The level of short-term (up to three months) inter-bank rates broadly corresponds to the marginal cost of banks' funds. However, since the Bank in its OMOs continues to deal primarily with the discount houses, its bill dealing rates can be out of line with inter-bank rates; the difference between the two rates represents the marginal cost of funds to the commercial banks. The level of banks' base rates tends to move in line with money market rates. A rise in the banks' base rates, the authorities believe, would lower the demand for bank lending and, in turn, would curb the growth in money supply.

If the objective of the OMOs is simply to *relieve any shortage or surplus of liquid funds* in the money market, then the Bank buys and sells money market instruments at a bill dealing rate that is equal to the existing level of short-term interest rates.

If the authorities wish to encourage the public to hold the public sector debt for a longer term, they will attempt to affect the *structure* of interest rates. While changes in the Bank's bill dealing rates will directly affect the level of short-term rates, these changes will also indirectly affect the structure of longer-term rates; they will do this by affecting market expectations as to the movements in longer-term rates, e.g. movement of short-term rates over the year (yield curve) will influence the one-year money market rate.

The OMOs are conducted by the Bank of England exclusively in the bill market via the discount houses, and in order to ensure an adequate supply of commercial bills – bills of exchange issued by commercial firms to finance short-term transactions – the authorities have increased the number (to over 100) of eligible banks, i.e. banks whose acceptances the Bank is prepared to rediscount.

2. In times of acute shortage of liquidity in the market, the Bank enters into REPOS agreements with the commercial banks directly.

3. All institutions in the monetary sector are obliged to keep with the Bank 0.4 per cent of their deposits in non-operational and non-interest bearing deposits. This requirement is not meant to affect the assets of the banks – although it does; rather, it is meant to provide the Bank with operational balances to assist it in its OMOs.

4. Under the 'dirty' floating exchange rate policy (i.e. the Bank intervenes in the market when it feels it to be necessary) pursued in the UK, the authorities seek to hold the exchange rate of sterling within a range which they believe to be in the best interests of the economy as a whole (currently the crucial rate is between sterling and Deutschemark). To prevent the exchange rate falling dangerously low, the Bank of England will seek, by direct intervention (i.e. buying sterling on the foreign exchange market), to raise short-term interest rates respectively to reduce the supply of, and increase the demand for, sterling on the foreign exchange markets.

The effectiveness of monetary control in the UK has not been an unqualified success. As far as the *manipulation of interest rates* is concerned, via OMOs, the interest rate policy has suffered due to two reasons.

1. The Bank of England cannot control *both* the money supply and the price of money, i.e. interest rates, simultaneously:
2. The demand for bank advances, at least in the short run, is often interest-inelastic.

UK interest rates at 11½ per cent are still well above those in other major countries, making UK firms less competitive internationally.

The attempts by the Bank of England to ease the acute downward pressure on the *foreign exchange value of sterling* by raising the level of short-term interest rates has attracted excessive inflow of foreign speculative and investment balances into the country. This has had adverse effects on efforts to control the growth of money supply. Fluctuations in the exchange rate have caused uncertainty to UK exporters and importers. The balance of payments position has progressively deteriorated and is expected to show a deficit of £20 billion, five times higher than 1989–90 Budget forecast. Inflation has reached an unacceptable level. The economic growth rate for the first half of 1989/90 was a mere annualised 1.5 per cent. During late 1990 and early 1991, it was negative.

The above analysis of the problems and after-effects of monetary policy which has sought to control interest rates, the money supply and the exchange rate, shows that the authorities cannot, in practice, achieve the intermediate monetary target of controlling all these variables *at the same time*, however much they might think otherwise.

On the positive side, the total national output growth has been until 1991 around 3 per cent, and the PSBR, as a percentage of the national output, has been steadily reduced, and for 1989–90 there was a balanced Budget, and since 1987–88 Budget there has been budget surpluses. Unemployment has steadily fallen, but is still around 7 per cent of the working population. Since the middle of 1990 it has been rising rapidly.

Recent examination questions

The following six questions have been asked in recent years on the topic of monetary policy and its relationship with fiscal policy. Before looking at the outline answers, spend ten minutes or so trying to identify the main points to be used in your answer to each question.

Question 1

To what extent is a successful anti-inflationary policy necessarily associated with an increase in unemployment? Illustrate your answer with reference to the economic experience of the UK during the past decade.

Question 2

(a) Outline the principal goals of economic policy.
(b) Consider the extent to which monetary policy in the UK has been successful in achieving these economic goals in recent years.

Question 3

In the 1988 UK Budget the Chancellor of the Exchequer indicated that the UK no longer had a Public Sector Borrowing Requirement (PSBR) but a Public Sector Debt Repayment (PSDR).

(a) Explain precisely what the Chancellor meant by this statement.
(b) Discuss the impact a PSDR will have on:
  (i) interest rates.
  (ii) the market for gilt-edged securities.
  (iii) the money supply.

Question 4

Outline the main changes in monetary control techniques that have occurred in the UK during 1980 and 1981. How have these changes affected the commercial banks?

Question 5

Describe the following and discuss their role in the operation of monetary policy:
(a) gilt-edged securities,
(b) commercial (eligible bank) bills,
(c) the sale of public sector assets.

Question 6

In seeking to achieve the ultimate objectives of monetary policy, the authorities can set *intermediate* targets.
(a) Discuss the *intermediate* targets that might be selected.
(b) List the techniques that could be used to achieve these targets.

Outline answers

Answer 1

(a) Explain alternative policies to control inflation:
- Deflation: via monetary policy and/or fiscal policy.
- Prices and incomes policy: to control aggregate demand and expenditure.
- Import controls: their effects on balance of payments deficit.

(b) Discuss causes of inflation:
- Cost-push: increased labour costs pushing up prices.
- Demand-pull: prices pulled up by too much money chasing too few goods.

(c) In the UK there has been some trade-off between inflation and unemployment.

Answer 2

(a) List clearly the traditional goals of economic policy:
- Full employment; stable prices; slight surplus in the current account of balance of payments; reasonable 'real' economic growth rate; satisfactory and stable exchange rate; a more equal distribution of income, between rich and poor people and between rich and poor areas.

(b) Explain the problems confronted by the authorities in achieving all goals simultaneously:
- Inherent conflicts among goals: control of inflation leads to rising unemployment and unsatisfactory exchange rate.
- Monetary policy, like fiscal policy, is an integral part of economic policy, and is not easy to isolate for analysis.
- MTFS and its link with PSBR and money supply.

Answer 3

(a)
- A PSBR is the *excess* of central government nationalised industries and local authorities expenditure over revenues. This has been the situation for many years in the UK, certainly since the Second World War.
- The emergence of the PSDR implies the *reverse*, meaning that National Debt can be repaid from the excess of revenue accruing to the public sector.

(b) (i) A PSDR implies that the private sector borrowers are not 'crowded out'; there is less pressure for borrowing *long-term* funds, and long-term interest rates should fall, other things remaining unchanged.

(ii) The gilt market will contract as the government requires to raise no funds to finance its activities, and repays existing debt.

(iii)
- Reference to the *counterparts* analysis shows that the sector from which gilts are purchased is crucially important. Bearing in mind that the government has withdrawn funds from the system. To the extent that gilts are purchased from the private sector (other than banks and building societies) there will be *no impact* on the money supply *once the cycle is completed*.
- Purchases from banks and building societies will *reduce* the money supply.
- Purchases from overseas residents, e.g. from sterling held overseas, will *reduce* the money supply.

Note: The recent (1988 and 1989) monetary growth has been due to bank and building society lending to the private sector.

Answer 4

(a) Principal changes in monetary control techniques during 1980 and 1981:
- *During 1980*: abolition of the 'corset' (actually 1979); phasing out of direct 'lender of last resort' lending by the Bank of England and the use of open market operations in the commercial bill market as an indirect method.
- *During 1981*: suspension of MLR; Bank of England to keep very short-term interest rates within an unpublished band; 1.5 per cent cash ratio on London clearers abolished; 0.5 (now 0.4) per cent cash ratio applied to all banks in the new monetary sector; all 'eligible' banks must keep secured loans, 4 to 6 per cent (reduced to 2.5 to 5 per cent) with discount houses (now abolished); creation of many new eligible banks.

(b) Effects of the above changes on commercial banks:
- Abandonment of corset: freer lending, visibly in mortgage field.
- Suspension of MLR: more flexible interest rates, with implication for bank base rates and the pricing of overdrafts.
- Emphasis by the Bank of England on intervention in the bill markets: upsurge in the use of commercial bill finance and keen competition on 'acceptances' from the new banks.
- Abolition of the reserve asset ratio: implication for bank balance sheets, able to assess liquidity requirements on prudential grounds in conjunction with the Bank of England.

Answer 5

(a) ● To finance the PSBR, the authorities can sell gilts to the:
  (i) M4 and building society private sector;
  (ii) banking sector;
  (iii) Bank of England;
  (iv) overseas sector.
- Sales to the M4 private sector together with the increase in PSBR have no effect on money supply, therefore keep monetary expansion under control.

(b) ● Commercial bills accepted by eligible banks become eligible bills, eligible for sale by the discount houses to the Bank of England to relieve cash shortages in the market.
- Dealing in eligible bills dominates the Bank's money market operations to smooth liquidity fluctuations and to influence short-term interest rates; the Bank provides relief to the market by purchasing the bills at rates consistent with interest rate policy.
- Dealing is usually in Bands 1 and 2 of the four maturity bands, but also sometimes in longer-term bills, if considered appropriate.

(c) ● Sale of public sector assets *reduces* the size of the PSBR, rather than finances it; therefore the amount of gilt sales is reduced by the amount of the net privatisation proceeds.

Answer 6

(a) Candidates for intermediate targets:
  (i) *Money supply*. Monetarists consider this as a very important target because of the close link between changes in the money supply and inflation. *Problem*: which definition of the money supply to target.

(ii) *Interest rates.* Interest rates play a significant role in controlling other intermediate targets. By effecting changes in interest rates, the authorities hope to influence consumer spending and business investment. *Problem*: it will be months before interest rate changes take effect.

(iii) *Credit.* There is a close relationship between the volume of credit and the level of expenditure because changes in credit cause changes in the money supply. *Problem*: unless *all* credit is targeted, disintermediation will result.

(iv) *Expenditure.* A target might be set for the nominal GNP growth. *Problem*: too many factors affect the GNP growth. PSBR, as a proportion of the GNP, may be targeted.

(v) *The exchange rate.* The connection between it and inflation and trade performance make it an obvious target. *Problem*: achieving the exchange rate target may mitigate against other objectives.

(b)
- The size of the PSBR and the sources of its finance.
- Direct intervention by the Bank to influence exchange rate.
- Manipulation of interest rates.
- OMOs.
- Moral suasion.
- Reserve requirements.
- Direct control on lending:
  - special deposits;
  - quantitative;
  - qualitative.

A tutor's answer

The following question deals with the theory and the practice of monetary policy. The specimen answer covers the full scope of the question. Try to make a relevant answer plan yourself before reading the specimen answer.

Question

(a) Outline the principal features of monetary policy as operated in the UK since 1979.

(b) To what extent have the overall goals of macro-economic policy been achieved in the UK since 1979?

Answer plan:

(a) (i) the ultimate objective of the monetary policy;

(ii) the policy framework to achieve that objective;

(iii) the implementation of the policy.

(b) An account of how monetary policy has fared in tackling:

(i) inflation;

(ii) economic growth;

(iii) current account of the balance of payments;

(iv) unemployment.

Specimen answer

(a) The main thrust of the monetary policy since 1979 has been towards securing a progressive reduction in monetary growth to contain and ultimately to eliminate inflation, thus providing a firm basis for economic growth. A steady decline in the PSBR as a percentage of Gross National Product, and in money supply growth, were projected for a number of years in advance, though these projections have been subject to upward revisions from time to time. Annual targets for various monetary and liquidity aggregates, and for the PSBR/GNP ratio have been adopted. Sterling's performance, as reflected by its exchange rate, has not been an explicit intermediate *target*. Rather it has become an increasingly important *indicator* of the success of monetary policy, particularly so from October 1985 onwards with the reduced emphasis on the behaviour of broad money.

The implementation of the policy has been achieved through: (i) controlling the size of the PSBR by expenditure cutbacks; (ii) Bank of England money market operations to influence the level of interest rates; and (iii) funding (or, for much of the period, overfunding), by selling public sector debt outside the banking system.

(b) The problem of *inflation* has been tackled very successfully over the past eight years, with the RPI falling from 18 per cent in 1980 to a little over 3 per cent in the first half of 1987. However, the inflation rate had risen to nearly 10 per cent by June 1990.

Economic growth in the period from 1983 to 1985 was restored to the long-term average of between 2 per cent and 3 per cent a year. This was near the EEC average, but low by comparison with the USA and Japan. Economic growth, however, slowed down during 1986, but there was some resurgence in 1987, achieving a growth rate of around 2 per cent by August 1989.

The *current account of the balance of payments*, aided by substantial oil revenues (except for the first nine months of 1986) has been in moderate surplus or near equilibrium from 1980 to 1985. It went into heavy deficit in March 1986, and performed rather badly until the rise in oil prices in the autumn of 1986. Britain, however, is currently a net importer of manufactured goods. By the end of 1989, the balance of payments deficit was approximately £20 billion.

The buoyant economic conditions during 1987–88 and increased government tax revenues and privatisation receipts resulted in the elimination of the *PSBR* and the emergence of a PSDR (Public Sector Debt Repayment) of over £14 billion in 1988–89.

In the 12 months to February 1989, M0 grew at 6.6 per cent per annum a substantial drop from 8.1 per cent annual growth in January 1989.

In common with the experience of most other countries in Europe and North America, the UK performance on *unemployment* has been disappointing. Despite the economic upturn between 1982 and 1985, the number out of work has remained on a stubbornly rising trend (except since the last quarter of 1986), reaching over three million by August 1986. The unemployment figures have fallen to below two million during 1989. There are economists who maintain that a reflationary monetary policy will break the logjam rapidly and reduce unemployment. There are others who claim that reflation will merely result in an upsurge in price and wage inflation. The stance of the current UK monetary policy was slightly expansionary until about the Autumn of 1988, when the inflation rate began to rise alarmingly and the brakes were applied on economic activity via the high interest rate policy.

A step further

This chapter and the chapters on 'Money and Inflation', 'Money Supply', 'Interest Rates' and 'Exchange Rates' are closely connected. It is essential for you to understand this linkage in order to gain an overall understanding of domestic monetary economics. The Chartered Institute of Bankers' *Examiners' Reports, Updating Notes* and 'Signpost' articles in *Banking World* are extremely useful sources for keeping abreast of various movements in monetary policy, and also in topics linked to monetary policy. In this connection, a study of *A Guide to Monetary Policy*, published by the Banking Information Service, is strongly recommended. Bank of England *Quarterly Bulletins* (BEQBs) give the up-to-date official figures and facts of the UK economy.

CHAPTER 8

Balance of Payments

Syllabus requirements

- The structure of the balance of payments accounts in general and of the UK in particular.
- Recent influences on the UK balance of payments.
- Causes and effects of changes in the terms of trade.
- Method of correcting current account disequilibrium.
- Difference between 'financing' and 'correcting' current account imbalances.

Getting started

A country imports those goods and services which it needs but is either unable to produce internally or which it can only produce at uncompetitive cost or of inferior quality. It pays for the imports of such goods and services largely by its foreign currency earnings from exports. The balance of payments of any country records the revenues and payments from all economic and non-economic transactions between its government, firms (including their foreign subsidiaries) and residents, and the governments, firms and residents of those countries with which it trades. The balance of payments is an account and, like any other account, it must balance.

The importance of the balance of payments position to a country is that if it has exported more goods and services than it has imported, then it is a creditor country and stands to receive payments in foreign currencies. These can be used to build up its currency reserves, to repay past overseas loans, to invest overseas and to give aid to less developed countries (LDCs) loans. Conversely, if it has imported more goods and services than it has exported over a period of time, then it is a debtor country, and has to make good the deficit by drawing on its currency reserves, by borrowing overseas, by selling its valuable assets and foreign investment and even by accepting foreign aid. A chronic balance of payments deficit for a country suggests to the rest of the world that it is unable to pay its way in international trade and investment, which reflects badly on its government, firms and citizens.

A country's foreign currency and gold reserves are finite and its ability to borrow overseas or to raise funds in some other ways is not without limit. Therefore, a country with a continuous balance of payments deficit runs the distinct risk of being treated as a bad debtor by its trading partners, who may refuse to sell it the goods and services it needs. If this happens, then its economic growth will be badly hit and the level of employment and the standard of living of its residents will fall significantly.

It is therefore of utmost importance for the government of a country suffering from a prolonged deficit on its external account to take such measures internally as will encourage its exports and discourage its imports, so that the deficit on its balance of payments is rectified and it is once again able to pay its way in the world.

Essential principles

Terms of trade

Over a period of time, the terms of trade compare the relative changes in the prices of a country's exports with relative changes in the prices of its imports. The changes in export prices are expressed as a percentage of changes in import prices, and then presented as an index, with some base year as 100. The terms of trade index of a country is determined by the following formula:

$$\text{Index of terms of trades} = \frac{\text{Index of export prices}}{\text{Index of import prices}} \times 100$$

The indices for both exports and imports start at 100 at a common starting date. If the index increases, compared to a base year at 100, the terms of trade are said to have 'improved', i.e. a given quantity of exports will purchase more imports than before. Thus, if the index of export prices of a country has risen over a period of years from 100 to 119, and its index of import prices has fallen over the same period of years from 100 to 97, then the terms of trade of the country are said to have improved over the period by the ratio 119/97 x 100 = 122.68 per cent. Since the terms of trade index in the base year was 100, then, in the above example, the purchasing power of a fixed bundle of exports rose over the period by 22.68 per cent, i.e. 22.68 per cent more imports could be purchased at the end of the period than were purchased by the same fixed quantity of exports in the base year. Note that the terms of trade refer to the multilateral trade of a country and not to its bilateral trade.

Changes in the terms of trade, i.e. relative changes in the prices of exports and imports, affect the *values* of exports and imports. Since values are quantities multiplied by prices, the relative elasticities of demand for exports and imports will be vital in determining whether the total receipts from exports or the total payments for imports will rise or fall as export and import prices change. If the overseas demand for a country's *exports is elastic* then, other things being equal, its total receipts from exports will be greater at *lower* export prices, i.e. when the terms of trade have 'deteriorated'. If the overseas demand for its *exports is inelastic*, then total receipts from exports will be greater at *higher* export prices, i.e. when the terms of trade have 'improved'. Similarly, if the domestic demand for its *imports is elastic* then, other things being equal, its import bill will be greater at *lower* import prices, i.e. when the terms of trade have 'improved'; if the demand for its *imports is inelastic*, its import bill will be greater at *higher* import prices, i.e. when the terms of trade have 'deteriorated'. Clearly the terms 'improvement' and 'deterioration' must be treated with caution when applied to the terms of trade.

There are gains to be made by countries specialising in the commodities they are relatively most efficient in producing, and exporting the surpluses for imports. However, if the terms of trade deteriorate, then the *exchange* advantage will be less than before. This does not mean however that the gains from trade will necessarily grow just because the terms of trade 'improve'. For instance, a rise in the price of exports may – unless demand for exports is inelastic – be associated with a fall in the *volume* of exports. Any cut in the volume of trade will clearly diminish the gains from specialisation and trade.

Changes in the prices of exports and imports result from various factors affecting the conditions of supply and demand for goods which are traded on international markets. *Producers* of a good for which there is a world-wide inelastic demand may exploit their *monopoly* position and raise the price of the product several times over, thereby improving their terms of trade. On the other hand, the major *buyers* of certain products may exploit their *monopsony* (buyer's monopoly) position by deliberately withholding demand, thereby causing the terms of trade of the suppliers of such products to deteriorate.

Shortages of food and raw materials in industrialised countries, or increases in demand for such commodities via higher real incomes or population growth, will tend to improve the terms of trade of *primary goods-producing* countries. On the other hand, technical progress may cause the terms of trade of primary goods-producing countries to deteriorate; for instance if the new information technologies economise on the need for raw materials in production.

Protectionism and other direct controls

In order to protect home industries and employment against foreign competition and to become self-sufficient in essential goods, a country may seek to protect itself against imports. Import barriers may take any of the following forms:

Import tariffs

When home products and foreign substitutes are equally priced, an import duty which is higher than any domestic excise duty is protective; it raises the price of foreign substitutes above the price of the domestic product, making home products more attractive.

Subsidies

The government gives direct grants to home producers to reduce their unit costs and give them a price advantage over imported goods.

Export premiums

Exporters are given rebates or refunds of taxation on exports to encourage the expansion of existing export industries.

Quotas

A specified volume or value of imports is allowed during a *given* period.

Physical controls

A complete embargo may be imposed on imports from certain countries.

Of the above protective methods, only import tariffs provide income for the government practising protection. In the UK, protection in one form or another has been practised since 1932. Protective measures are often 'hidden', in the form of credit guarantees, cheaper finance to exporters, import deposits and excessive documentation against imports.

Most trading countries accept that an international trade free from protection will benefit all participants. To free international trade from trade barriers, associations such as the General Agreement on Tariffs and Trade (GATT) have been set up. Although GATT, with over 100 member countries, has succeeded in reducing import tariffs to an appreciable extent, the aim of complete free trading among members still remains an ideal.

Protection need not be confined to a single country, but may be extended to cover a group of countries, e.g. the 12 member countries of the EC enjoy free trade amongst themselves but have a protective wall around themselves and the rest of the world.

Rectifying imbalances in the balance of payments

As we have already noted, no country can continue to have a balance of payments deficit year after year. However, no country may continue to have a balance of payments *surplus*, for at least two reasons.

1. It means that such a country is continuously selling more to the rest of the world, and buying less from it. This is likely to mean that the export earnings of *other countries* in the surplus country's currency are less than is required; therefore they will become less and less able to buy and pay for the surplus country's exports. It may even be in the surplus country's own interest to work off its surplus by increasing its imports from the rest of the world.
2. If the surplus country refuses to increase imports, it may lead other countries to erect trade barriers against its exports via prohibitive import duties, stringent import quotas or even an embargo on its exports.

Rectifying a balance of payments surplus

Under freely floating exchange rates (see Ch.9), the adjustment should be automatic via the market mechanism. The demand for the surplus country's currency will be high, because the rest of the world will need its currency to pay for their imports; this will push up the exchange rate of the surplus country's currency, making its exports expensive and its imports cheaper and more attractive. The higher exchange rate will, other things being equal, tend to eliminate the surplus and bring about an automatic equilibrium in its balance of payments. If 'other things' are not equal, e.g. there is inelastic demand for its exports, then the government of the surplus country will need to take deliberate policy action to discourage exports and the inflow of capital, and to encourage imports and the outflow of capital.

The following are possible policy measures which the government may take to correct a *surplus* on its balance of payments on current account.

Expansion of home demand

This may be achieved by reducing taxes, lowering interest rates, lifting credit restraints and increasing public expenditure. The increase in home demand would divert export production to the home market and increase the level of imports, thus reducing surplus on visible trade. The extent to which resources switch to home demand will depend on the elasticity of domestic supply, i.e. how quickly domestic supply can meet increased home demand.

Allow its exchange rate to rise

That is, let the exchange rate appreciate under floating rates, revalue under fixed exchange rates. Adjustment through the exchange rate mechanism involves changes in prices, so that the elasticities of demand for imports and exports will be crucial. If the demand for *imports* is elastic, then the total amount of foreign exchange paid out on imports will be greater at a lower domestic price, i.e. after appreciation (or revaluation) of the domestic currency; similarly, if the demand for *exports* is elastic, the amount of foreign exchange received for exports will be lower at the higher overseas price, i.e. after appreciation (or revaluation). The policy objective here is to increase total import payments and to decrease total export revenue.

Free imports from restrictions, and place restrictions on exports

Import restrictions, such as import quotas, restrict the volume of imports; *removal* of such restrictions will markedly increase imports. By the same reasoning, placing export quotas, especially if the demand for exports is inelastic, will quickly achieve a reduction in the volume of exports. However, some countries, for instance, those who produce and export oil, may prefer to place a tax on exports; this will not only reduce exports, but will at the same time benefit the National Exchequer.

Reduce net 'invisible' earnings

This may be achieved by a variety of measures, such as giving grants to developing countries, or by encouraging residents to take holidays abroad and to send gifts to relatives and to charities overseas. Note that giving *loans* to developing countries will mean that interest on loans will increase the surplus on current account.

Rectifying a balance of payments deficit

A deficit country will need to adjust its current and/or capital accounts.

Adjustments on current account

A number of measures may be adopted:

1. Depreciation or devaluation of the exchange rate of the domestic currency

This means a fall in the exchange rate. Other things being equal, this will make imports expensive and therefore less competitive with domestic goods, and make exports more competitive in overseas markets. The extent of the reduction in imports and increase in exports will be determined by the relative elasticities of demand for imports and exports. If the price elasticity of demand for imports is elastic, i.e. if the percentage change in quantity of imports demanded divided by the percentage change in price of imports (consequent upon depreciation/devaluation) results in greater than one, then a rise in import price will cause a more than proportionate fall in the quantity of imports. The *value* of imports (quantity of imports x price) will then be less than it was *before* the depreciation/devaluation. If, however, the price elasticity of demand for imports is inelastic, then depreciation/devaluation will cause the value of imports to be greater than it was prior to the fall in the exchange rate. A similar calculation will derive the price elasticity of demand for exports. Note that the calculation of the relative elasticities of demand for imports and exports is vital in order to determine precisely the extent to which the exchange value of the national currency must fall in order to achieve the desired level of import reduction and export expansion.

The factors which determine the demand elasticities for imports and exports are:

(a) the availability of close substitutes in terms of price and quality; such substitutes tend to make demand elastic;
(b) the time scale; in the short term, both demand and supply tend to be less elastic than they are in the long term.

If the *sum* of price elasticities of demand for exports and imports is *greater than one*, i.e. elastic, then a fall in the exchange rate will improve the balance of payments.

2. Deflationary policies

These may take the form of higher taxes and interest rate, tighter hire purchase regulations and constraints on lending, and reductions in government expenditure. The intention of all such policies is to reduce aggregate domestic demand, thereby reducing demand for imports as well. Further, as domestic demand is reduced, so will be the pressure on domestic prices, which may then fall; a lower rate of inflation will improve the competitiveness of exports and domestic import substitutes. Note that deflationary policies to correct the current account deficits of member countries, are an integral part of International Monetary Fund (IMF) corrective measures.

3. Direct control measures

These may involve import controls or export subsidies. However, direct measures run the risk of retaliation by trading partners, and may contravene the rules and regulations of trade associations of which the deficit country may be a member, e.g. the General Agreement on Tariffs and Trade (GATT), the EC, etc. The success of direct controls will largely depend upon the willing cooperation of trading partners.

4. Exchange controls

If stringently applied, these will place restrictions on the access to foreign currency by domestic residents. Buying foreign goods or foreign services has a negative effect on the current account; exchange controls may help reduce either or both, thereby reducing any current account deficit. However the effects of exchange controls on the capital account are often more dramatic, and it is to the capital account that we now turn.

Adjustments on capital account

A number of measures may be adopted:

(a) Higher interest rates encourage a greater inflow of currency; for example foreign short- and long-term investment may be attracted by higher returns. Higher interest rates may also discourage outflows of currency to other financial centres.
(b) Lower taxation on profits and an easier repatriation of capital and profits may attract even more foreign investment capital.

Financing a current account deficit

The deficit must be financed. The following methods may be used to obtain foreign currencies to finance the deficit.

(a) Attract overseas capital, by higher interest rates and good prospects of high profitability, into factories, equipment, etc. or indirect portfolio instrument in purchasing stocks and shares.
(b) Draw on official currency reserves.
(c) Borrow from the IMF and/or eurocurrency markets, without creating future repayment problems.

If the deficit is temporary and not unbearably large, then it need not be unfavourable to the country concerned. Since the economy is importing more than it is producing, there is some short-term gain in living standards. If the economy is coming out of recession it will need more imports than exports, i.e. a deliberate current account deficit in the short term in order to have a surplus in the long term.

Useful applied materials

The structure of the UK balance of payments accounts

There are three components of the UK balance of payments accounts:
(1) current account;
(2) external assets and liabilities (capital account);
(3) balancing item.

Current account

There are two sections in this account:
(a) *The visible trade balance (or balance of trade).* An excess of exports of *goods* over imports of *goods* results in a surplus balance of trade (+); an excess of imports of goods over exports of goods results in a deficit balance of trade (−). A surplus on visible trade means, other things being equal, an inflow of foreign currency; a deficit means an outflow of foreign currency.
(b) *The invisible trade balance.* The 'invisible' earnings of a country result from the sale of *services* (banking, shipping, tourism, insurance and other financial services); the receipt of transfer payments (e.g. receipts by residents of monies transferred by relatives abroad, and more recently payments to the EC and refunds from them); the receipt of interest (payments from abroad for investments held abroad); and the receipt of profits (from successful trading by overseas subsidiaries) and dividends and interest (from the ownership of the share capital of foreign firms and their subsidiaries). The 'invisible' payments are in respect of the above items, but in reverse.

A surplus (+) on the 'invisible' trade balance suggests an excess of 'invisible' receipts over 'invisible' payments, and a deficit (−) on the 'invisible' trade balance suggests an excess of 'invisible' payments over 'invisible' receipts. As with the visible trade balance, a '+' or a '−' on the invisible balance will, other things being equal, result in an inflow or outflow respectively of foreign currency.

The *current account* is the sum of the visible and invisible trade balances; it represents the UK's claims against or indebtedness to the rest of the world on the current basis.

External assets and liabilities

Capital transactions include *official* capital transactions (inter-government and inter-governmental agencies; e.g. loans, grants and subscriptions), and *private* capital transactions (long-term and short-term, direct and indirect, investment and speculative balances): purchases of and sales to overseas governments and public bodies' stocks, business company securities, etc.

Private long-term balances are attracted overseas by the prospect of greater profits on investments; private short-term funds (hot money) are attracted overseas by the prospect of short-term gains, either because of interest rates differentials, or because of the possibility of exchange rate movements in the leading international financial centres. In addition to the above capital transactions, there are borrowings and lendings by banks and other financial institutions, and import and export credits, i.e. importers delaying payments or exporters allowing delayed payments. The changes in external assets and liabilities are added to the current account balance and, in theory, the total of the two components should result in a zero balance.

Balancing item

In practice, the total of the current account and changes in external assets and liabilities do not result in zero; any unidentified items form the *balancing item*. The balancing item balances the difference between the *actual* amount of currency received by the monetary authorities of a country and the amount that they *should* have received as recorded in the current and capital accounts. The imbalance between what has been received, and what should have been received results from errors and omissions in the recording of payments. If the balancing item is positive (+), then *more* foreign currency has actually been received than the recorded items show; if it is negative (−), then less foreign money has actually been received than the recorded items show. Over a number of years, + and − values of errors and omissions largely tend to cancel each other out.

If there is no balancing item then the sum of the current account and external assets and liabilities *will* be zero because of an extension of double-entry bookkeeping, i.e. every debit must have a credit, which can either be a current account item or involve an external asset or liability. For example, exports for cash involve the current account (the receipts from the exports) and also an increase in an asset (cash). If the exports are financed by a loan then this loan is an asset. When interest is received on the loan then invisible exports (and cash) rise. When the loan is repaid then there is a switch on the composition of the assets from the loan to the cash received. All the debits should equal all the credits.

Table 8.1 shows the UK balance of payments accounts constructed according to the method described above.

After the abolition of exchange controls and the coming on stream of North Sea oil at the end of 1970s, UK investment overseas has been increasing strongly. Foreign investment in the UK, however, did not really increase until after 1985, with the most marked increase being in direct investment by non-oil companies. The main reasons for this rise in inward investment are the UK's continuing high rate of economic growth (until 1989), the approach of the single European Community Market (in 1993), and relatively high interest rates (since the last quarter of 1988). (See p.137: Exchange controls.)

In recent years the large positive balancing item, which can also be revised drastically, has caused the accuracy of the data to be questioned. For example, it was published at £3.5 billion for 1987 in January 1988, but in March 1988 it was revised up to £12.4 billion for 1987. These uncertainties over the balancing item – the figure for unidentified items, which the then Chancellor of the Exchequer called 'another name for errors and omissions', led him to qualify the £14.6 billion current account deficit for 1988 with 'whatever the true figure is, it is undoubtedly large'.

Table 8.1 UK balance of payments accounts

	£ million			
	1986	1987	1988	First two quarters of 1989
1. *Current account* (exports and imports of goods and services, investment income and transfers).				
Visible trade				
(Credits) Exports of merchandise	72,656	79,421	80,602	44,336
(Debits) Imports of merchandise	82,020	90,350	101,428	56,147
(a) Visible trade balance =	−9,364	−10,929	−20,826	−11,811
Invisibles				
Services (insurance, banking, transport, travel)	6,247	5,682	4,165	2,171
Interest, profits and dividends (including overseas subsidiaries)	5,364	4,987	5,619	1,631
Transfers (including payments and receipts from EC budget)	−2,181	−3,411	−3,575	−1,632
(b) Invisible balance =	9,430	7,258	6,209	2,170
Current balance ((a) + (b)) =	66	−3,671	−14,617	−9,641
2. *Transactions in UK external assets and liabilities (inward and outward investments).*				
Assets (− = increase)				
UK direct investment overseas*	−11,304	−18,615	−15,219	−8,770
UK portfolio investment overseas**	−23,068	+2,702 (fall)	−9,718	−14,783
Bank and other lending overseas	−54,689	−55,200	−21,484	−14,231
UK government external assets	−509	−796	−891	−356
UK governemt official reserves	−2,891	−12,012	−2,761	+2,636 (fall)
Total transactions in assets =	−92,461	−83,921	−50,073	−35,504
Liabilities (+ = increase)				
Overseas direct investment in UK	+4,846	+8,108	+7,346	+9,233
Overseas portfolio investment in UK	+8,135	+10,440	+4,639	−12 (fall)
UK bank and other borrowing from overseas	+68,210	+56,136	+39,522	+28,787
UK government borrowing from overseas	+178	+1,570	+902	+28
Total transaction in liabilities =	+81,369	+76,254	+52,409	+38,036
Summary				
Increase in assets	−92,461	−83,921	−50,073	−35,504
Increase in liabilities	+81,369	+76,254	+52,409	+38,036
Net change	−11,092	−7,667	+2,336	+2,532
3. *Balancing item.*	+11,026	+11,338	−12,281	+7,109
Balance on current account	+66	−3,671	−14,617	−9,641
Difference	nil	nil	nil	nil

* Direct: Investment in houses, factories, warehouses, etc.
** Portfolio: Investment in stocks, shares and other financial securities.
Source: Press release for 1989 data.
Note: Another and, according to the CIB Chief Examiner, acceptable way of presenting the UK Balance of Payments Accounts, is shown in Table 8.2.

Table 8.2 UK balance of payments accounts (alternative)

1. *The current account:*		
(a) Balance of trade		
Exports (visibles)	(+)	
Imports (visibles)	(−)	
		Visible trade balance (±)
(b) Invisibles		
Services (insurance, shipping, banking)	(±)	
Interest, profits, dividends	(±)	
Transfers (remittances to and from residents and governments including to and from EC budget)	(±)	
Transport and travel	(±)	
Government services (consular, diplomatic, troops)	(±)	
		Invisible trade balance (±)
		Net current balance (±)

2. *Investment and other capital flows:*

Inward flow (+)	Outward flow (−)
Overseas investment in the UK:	Official long-term capital
private sector	UK private investment overseas
public sector	Import credits
Overseas currency borrowings by UK banks	Export credits
* Exchange reserves in sterling	
* Other external and money market liabilities in sterling	
Other transactions	
(+)	(−)

Net investment and other capital flows balance (±)

3. *Total currency flow:*		
Net current balance	(±)	
Net investment and other capital flows balance	(±)	
		Net currency flow (±)
4. *The balancing item* (±)		
5. *Official financing:*		
Net currency flow	(±)	
Balancing item	(±)	
		Balance for official financing (±)
Sources of official finance (a) (b)		
(i) Overseas monetary authorities:		
International Monetary Fund	(+) or (−)	
Central banks	(+) or (−)	
Others	(+) or (−)	
(ii) Foreign currency borrowings by:		
The UK government	(+) or (−)	
Public bodies	(+) or (−)	
(iii) The UK official reserves	(+) or (−)	
Total official financing	nil	

Note:
(a) The balance of payments is an account, and like any other account it must balance: the function of official financing is to achieve that balance.
(b) In the context of official financing:
a '−' sign is a favourable entry because it reflects a positive net currency flow; a '−' sign here means either an increase in assets or a reduction in liabilities. For instance a balance of payments surplus can be used to increase official reserves or to pay off previous borrowing.
A '+' sign is an unfavourable entry because it reflects a negative net currency flow; a '+' sign here means either a decrease in assets or an increase in liabilities. For instance a balance of payments deficit can be financed by running down official reserves or by extra borrowing.
* These two entries, under the Capital Account, are called 'Sterling Balances', and are highly sensitive to interest rate differentials and exchange rate movements. Holders of these balances are always seeking capital gains from such differentials and movements.

The critical element in the UK balance of payments for 1988 was the £39 billion borrowed from overseas by the UK banks and non-bank private sector because it was this money which financed the 1988 current account deficit. If this kind of borrowed money begins to be withdrawn because the overseas investors lose confidence in the strength of our UK economy and the stability of sterling, then a 'hard landing' for sterling will be inevitable, involving depreciation, high inflation and more unemployment, causing recession in the UK economy.

Between mid-1980 and Easter 1984, the UK enjoyed 15 successive quarters of current account surpluses, but now it is faced with an even longer succession of deficits. The main cause of this deterioration has been the substantial increase in the deficit on the *visible trade*.

The expected decline in North Sea oil production has begun but further cut-backs have resulted from the Piper Alpha disaster. Not only has output fallen but so has price. Export revenues from oil have fallen by about 36 per cent in 1988 compared with 1987. Between 1985 and 1988, the volume of non-oil exports rose by 14 per cent but the volume of imports rose by 29 per cent. The current account quarterly deficits have been as high as £3 or £4 billion during this period.

In the invisibles, under 'Services', only the 'financial and other services' sub-section is in substantial surplus, all other sub-sections are in deficit. 'Interest, Profits and Dividends' section is also in substantial credit, largely due to heavy investment overseas since the beginning of the 1980s. The 'Transfers' section is in slight deficit in both the government and private sub-sections. The government's deficit is increased by net transfers to the EC.

By keeping the UK interest rates higher than the USA, Germany and Japan, the Chancellor has been able to attract sufficient short-term funds from overseas, so that *financing* the deficit has not proved a problem; much will depend upon overseas investors maintaining their confidence in the authorities' ability to manage the economy satisfactorily.

Correction of the huge deficit is being undertaken solely through the rate of interest, which is kept at a high enough level not only to finance the deficit but also to reduce domestic demand in order to lower inflation. However, the problem with the high interest rate policy is that it leads to high rates of exchange, which worsen the trade deficit by making exports more, and imports less, expensive.

Exchange controls

When, in the past, exchange controls operated in the UK all private sector's foreign currency earnings had to be exchanged for sterling at the Bank of England, and only the Bank authorised withdrawals from the currency reserves to the UK importers, investors, banks and tourists. The objective of exchange controls was two-fold: to keep the balance of payments out of deficit and to ration currency reserves according to the national priorities. However, the major problems with exchange controls were the development of black markets in 'hard' currencies (i.e. the currencies which were hard to get because their countries of origin were running balance of payment surpluses), the frustration of firms who could not import the required raw materials to carry through their expansion projects and the inability of investors and banks to obtain the best returns from their activities in the international markets. In October 1979, the new government, because of their strong commitment to the free operation of market forces on the domestic and international levels, abolished exchange controls in the UK. The abolition of exchange controls has led to an increase in investment overseas as large institutions broadened their portfolios of asset holdings. This has resulted in increased receipts of interest, profit and dividend payments

(IPD) in the UK balance of payments invisible account. By the end of 1988, the net external assets of the UK private sector were approximately six times higher than they were in 1979. The increase in UK capital outflow is now producing substantial IPD earnings, which will be a major support to the balance of payments as the North Sea oil production declines.

Recent examination questions

The questions on this topic tend to be repetitive. The following six questions from recent CIB exams are good examples of the types of question which are commonly asked. Try to spend ten minutes or so in preparing your own outline answers to each question before reading the outline answers provided.

Question 1

(a) Distinguish between the concepts of balance of (visible) trade and terms of trade.
(b) Analyse how changes in the terms of trade help to determine a country's balance of trade.

Question 2

Is a deficit on a country's visible trade account necessarily of concern to its government? Discuss the ways in which a deficit may be corrected.

Question 3

In what sense do a country's balance of payments accounts always balance? How will the operation of a truly floating exchange rate regime affect the balance for official financing?

Question 4

Explain, with regard to a country's balance of payments:
(a) How overall balance is achieved if the current account is in surplus;
(b) Why and how a country might seek to reduce its current account surplus.

Question 5

The figures below are taken from the annual balance of payments of Ruritania. Prepare:
(a) Ruritania's balance of visible trade.
(b) Ruritania's balance of payments on current account.
Do these figures support the contention that Ruritania is a developing economy, and not highly industrialised? Give reasons for your answer.

	Million Rurits
Banking earnings (net)	– 30
Capital movements (net flow)	+ 1,280
Insurance earnings (net)	– 20
Interest paid abroad	– 1,400
Interest received from abroad	+ 30
Manufactured goods:	

exports	+ 120
imports	– 2,000
Raw materials and fuel:	
exports	+ 3,000
imports	– 1,000
Shipping earnings (net)	– 80
Tourists earnings (net)	+ 100

Note: There were no changes in Ruritania's official reserves during the year.

Question 6

What do you understand by the 'invisibles' section of a country's balance of payments accounts? Assess the importance of and recent influences on the invisibles account of the UK.

Outline answers

Answer 1

(a) Balance of visible trade: the value of exports *minus* the value of imports of goods for a given period. The balance can be in surplus or deficit.

- Terms of trade. Changes in export prices expressed as a percentage of changes in import prices of a country during a given period; then expressed as an index, with some base year = 100.
- The concept of terms of trade measures the purchasing power of a fixed 'bundle' of goods exported in terms of goods imported. Terms of trade refer to multilateral, not bilateral trade.

(b) The effect of changes in terms of trade on the balance of trade:

- Elasticities of demand for exports and imports are crucial:
  - (i) if elastic, then total receipts will be greater at lower prices. This means that a **lower** price for exports will help raise export earnings and a **higher** price for imports will help cut import spending – i.e. unfavourable terms of trade will help the balance of payments.
  - (ii) if inelastic, then total receipts will be greater at higher prices. A higher export price/lower import price will help the balance of payments – i.e. favourable terms of trade.

Answer 2

A deficit on visible trade is not necessarily of concern to the government. Of importance are:

- The position on the current (i.e. visibles + invisibles) and capital accounts in the balance of payments.
- The sign and size of the **overall** balance for official financing; only if this is negative will there be a need for official financing via running down reserves and/or borrowing overseas.
- Whether the deficit on visible trade is temporary or permanent.
- The stage of development for the national economy.

The main ways of correcting (not financing) a balance of trade deficit:

(a) By devaluation (fixed exchange rates) or depreciation (floating rates) of the exchange rate. Success depends on: adequate price elasticities of demand for exports and imports, no competitive devaluation or depreciation; no offsetting increase in wages, profit margins, or indirect taxes.

(b) By deflationary policies: higher taxes and interest rates, and less attractive hire purchase terms; more attractive saving schemes; a credit squeeze.

(c) By direct measures: import controls; export subsidies.
Success will depend upon no retaliatory measures by trading partners.

Answer 3

The balance of payments accounts always balance in an *accounting* sense: balance of payments accounts include visible trade balance, 'invisible' balance and the balance of investments and other capital flows; the sum of these, along with the balancing item, produces the balance for official financing.

- The value of official financing will be equal, but opposite in sign (plus or minus), to the balance for official financing; this preserves the accounting identity.
- Under freely floating rates, the balance for official financing should be zero, because the movements in the exchange rate should be such as exactly to counterbalance the deficit/surplus position on current and capital accounts; there may of course be time lags before, say, the fall in exchange rate can eliminate a deficit in the balance for official financing.

Answer 4

(a) Equilibrium is achieved by some or all of the following:
- capital outflows (direct or portfolio);
- other external assets and liabilities transactions;
- reserve accumulation;
- balancing item.

(b) A country may seek to reduce a current account surplus because of:
- pressure from trading partner countries with current account deficits;
- reduced ability to import by trading partners;
- foreign currency reserve accumulation generating inflation.

The surplus can be reduced by:
- revaluing the currency in order to raise export and lower import prices: success will depend upon the elasticities of demand for export and imports;
- boosting domestic demand in order to attract imports and divert potential exports to the home market;
- removing any import restrictions or export encouragements in force;
- giving aid to less developed countries.

Answer 5

	Dr. (million Rurits)	Cr. (million Rurits)
(a) Balance of visible trade		
Exports of manufactures		120
Exports of raw materials/fuel		3,000
Imports of manufactures	2,000	
Imports of raw matrial/fuel	1,000	
	3,000	3,120
Visible trade surplus		120
(b) Invisibles		
Banking	30	
Insurance	20	
Interest paid	1,400	
Interest received		30
Shipping	80	
Tourism		100
	1,530	130
Deficit on invisibles	1,400	

Balance of payments on current account = visibles + invisibles
= + 120 − 1,400
= − 1,280

Capital inflow was 1,280 million Rurits, because official reserves were unchanged.

Ruritania is a developing country because:

- greater reliance on exports of raw materials and less on exports of manufacturers;
- low earnings from commercial services;
- large interest payment on current account and heavy borrowings on capital account;
- sizeable tourist earnings suggest unspoilt countryside, 'golden' beaches, lower price level, etc.

Answer 6

The 'invisibles' section of a country's balance of payments shows:

- The net receipts or payments in respect of commercial services, transport, interest, profit, dividends, and tourism in the private sector.
- Overseas grants and aid, by the government.
- Transfer payments: private (to relatives abroad); government (e.g. the UK payments to the EC).

The importance of recent influences on the invisibles account of the UK:

- In the earlier 1980s, the relatively strong sterling exchange rate had a negative effect on inward travel and a positive effect on outward travel (i.e. deterioration of tourism section of the account).
- A major portion of investment in the North Sea oil was by overseas oil companies, which led to large payments abroad of profits and dividends.

- The abolition of exchange control led to an increase in investments overseas as large institutions broadened their portfolio of asset holdings. This resulted in increased receipts in the UK of interest, profits and dividends. It is now rising only slowly, due partly to increases in interest earned on the government's official reserves.
- A sharp deterioration in the transfer account, despite rebates, because of payments by the UK to the EC. The deficit or transfers in 1988 exceeded the UK net earnings from services.
- The heavy fall in the exchange rate of sterling at the end of 1984 and in early 1985 has had a positive inward and negative outward travel effect.

A tutor's answer

The following question has been chosen for the specimen answer because variants of this question are most frequently asked on the topic of the Balance of Payments. You will notice from the answer plan that it is essential that you avoid confusing the two elements of the question.

Question

In which ways can a deficit on the current account of a country's balance of payments be:
(a) financed;
(b) rectified?

Answer plan:
- Definition of the 'current account' within the balance of payments (briefly).
- How does a deficit on current account occur (briefly)?
  - (a) Deficit may be financed by:
    - (i) private capital inflows;
    - (ii) sources of official finance.
  - (b) Deficit may be corrected by:
    - (i) devaluation/depreciation;
    - (ii) deflation;
    - (iii) direct controls.

Specimen answer

The current account of a country's balance of payments consists of:
(i) *The balance of trade*. This is the difference between the value of good exported and the value of goods imported; this balance may be positive (+) or negative (−).
(ii) *The invisible balance*. This shows the net receipts (+) or payments (−) in respect of services, transfer payments, and interest, profit and dividends.

A deficit on the current account occurs when (a) + (b) is negative. It implies that the country is a debtor on its external current account transactions with its trading partners, and suggests a poor performance in buying and selling goods and services with the rest of the world.

A current account may be *financed* by:

1. Private capital inflows. If the country in question offers good prospects for high profitability, then overseas private *long-term* investment, in foreign currencies, will be

attracted into the country. The long-term overseas investment may be direct investment into factories, equipment, etc. or it could be indirect portfolio investment, in purchasing stocks and shares in the country. If the country offers opportunities of interest-rate differential gains or capital gains due to exchange rate movements, it may attract *short-term* private capital (hot money). The net receipts of foreign currencies from long-term and short-term foreign capital will help reduce the deficit on current account.

2. If the current account deficit is not wholly financed by the inflow of private capital, then the government of the country will need to tap the three main sources of official finance:
   (a) transactions with overseas monetary authorities and the International Monetary Fund to obtain supplies of the currencies needed;
   (b) borrowing, by the public sector, of foreign currency in the international financial market;
   (c) reducing official reserves of the country.

The country may take three main measures, singly or in a 'mix', to *rectify* the deficit on its current account.

1. By devaluation or depreciation of the exchange rate of its currency. This would make exports cheaper and imports more expensive. The effectiveness of this approach depends on:
   (a) the relative price elasticities for exports overseas and for imports at home; the greater than one the **sum** of these elasticities, the more favourable the impact of a fall in the exchange rate on the balance of payments (this is Marshall and Learner theory).
   (b) no competitive devaluation or depreciation by trading partners.

   There will tend to be a time lag of 18 months or so before the fall in the exchange rate has its full impact on export sales and import purchases ('J' curve effect). A depreciation/devaluation of a currency may initially lead to a balance of payments deficit. Subsequently, however, the current account should, depending on elasticities, move into surplus, – hence the name 'J' curve: falling to begin with, then rising.
2. Using deflationary policies (increasing tax rates and interest rates, credit squeeze, etc.), will reduce aggregate domestic demand in general, thereby dampening the demand for imports. Furthermore, deflationary policies will tend to lower the domestic rate of inflation which, in turn, will improve the competitiveness of its exports and its production of import substitutes.
3. By using direct controls, involving either import tariffs and other controls, or export subsidies. However, direct measures run the risk of retaliation, and may prove to be self-defeating. The success of direct controls will depend upon the willing cooperation of the trading partner countries.

A step further

The topic of balance of payments is an important area, both for examination questions and also for practical bankers in the international arena, who may have to evaluate a country's economic performance for credit assessment purposes. You are expected to be able to appreciate *recent* influences on the constituent parts of the UK balance of payments accounts. You need to keep abreast of developments by reading current banking journals, financial reports, The Chartered Institute of Bankers *Examiners' Reports* and *Updating Notes*. The UK government releases a monthly balance of payments statement, which is the basis for comments by the quality press, television and radio programmes. Look out for this media coverage of the monthly balance of payments statement.

CHAPTER 9

Exchange Rates

Syllabus requirements

- Need for foreign exchange rates.
- Theories and determination of foreign exchange rates.
- Factors which cause changes in foreign exchange rates.
- Types of foreign exchange rate systems.
- European Monetary System.
- European Currency Unit.
- Relationship between foreign exchange rates and interest rates.

Getting started

'Foreign exchange' generally means any currency other than your own. The 'foreign exchange rate' of a currency implies the exchange value of the currency (its price) in terms of other currencies and, like any other price, it is determined by the supply of and demand for the currency on the 'foreign exchange markets'. Foreign exchange (forex) markets provide an international system of buying and selling claims to currencies immediately (spot) and in the future (forward) involving a world-wide group of banks, brokers, commercial companies and other financial institutions.

The need for foreign exchange (i.e. foreign currencies) arises for many reasons. A country, its business companies and citizens may require foreign currencies to pay the purchase price for imported goods and services, to invest in other countries, to provide for its tourists going abroad and to sustain the sending of gifts and other payments overseas.

If the bilateral (between two currencies) and multilateral (among all currencies) exchange rates are absolutely fixed on the forex markets, then there will be certainty in trade payments; for instance as regards imports, it will be clear how much the buyer in the domestic country needs to pay in terms of his currency, and how much the seller in the foreign country will receive in terms of his currency. However, the domestic purchasing power of the currencies does not remain static, mainly due to inflation rate and interest rate differentials and major changes in the supply and demand of currencies (e.g. via balance of payments deficits and surpluses and consequent changes in international indebtedness). These factors put too much pressure upon the central banks to hold the absolutely fixed exchange rate parities. Hence absolute certainty may have to be replaced by the compromise of relative certainty, i.e. the absolutely fixed exchange rate system is replaced by one in which there is some movement of the exchange rate between specified upper and lower limits. However, international circumstances may make it difficult even to uphold a system with this degree of flexibility in exchange rates. If so, then the monetary authorities of individual countries have no option but to allow the exchange value of their respective currencies to be determined by supply and demand on the forex markets, i.e. to accept a system of freely floating exchange rates. The authorities may still intervene in a free exchange rate system, buying or selling their own currencies to affect the exchange rate. Such a 'managed' system can be compared with a 'pure' system in which no intervention takes place.

The international monetary system, whether of fixed, managed or pure floating exchange rates, exists to facilitate international trade and the settlement of debt; it is the international counterpart of the national monetary systems of the trading countries.

Essential principles

The basis of bilateral and multilateral trade

The objective of *bilateral* trade is to regulate trade with each single country in such a way as to secure an exact balance of trade with it. The need for bilateral trade arises where one currency cannot be easily converted into other currencies, so that the earnings from trade with one country cannot be used to pay for goods and services imported from other countries; the only way to pay for imports is then by exports. Bilateral trade, therefore, is completely controlled by inter-governmental agreements.

Under *multilateral* trade, a country aims, not at exactly offsetting imports and exports with each single country, but at a general balance of trade. Multilateral trade is not possible without the 'convertability' of one currency into other currencies. Only then can countries use their surplus earnings from one country to offset deficits with other countries, so that a multilateral trade system becomes possible. The basis of multilateral trade is the theory of *comparative cost advantage*. Under this theory countries specialise in those economic activities in which they have a relative advantage in terms of efficiency over other countries. Specialisation, based on comparative cost advantage, reduces costs of production, and international trade not only passes on this advantage to consumers in other countries, but also widens their choice of goods and services.

Multilateral trade makes possible international investment, so that investors in one country can take advantage of national differences in yields on investments and can reduce overall investment risk by diversifying their investment portfolios. Investment capital can then flow to countries with projects offering the highest projected returns; these may be low cost centres of production, which can then expand at the expense of other countries where costs are higher. Thus multilateral trade, unhindered by tariffs, exchange controls and other artificial barriers, can lead to an efficient, world-wide use of resources.

International trade and investment are therefore only possible if suitable means are available for international payments. Most international trade nowadays is settled by using national currencies, either the currency of the exporter, importer or one of a limited number of 'hard' currencies that command general confidence and are widely accepted in international payments.

Operation of foreign exchange markets

Traders and investors must be able to buy and sell national currencies if they are to make international payments. The forex markets have developed to allow this. Trading in these markets determines the rates at which one currency can be exchanged for others. The forex markets play a central role in facilitating international trade, and their smooth functioning is essential for the expansion of trade and investment.

National currencies are bought and sold in major financial centres, e.g. New York,

Singapore, Hong Kong, Tokyo, Frankfurt, Paris and London. Foreign exchange buying and selling, however, take place in all countries. London is one of the largest centres of activity with several hundred institutions, mainly banks, dealing in foreign exchange, and with more currencies actively traded than in any other major centre. Foreign exchange dealers in forex markets do not meet in a particular location but keep in touch via telephone, telex and other more sophisticated forms of electronic communication. Exchange rates adjust continually, depending on the balance between orders for buying and selling currencies, and instant communications, combined with extreme competitiveness, ensure that exchange rates in different financial centres keep closely in step.

The main brokers and dealers in these markets are: (a) *Commercial banks* who deal on behalf of their personal and corporate customers, and also on their own account to 'square' their positions daily in major currencies and to make arbitrage profits arising from exchange rate differentials on various centres; (b) *Business companies* who make and receive currency payments for their international trade transactions, and for investments, particularly in buying overseas subsidiaries; (c) *Central banks* who buy and sell their national currencies to assist their exchange rates to move up or down in accordance with their economic objectives.

Inconsistencies between exchange rates, if they appeared, would be quickly exploited by a process known as *arbitrage*. This involves buying currencies in the financial centres where they are quoted more cheaply and selling them on forex markets where they are quoted at a better rate. The overall result of arbitrage is that the exchange rates soon adjust and come into line in each centre until there is no incentive for arbitrage (see below).

There are two basic types of foreign exchange transactions; spot and forward. Currency is bought and sold for prompt delivery (i.e. two working days hence) in the *spot* market; currency is bought and sold for delivery at a specified future date in the *forward* market. Forward contracts can reduce or even eliminate the risk of adverse movements in exchange rates, which may upset the profitability of importers and exporters. The extent to which importers and exporters choose to avoid exchange risk by using the forward market depends partly on their expectations of future movements in spot rates compared to the cost of covering forward, and partly on their own attitude to risk.

Whereas arbitrage exploits the inconsistencies between exchange rates quoted on various centres, *speculation* aims at profit-making from the expected movements in exchange rates; for example, by selling a currency on the spot market in the hope of buying it later at a lower rate of exchange, or by buying a currency on the spot market in the hope of selling it later at a higher rate. Like arbitrage, speculation on forex markets hastens the realignment in exchange rate differentials on different forex markets, by anticipating changes; thus, in this sense, both arbitrage and speculation are market forces which help forex markets regain equilibrium quickly, so that it can be argued that these market forces serve an economic purpose. However, in recent years, the amount of speculative balances has increased substantially, both in volume and volatility. Movements of such balances in response to anticipated changes in exchange rates in the forex markets can *overcompensate* for any possible degree of non-alignment, thereby causing much greater short-term volatility in exchange rates. This will place intense pressures on the central banks of the countries whose currencies are the object of speculation, whether for appreciation or depreciation.

The determination of exchange rates

Since the exchange rate of a currency is its price on the forex markets in terms of other currencies, it is determined by its demand and supply conditions on the forex markets:

instant communications and extreme competitiveness among the forex markets make them almost perfect markets. The demand for, and supply of, a country's currency are derived from the country's balance of payments position; if it is a surplus country, i.e. if the value of its exports of goods and services and capital inflows (demand for its currency) is greater than the value of its imports of goods and services and capital outflows (supply of its currency) then the demand for its currency will be rising relative to the supply. The forex markets will then quote the currency at a higher exchange rate. On the other hand, if it is a deficit country, the supply of its currency will be rising relative to the demand and the forex markets will quote a lower exchange value for it. There are two main theories which seek to explain the determination of exchange rates: one relates to the current account, and the other to the capital inflows and outflows.

1. The purchasing power parity (PPP) theory

In its original form the theory states that the equilibrium exchange rate between one currency and another is that rate which equalises the domestic purchasing powers of the two currencies. If, for example, £1 buys the same amount of goods and services in the UK as do 10 francs in France, then, according to PPP theory, the equilibrium exchange rate must be £1 = 10 francs. If this were not the case, there would be strong incentive to import goods from the 'cheaper' country, which would lead to a deficit on the current account for the 'expensive' country; as the supply of its currency increased in settling its current account deficit, the forex markets would mark down its exchange rate. The incentive for importing goods and services from the 'cheaper' country would only disappear when the sterling/franc exchange rate becomes equal to £1 = 10 francs.

The PPP theory was originally developed to explain the values of exchange rates in the long run. However, there are many problems associated with this theory in its original form. For instance, the theory ignores transport and insurance costs and import duties. More importantly, it depends on the extent to which the goods and services involved may enter into international trade; there are many goods and services which are traded internally, but which *cannot* be traded internationally, e.g. houses, haircuts. The theory has been refined to take account of differences in patterns of consumption and levels of income in different countries. Nevertheless, the problem of devising baskets of goods and services which reflect common consumption patterns in different countries yet which only include goods which are traded internationally, has limited the usefulness of the theory in predicting exchange rates. Since the relative costs and prices of *non-traded* goods and services can vary between countries, a comparison of *general* price levels is not therefore a reliable way of determining the exchange rate equilibrium.

However, the theory has a broad relevance in times of differing inflation rates in the domestic economies of trading partners. If a country's inflation rate significantly exceeds that of its trading partners then, generally speaking, its exports will become uncompetitive at any given exchange rate; as a result it may encounter balance of payment problems, and, under a floating exchange rate system, the exchange rate will fall.

2. The portfolio balance theory

This theory emphasises the importance of interest rate differentials on the financial centres, and their impact on international investment and speculative capital flows, as a major determinant of exchange rates. It is assumed that large sophisticated investors are aware of interest rate differentials and move funds to take advantage of higher yields; also that they seek to reduce overall investment risks by diversifying their investment portfolios. The inflow of these funds into financial centres offering higher yield increases the demand for the currencies of such centres, so that the exchange rates of these currencies rise on the forex markets.

Different types of exchange rate systems

National monetary policies of the trading partners are to some extent inter-dependent, on account of the exchange rate links between their currencies. Therefore changes in national monetary policies, even if in pursuit of internal objectives, put pressure on the international exchange rate system in operation.

There are two main exchange rate systems, absolutely fixed and freely floating.

1. Absolutely fixed exchange rates

The central bank of each country is obliged to intervene to increase or decrease the supply of its currency by selling or buying it, on the forex markets, using the national gold and foreign currency reserves, so that its exchange rate is maintained at a predetermined exchange parity with certain other currency or currencies.

Advantages of fixed exchange rates

(a) They largely eliminate uncertainty in international trade and investment, and therefore encourage both by ensuring that the exporters' profits, importers' payments and investors' income and capital remain stable.
(b) They impose discipline on governments to pursue sound monetary and fiscal policies.

Disadvantages of fixed exchange rates

(a) Unbearable pressures build up on the central banks of those countries whose inflation rates and economic performance drastically worsen relative to their trading partner countries, and this may lead to the stigma of 'devaluation', i.e. lowering the exchange parity of the national currency. Of course, before devaluation the governments concerned will employ monetary and fiscal measures to curb inflation and improve balance of payments in order to defend the predetermined exchange parity.
(b) Central banks need to hold large amounts of gold and foreign currency reserves to neutralise exchange rate fluctuations.
(c) If a currency is suspected to be weakening or strengthening, speculation may build up and may in fact cause its devaluation or 'revaluation', i.e. raising its exchange parity.

2. Freely floating exchange rates

The exchange value of each currency is determined not by the monetary authorities but by the market forces of supply and demand for each currency on the forex markets. In a 'pure' float, the central banks take no action, whatever the exchange values quoted for their respective currencies.

In between these two extremes, there are a number of compromise arrangements:

(a) *Fluctuation limits around parity values* – the international trading community agrees that exchange rates can vary within specific bands either side of an agreed central parity; the central banks only intervening on the forex markets to ensure that the foreign exchange value of their currencies remains within the agreed bands.
(b) *'Dirty' floating* – the monetary authorities profess to follow freely floating exchange rates policies, yet intervene, behind the scenes, to limit the fluctuations in the exchange rates of their currencies to such levels as are most beneficial for their own economies. This is sometimes called a 'managed' float.
(c) *Crawling peg* – the monetary authorities, instead of declaring and maintaining a fixed parity, allow the parities to adjust from time to time, i.e. a system of 'gliding' fixed parities.
(d) *Direct foreign exchange control* – each central bank states the terms and conditions for the release of foreign exchange. An extreme type of direct control is 'counter trading', i.e. all foreign trade transactions are undertaken as purely bilateral barter arrangements.

Advantages of freely floating exchange rates

(a) Since there are no fixed exchange parities to defend, there is no need for large gold and foreign exchange reserves.
(b) Imbalances in balance of payments are *automatically* corrected by the movements in exchange rates: a deficit country's exchange rate will depreciate, making its exports more and its imports less attractive, and the reverse in the case of a surplus country.
(c) Countries with freely floating exchange rates can pursue unfettered national economic policies.

Disadvantages of freely floating exchange rates

(a) For the automatic adjustment of balance of payments imbalances, it is essential that the elasticities of demand for exports and imports are sufficiently elastic, which may not always be the case.
(b) Unfettered national economic policy aimed at economic growth may lead to inflation which will cause the exchange rate to depreciate and import prices to rise, causing a further rise in inflation; such economic freedom may therefore be more illusory than real.
(c) Uncertainty caused by fluctuating exchange rates discourage international trade and investment.
(d) If 'free' floating becomes 'managed' floating, there will be need for substantial gold and foreign currency reserves.

Fixed versus floating exchange rates

If the fixed exchange regime is to function satisfactorily, it is essential that all countries under this regime should ensure that they do not let their interest rates, inflation rates and monetary expansion rates move too far out of line with those prevailing elsewhere within the regime. Those countries which are unwilling or unable to abide by the strict discipline of fixed exchange rates will find their price levels rising above those of the countries which *are* adhering to such discipline; their exports will become less, and imports more, competitive, leading to rising balance of payments deficits year by year. In order to defend the fixed exchange rate parities, the central banks of these countries will have to continue buying their own currencies on an increasing scale, spending their foreign exchange reserves, until their reserves fall dangerously low. The monetary authorities may then be forced to devalue their currencies by declaring lower exchange parities, in order to avoid continuous intervention on the forex markets. There is a stigma of mismanagement of the economy attached to 'devaluing' under a fixed exchange rate regime, which countries under such a regime will try to avoid at almost any cost. The strongest argument in favour of fixed exchange rates is that, since currencies will be accepted at known and fixed exchange rates, there will be certainty in international payments and receipts. Fixed exchange rates will eliminate exchange risks and thereby promote international trade and investment.

With fixed exchange rates, however, inflation in the economies of some trading partners will be 'imported' into other, non-inflation, economies, unless the demand for imports is relatively price elastic, and cheaper domestic import substitutes are preferred.

Fixed exchange rates also provide speculators with a one-way option. Currencies which are perceived to be potentially weak can safely be sold in the knowledge that the relevant national central bank will be a buyer in order to maintain the parity (or at least until there is devaluation). Conversely, strong currencies can be bought with confidence, because their central banks will sell the national currencies to keep the exchange rates down and maintain the parity.

In stark contrast to the fixed exchange rate regime, there is the freely floating system. With freely floating, market determined, exchange rates, it is claimed that there will be less need for official reserves; this follows since (a) there will be no exchange parities to defend, and (b) balance of payments' imbalances should be automatically corrected by movements in exchange rates. Furthermore, with no fixed regime rules to obey, national governments will be able to pursue independent domestic economic policies, aimed at higher growth and employment. Individual economies will be insulated against 'imported' inflation. The economies with the higher inflation rates will tend to experience an automatic fall in their exchange rates. This will reduce their export prices, making imports into the non-inflation economies somewhat cheaper.

However, these theoretical advantages of floating exchange rates do not always fully materialise. For instance, if the adjustment of balance of payments imbalances is to be automatic, it is essential that the elasticities of demand for imports and exports are sufficiently high to support the automatic adjustment process. Again, even though there is no exchange rate parity to defend, countries are not always free to follow independent monetary policies. For example, rapid growth may bring about higher imports and a fall in the exchange rate; even if this raises import prices and curbs the growth in imports, it may stimulate domestic inflation so that the 'cost' of this policy is still too high, despite balance of payments equilibrium.

There will be less need for official reserves or international borrowing only if the exchange rates are *truly* floating. If floating is 'dirty', i.e. managed, there will still be a need for official reserves so that the authorities can intervene on forex markets.

The principal weakness of freely floating rates is that they might discourage international trade and investment. It is not so much the flexibility in current exchange rates that discourages trade and investment; rather it is the uncertainty about future exchange rate movements which might have this effect. If, however, movements in exchange rates were easily predicted, then traders and investors could take them into account when planning overseas business and investment.

Influences causing exchange rate movements

If a country's inflation rate significantly exceeds that of its trading partners then, in due time, its exports will become uncompetitive and as a result it will face a balance of payments deficit and in the long term its exchange rate will fall against the currencies of its trading partner countries. The *Purchasing Power Parity* theory of exchange rates states that the equilibrium exchange rate between one currency and another is that rate which equalises the domestic purchasing powers of the two currencies.

Despite the *purchasing power parity* theory – which states that competition in trade will tend to compensate for *differences in national inflation rates*, i.e. that exchange rates will be constant in real terms – there is little evidence that the real exchange rates do in fact tend to be stable. Real exchange rates have varied markedly over both short and long periods. It may be that in the *very long term*, say 15 to 20 years, the forces represented by the purchasing power parity theory may become dominant and create stability in real exchange rates, but it is a largely unproven hypothesis.

It is likely that some of the longer-term movements in real exchange rates which occurred between 1972 and 1980 were partly due to a movement towards more diversified reserve currency portfolios, following the collapse of the UK dollar-dominated Bretton Woods regime. It is also possible that the transfers of wealth towards OPEC (Organisation of Petroleum Exporting Countries), due largely to the huge oil price increases, had a significant impact on global currency preferences: a few major oil producers were then able to place, or withdraw, huge sums in financial centres and currencies of their choice. For the UK, the advent of North Sea Oil certainly raised the demand for sterling from the early 1980s; hence the title, 'petro-sterling'.

The comparison of data on various countries' *balance of payments positions* indicates that changes in the current account balances have frequently influenced exchange rate movements in the short term. This would suggest that the current account does have an impact on the longer-term value of a country's exchange rate.

Short-term movements in exchange rates appear to have been linked to *relative interest rates*, but this relationship has sometimes been positive and sometimes negative. A *positive* relationship has prevailed most frequently in recent years, as monetary authorities have followed an interest rate policy directed more towards domestic rather than external objectives. A high relative interest rate has tended to raise the exchange rate of the currency in question. Where there has been a *negative* relationship, e.g. where a high relative interest rate has been associated with the exchange rate remaining constant or falling (as happened in the UK in 1985), it has perhaps been due to *expectations* of a still greater rise (or fall) in interest rates.

In addition to the above influences on exchange rate movements, there are other influences, such as the stance of economic policy (expansionary or deflationary) and the level of economic activity. However, these influences will reflect themselves in both the balance of payments current accounts and in interest rates.

In **summary**, then, exchange rates may be influenced by relative inflation rates, by relative current account positions, by relative interest rates, by relative economic stances, and by a range of other factors, such as the degree of official intervention on forex markets, and political developments. In the forex markets, though, it is often merely 'expectations' as regards one of the above that causes movements. (See also 'A tutor's answer' at the end of this chapter.)

The European Monetary System and its origin

It became clear to the European countries that despite the wider fluctuation bands around central rates introduced in 1971 under the Smithsonian agreement, the fixed exchange rate system could not be saved. In an attempt to keep the narrowest possible exchange rate fluctuation among themselves, ten European countries moved in the opposite direction in April 1972. They introduced narrower cross exchange rates against each other's currencies (1.12 per cent either way), while maintaining the wider band (2.25 per cent) against the US dollar. This arrangement was quickly nicknamed the 'Snake in the Tunnel.' The Snake aimed at reducing uncertainty as regards the exchange rates of the members by limiting the extent of fluctuations against each other. This took place at a time when most major currencies were beginning to show signs of abandoning the Bretton Woods/Smithsonian arrangements prior to floating against each other. However, balance of payments imbalances, largely due to the oil crisis in 1973, caused volatile exchange rate fluctuations, making it very difficult to maintain par values within the narrow bands of the Snake. Despite currencies entering and leaving the Snake at various times, it remained in existence until 1979, when the Snake was replaced by the European Monetary System (EMS).

The EMS

The EMS was established by the Brussels Resolution dated 5 December 1978, signed by all EEC countries, and was implemented on 13 March 1979. The objectives of the EMS were to combat the international monetary instability caused by the weakness of the US dollar in the 1970s, to establish a zone of monetary stability in Europe, to assist in drawing together the monetary and economic policies of EEC countries, to promote inter-community trade by stabilising exchange rates and to achieve, in the long run, Economic Monetary Union (EMU).

The EMS has two major elements:

1. An exchange rate intervention system which attempts to preserve stability between the different currencies participating in it. It organises exchange rate relationships between the participants according to a system of stable parities, but ones which can be adjusted when necessary. It allows for periodic realignments and permits margins of fluctuation between currencies. Thus the EMS is a 'movable peg' exchange rate system for the participating currencies.

   The heart of the EMS is the *European Currency Unit* (ECU), which is a weighted 'basket' of 12 EC currencies, of which drachma and escudo are not members of the exchange rate mechanism (ERM, see below) of the EMS; the weight of each currency is determined by the economic strength of the country concerned. The currencies and their weights are reviewed every five years – the last review was in September 1989, when the currencies of Spain and Portugal, joined the ECU basket.

   With effect from 21 September 1989 the currency composition and weight percentage of each currency are shown in Table 9.1.

   Each currency participating in the exchange rate mechanism (ERM) of the EMS has an ECU-related central rate, and these values determine a grid of bilateral central rates between the members. Every country must maintain a margin of + or – 2.25 per cent on either side of its bilateral rate. Spain and Britain are exceptions, because of the weakness of the peseta and sterling, and at present their intervention limits are roughly 6 per cent on either side of their central rates. If a currency reaches its upper or lower bilateral intervention point in relation to another currency, its central bank must intervene on the forex market to buy or sell its currency for ECUs, to raise or lower its exchange rate respectively. The EMS supplements the compulsory intervention rules with a 'divergence indicator', which is based on the ECU as the common numeraire, and which gives countries a forewarning that their currencies are getting out of line from the Community average. If a currency moves to 75 per cent of its maximum spread of divergence in relation to the Community average, then it is an 'early warning' to the country concerned to take corrective monetary and/or fiscal measures before the compulsory intervention points are reached. Therefore all participant currencies are pegged against the ECU directly and against each other indirectly. Clearly ERM is the cornerstone of the EMS, and is vital to the achievement of EMS objectives.

Table 9.1 Currency units and weights in ECU baskets

Currency	Units	Weight (%)
Deutschemark	0.6242	30.10
French franc	1.332	19.00
UK sterling	0.08784	13.00
Italian lira	151.8	10.15
Netherlands guilder	0.2198	9.40
Belgian franc	3.301	7.60
Spanish peseta	6.885	5.30
Danish kroner	0.1976	2.45
Irish punt	0.008552	1.10
Greek drachma	1.44	0.80
Portuguese escudo	1.393	0.80
Luxembourg franc	0.13	0.30
		100.00

2. Each member country of the EEC (including the UK) makes 20 per cent of its gold and dollar reserves available to the European Monetary Cooperation Fund (EMCF) in return for ECUs. EMCF is empowered to lend to those member countries which are unable, by economic measures to correct excessive divergences. The EMCF credit facilities available to such member states are as follows; unlimited amounts up to ten weeks; ECU 14 billion up to nine months, ECU 11 billion from two to five years. *Note*: While intervention is carried out through national currencies, debts are settled in ECUs. Thus EMS is an improvement on the old Snake arrangement which was simply an exchange rate agreement.

EMS failures

The staunch critics of the EMS point to its lack of success in achieving fully many of its objectives. For instance, critics question how the EMS can bring about a zone of exchange rate stability when, in its first ten years of existence there were 11 (four of them major) realignments of exchange rate parities! There have been differences in inflation rates and in balance of payments performances among member countries; the fact that such differences continue to exist may suggest further realignments. The EMS has failed in leading the member states towards the objective of Economic Monetary Union (EMU), in which the economic policies of the members are fully harmonised. The ECU has not become a major 'reserve' asset for the EC countries, and the EMCF has not developed, as was expected, into a fully-fledge European Monetary Fund (on the pattern of the International Monetary Fund).

EMS successes

The supporters of the EMS counter-argue, emphasising the degree of success the EMS has been able to achieve in moving towards its objectives. For instance, it has survived, despite the 11 realignments, because it has an in-built flexibility, which the IMF did not possess and which caused the downfall of the latter. The member states are *beginning* to accept the need for convergence of their economic policies, e.g. French monetary policy is now much closer to the monetary policies of Germany and the UK.

It is true that the EMCF has not developed in importance as was expected, and that the hopes of it becoming a fully-fledged European Monetary Fund have been shelved indefinitely. However, the ECU has remained stable, due largely to the stabilising influence of the EMS, despite massive exchange rate swings and interest rate fluctuations. This is because stronger, more stable currencies comprise a greater proportion of the basket (see table above), than do the weaker, more volatile currencies. Thus the overall stability of the ECU is very marked, and its fluctuations are more muted because of the combination of weak and strong currencies. In addition, 10 of the 12 constituent currencies are members of the ERM of the EMS which maintains the parity of the member currencies within the agreed range. The combination of these two factors enhances the stability of the ECU. The ECU has gradually become a fully-fledged financial instrument used by banks, businessmen and governments for accounting, investment, savings and payments purposes. The ECU is not far short of becoming a reserve asset for the EC countries and is now a major currency for loans and bond issues. Companies, too, now often insist on paying or being paid in ECUs. This removes the risk of one currency fluctuating far from the other currencies – a weighted average of currencies is inherently more stable than just one currency (see below).

The EMS, unlike the IMF, is not an institution in its own right. It has no real teeth to force member states to pursue some prescribed monetary and fiscal policies. A basic precondition for the successful operation of the EMS is that there is convergence of economic policies and performance of member countries; *how* they achieve this convergence largely rests with their own respective governments.

Absolute rigidity in exchange rate commitments by member countries who are *not* at the same level of economic performance is a recipe for failure. The strength of the EMS lies in its pragmatic flexibility which allows for differences in the economic performances, inflation rates and balance of payments positions of member states by explicitly permitting currency realignments.

European Currency Unit (ECU)

In 1987 the ECU Banking Association launched the ECU clearing system, to operate with a final complement of some 30 commercial banks. All clearing members have settlement accounts with the common clearing bank – the Bank for International Settlements in Basle (see Ch. 10).

The ECU has a powerful attraction for citizens of countries with weak currencies. These include currencies which have been devalued in the past, or are likely to be devalued in the future, e.g. the currencies of Belgium, France and Italy. By denominating deals in ECUs, buyers are increasingly availing themselves of the protection offered by an ECU against the down-grading of their own national currencies.

As a basket currency ECU smooths out interest and exchange rate fluctuations of the currencies of which it is composed, thus offering some protection against those fluctuations. The relative stability is attractive to both borrowers and lenders. This is because the spread of the basket over a number of stronger currencies means that the dramatic changes which occasionally occur between two currencies are spread over all the currencies in the basket. This also means that those countries with strong currencies do not have any great incentive for going into ECU denominated investments. For instance, in Germany, ECU issues are not authorised. On the other hand, countries with weak currencies greatly benefit from ECU-linkage. For example, Italy has authorised the use of ECU as an official foreign currency, and up to 20 per cent of Italian export invoicing is in ECU.

The ECU has been one of the main beneficiaries of the massive exchange rate swings and interest rate fluctuations, in recent years. For instance, firms with subsidiaries in several EC countries can avoid the problem of dealing in several different currencies by using ECUs. Due to its relative stability against most EC currencies, it has been used increasingly by business companies as a hedging instrument against foreign exchange rate fluctuations. For example an exporter whose receivables are in EMS currencies in broad proportion to the ECU basket can clearly be seen to hedge the exchange risk by invoicing in ECU. The ECU is gaining in importance and its use will continue to increase. Some knowledge of the ECU for those living in rural areas of the UK will be of particular relevance, since the EC is likely to pay support payments to farmers in the ECU in future.

In the autumn of 1988 the UK government issued ECU Treasury bills, which are similar to conventional Treasury bills but denominated and payable in ECUs. Arrangements have been made to ensure secondary market liquidity through the qualified intermediaries, e.g. commercial banks. According to the then Chancellor of the Exchequer, the ECU Treasury bill 'introduces a useful new facility. It widens the options for managing the UKs reserves and will establish London's position as the centre of the ECU market, which we wish to see develop further'. The amount of ECU Treasury bills outstanding in March 1991 was £3.6 bn.

ECU interest rates parallel those in the domestic market for the major currencies, reflecting the weights of these currencies in the ECU basket. On 21 September 1989 they were about 9.5 per cent to 9.75 per cent, for deposits of between one month and one year. ECU exchange rates, which are the same for official and private ECUs, are published in the financial press. By linking via a major currency, say, the US dollar, exchange rates can be calculated for most major currencies.

The reasons why the UK did not joined the ERM or the EMS

The Bank of England pointed to the following factors, in June 1983, which have kept the UK out of the ERM:

1. The UK has had an alternative financial anchor in its firm adherence to a policy of money supply control, as outlined in the UK government's Medium Term Financial Strategy; hence it has not been felt necessary to have a second anchor for sterling in the ERM.
2. Sterling, as a petro-currency, is particularly exposed to fluctuating pressures, especially

those related to oil price movements and expectations. These tend to push sterling in the *opposite* direction from other European currencies, and have made sterling the 'odd man' out of the currencies participating in the ERM.

3. When conditions do become appropriate for sterling's entry into the ERM, then the UK will fully participate in the ERM of the EMS; but that time has not yet come!

However, the House of Lords European Community's Committee concluded, in the autumn of 1983, that the UK should participate in the ERM of the EMS *as soon as possible*, because the UK would then have more influence on the system's development as a full member; this is important both for the UK's more general role within the EEC and also because the EMS is likely to be an important element in attempts to reform the global exchange rate system. Similar conclusions were reached by the House of Commons enquiries in 1985.

The Confederation of British Industry which, until the buffeting of the pound in the forex markets in 1985, resolutely opposed the UK's entry into the ERM, changed its mind dramatically; it now strongly supports the UK's full commitment to the ERM of EMS. The reasons it gives for the change of mind are as follows:

(a) The credibility of the UK within Europe is being increasingly undermined by the government's refusal to participate in an important part of community policy, viz. the ERM.
(b) The volatility of the exchange rate for sterling would have been averted had sterling been committed to the ERM, at least as regards ERM members, with whom the UK now conducts over 50 per cent of its trade.
(c) The major argument which has kept the UK out of the ERM has been that the membership would lead to higher interest rates in order to keep sterling within the prescribed bands; this argument has been undermined because had the UK been within the prescribed band system of the ERM it would never have been necessary to raise interest rates in 1989 by anything like the 15 per cent to curb inflation.
(d) The addition of sterling as an important trading currency would give the ERM still further weight against the US dollar.

It is also worth noting that, despite the monetary targets in the government's Medium Term Financial Strategy, money supply expansion has often overshot the MTFS targets, suggesting that the anchorage of sterling to money supply control targets has not been completely effective.

However, the mere fact of joining the EMS would not make speculators go away. It is far from certain that the central banks have the means or the determination to withstand any major speculative forays between two major traded currencies, e.g. sterling and the Deutschemark.

The arguments *for* and *against* locking the pound sterling within the ERM, which only allows the member currencies a relatively small degree of fluctuation, can be tabulated as follows:

Arguments against joining the ERM

1. Sterling is one of the main investment currencies and large inflows of investment funds can cause unhealthy increases in its exchange rate which might not be easy to correct.
2. Unlike other EMS currencies, sterling is still vulnerable to fluctuations in oil price.
3. The comparatively high inflation rate in the UK would involve excessive direct official intervention to sustain parities with other EMS currencies.

4. The UK government would lose a degree of autonomy over the national economic measures.
5. Given the importance and strength of the German mark and sterling, the two currencies might prove awkward partners in the same parity structure.
6. Even those who support sterling's entry into the ERM are not certain of the rate at which it should join.
7. With the UK interest rate comparatively high and the balance of payments deficit so deep, this is not the right time to lock-in sterling in the fixed exchange rate parities of ERM.

Arguments for joining the ERM

1. UK's oil production has peaked, and sterling's petro-currency status is not so significant now.
2. Anti-inflationary policies of the other ERM members have reduced their inflation rates below that of the UK.
3. Well over 50 per cent of UK trade is with EC countries; a stable sterling would benefit UK importers and exporters.
4. The conduct of the MTFS in the UK has neither fully controlled the inflation rate nor the exchange rate fluctuations; the anchorage of ERM may help achieve both these to a greater degree.
5. If the UK does not join the ERM now, it is in danger of being isolated in the EC and, as such, it will not be able to influence changes and developments in the EMS.

EMU, EMS, ERM

There are three possible levels of integration in Europe: European Monetary Union (EMU); European Monetary System (EMS); and Exchange Rate Mechanism (ERM). EMU is the most radical. Its aim is *a single currency* for the EC, which would involve a high degree of economic policy coordination and therefore the sacrifice of considerable economic autonomy by individual countries. UK is the least positive EC member country towards the EMU. The EMS aims for *exchange rate* stability within the EC, and convergence of economic and financial policies, but to a lesser degree than required by EMU. UK is a member of EMS but has failed to benefit fully by refusing to join the ERM. Exchange rate stability among ERM members has been a feature of recent years, and of especial note is the fact that price rises and exchange rate volatility in Italy and Spain – two traditionally inflation-prone countries – have moderated significantly in recent years. In addition, the inflation differential between France and West Germany, which stood at 6.7 per cent in 1979 when the EMS was launched, narrowed to 1.6 per cent in 1989, representing a further success of the system.

The Prime Minister has committed the UK to enter when certain conditions are met – including lower inflation in the UK and the abolition of the few remaining exchange controls in the EC. A possible solution would be for the pound to enter the ERM subject to a margin of 6 per cent on either side of the central rate, as is permitted for Spain.

Note: On 8 October 1990, the UK joined the ERM of the EMS.

The relationship between interest rates and exchange rates

Earlier in this chapter, under the portfolio balance theory, it was stated that high interest rates will attract inflows of capital from lower interest rate economies, which in turn will raise the exchange rate of the former. Note that it is changes in the interest rates in a country *relative* to interest rates in other countries that is the key factor in determining exchange rates.

Interest rates may be raised to reduce outward capital movements and/or to attract capital back. However, the relationship between interest rates and exchange rates extends further. The interest rate is the price of *borrowing* money, whereas the exchange rate is the price of *buying* currency. The relationship between interest rate and exchange rate, although indirect, is nonetheless significant in equalising interest differentials between major international financial centres.

The interest rate and exchange rate link may be shown by the following example. Suppose that DM interest rate is 5 per cent p.a. and £ interest rate if 10 per cent p.a., then by switching funds from DM to £, interest gain of 5 per cent can be made, *but* there is an exchange risk of £ appreciating and causing a capital loss in the converted DM receipts. This risk can be eliminated by paired forward transactions: (1) buy £ and sell DM *spot*, and invest at 10 per cent p.a.; (2) buy DM and sell £ 12 months *forward*. Transaction (1) is at spot exchange rate. Transaction (2) is at spot exchange rate plus/minus forward discount/premium margin. Thus the difference between the two is the forward margin. If the forward margin is not equal to the difference in DM and £ interest rates, an arbitrage exists, which will be exploited until the difference between transactions (1) and (2) equal forward margin.

Arbitrage in the forex markets involves buying and selling currencies to take advantage of exchange rate differentials between currencies.

Suppose a London exchange dealer notices that in New York the dollar/sterling rate is being quoted at £1 : $1.55, whereas in London the dollar/sterling rate is £1 : $1.44. He will at once realise that by buying 'cheaper' dollars with pounds in New York and by selling 'dearer' dollars for sterling in London, he will make a quick profit. Thus arbitrage will drive up the dollar/sterling exchange rate quoted in New York and push down the dollar/sterling rate quoted in London; once the exchange rates in the two financial centres equalise, there will be no incentive for arbitrage. The London dealer will, of course, take into account the *cost* of his buying and selling dollars to decide whether arbitrage is worthwhile. On account of arbitrage opportunities, rates quoted in different financial centres are generally only *slightly* different, but not by enough to trigger arbitrage

The movement of *long-term* funds between countries will largely depend upon factors such as political stability and the long-term profitability potential of the project which is being financed. Therefore, movements in exchange rate play a less important part in long-term overseas investment decisions.

The relationship between interest rates and exchange rates means that governments can intervene in two ways:

1. By directly buying and selling their currency in the markets.
2. By raising or lowering interest rates.

It may be the latter which has the major impact on their exchange rate. (See p.72.)

Investment portfolio approach

Suppose there are two alternative investment possibilities, say either in dollars or DM deposits. The expected relative return will be influenced by the *known* interest rates differential plus the *expected change* in the exchange rate of the DM against the dollar. These are of course connected. An increase in US interest rates will, other things being equal, raise the dollar's exchange rate against the DM, due to increased demand for the dollar and increased supply of the DM.

Thus the *appreciation* of the dollar, despite the huge US federal budget deficit and its higher inflation rates than those of Germany and Japan, its main trading partners, can best be explained in terms of the higher levels of US interest rates in recent years.

The relatively high US short-term interest rates were due to two factors: (i) a tight domestic monetary policy to contain inflationary pressures; and (ii) the need for a substantial inflow of foreign capital to finance the budget deficits. Therefore, higher US interest rates, according to the investment portfolio theory, have led to the high exchange rate of the dollar (itself a factor in the high US current account deficits) and, by causing large inflows of overseas capital, to the huge surplus in the US *capital* account.

In addition to high interest rates, there have been other factors which have led to the movement of overseas capital into the USA: the purchase of dollar assets by Japanese investors after the liberalisation of Japanese exchange controls; the rapid growth in the US economy in 1983–84; and the slowing down of US bank lending overseas following the international debt problem.

However, in explaining exchange rate behaviour, the investment portfolio approach cannot be considered in isolation from other economic fundamentals, such as the current account position, inflation rate differentials and the level of economic activity.

Sterling trade weighted exchange rate index (SERI)

In times of floating and rapidly moving exchange rates, it can be misleading to focus on the rate of exchange for sterling against any *one* currency. For example, the strength of the US dollar in the early months of 1985 had tended to obscure sterling's relative stability against other currencies. The SERI measures the overall change in the value of sterling against other currencies *as a whole*. SERI therefore is a better indicator of the average exchange rate of sterling, and of the impact of exchange rate movements on UK trade competitiveness or inflation, than is any individual rate such as the dollar/sterling rate. SERI is calculated by taking a *weighted* average of the sterling exchange rate against 17 other currencies, including the dollar. The weighting reflects the importance of the individual currencies to UK trade. To make it easier to monitor sterling's overall movements, the SERI is calculated and published every hour by the Bank of England, with 1975 as its base date. The trade-weighted index takes into account the importance of each country's trade with the other countries in the basket by utilising a weighting system.

Recent examination questions

The following seven examination questions should give you a good idea of the breadth and depth of knowledge required to answer questions on this topic satisfactorily. After you have read this chapter carefully, spend ten minutes or so making answer plans for each question. Only then turn to the outline answers given below.

Question 1

(a) To what extent does the theory of purchasing power parity explain a change in a country's exchange rate?

(b) Examine the consequences of a depreciating exchange rate on a country's:
  (i) Current account of the balance of payments;
  (ii) Inflation rate.

Question 2

Discuss both the desirability and the feasibility of a return to world-wide fixed-exchange rates such as operated under the so-called Bretton Woods system.

Question 3

(a) Outline the main objectives of the European Monetary System (EMS).

(b) What economic conditions are essential for the objectives of the EMS to be achieved?

(c) Discuss the case for and against full UK entry into EMS.

Question 4

(a) Outline the reasons which might lead a central bank to intervene on foreign exchange markets.

(b) Apart from imposing exchange controls, how might a central bank intervene to influence the exchange rates?

(c) Can central bank intervention succeed in stabilising a country's exchange rate in the long term? Give reasons for your answer.

Question 5

Following the breakdown of the so-called Bretton Woods system in the 1970s most major currencies were allowed to float. To what extent have the theoretical advantages of floating exchange rates been borne out in practice?

Question 6

Discuss the factors which determine changes in the foreign exchange rate of a country's currency.

Question 7

(a) What is meant by measuring changes in a country's exchange rate on a 'trade-weighted' basis?

(b) What are the fundamental factor's underlying currency performance?

(c) Between late 1980 and early 1985, the index of the US dollar's trade-weighted exchange rate rose by almost 70 per cent. To what extent did this appreciation, and subsequent developments, reflect the fundamental factors underlying currency performance?

Outline answers

Answer 1

(a) *PPP theory*: exchange rates are determined by the *relative* domestic purchasing power of each currency. It attempts to explain a depreciation of a currency *simply* in terms of different rates of inflation for traded goods; that is its weakness.

- In the short term, this would not be an adequate explanation since interest rate differentials, balance of payments performances, government intervention, and relative costs and prices of non-traded goods included in the domestic price level would need to be considered.

(b) (i)
- A depreciating exchange rate tends to increase a current account surplus or decrease a deficit, after the 'J-curve' effect.
- Home-produced goods become cheaper in international markets, while imports become dearer.
- The extent of improvement in trade performance depends on the elasticity of demand for traded goods.
- The invisible account, in the current account may also improve from increase in, say, tourism.

(ii) Since the price of imported goods and raw materials has increased due to the depreciation, inflation will increase; the extent will depend on second-round effects and the domestic monetary and fiscal policies.

Answer 2

Arguments for fixed exchange rates:
(i) provide a measure of certainty; favourable to the growth of world trade;
(ii) individual countries prevented from pursuing inflationary policies by the need to avoid excessive upward pressure on their exchange rates.

Arguments against fixed exchange rates:
(i) preclude independent domestic policies, requiring deflation rather than devaluation to correct balance of payment deficits;
(ii) large holdings of official reserves essential to defend the fixed rate.

Feasibility of a return to fixed exchange rate system: Bretton Woods system of fixed exchange rates broke down because of:
(i) differences in inflation rates; and
(ii) large imbalances in the balance of payments.

These two factors have increased since the breakdown of Bretton Woods.

Bretton Woods-type exchange rate system is unlikely to be durable.

Frequent realignments, even in the 'fixed' exchange rate parities in the EMS, cast doubt on the durability of a fixed exchange rate system.

Answer 3

(a) *Objectives of EMS*:
- Medium term: to achieve a zone of exchange rate stability in Europe.
- Long term: to achieve European economic and monetary union.

(b) *Necessary conditions*:
- A high degree of economic coordination which will:

- nearly equalise the inflation level in member states;
- reduce interest-rate differentials; and
- eliminate large balance of payments imbalances.

(c) (i) *For UK entry*:
- Over 50 per cent of the UK's foreign trade is conducted with EC;
- Exchange-rate stability would benefit UK exporters and importers;
- Stability against strong DM would help contain inflation; and
- Prospects of UK becoming isolated in European monetary developments (e.g. establishing of a common currency and a central bank).

(ii) *Against UK entry*:
- Loss of economic independence.
- The importance of DM and sterling in international trade and investment might make them uncomfortable partners.
- Although the UK's oil production has peaked, sterling is still vulnerable to oil price movements.
- Not easy to establish the appropriate rate at which entry should occur.
- No consensus on when the time would be right for entry.
- Entry may lead to excessive intervention by the Bank of England. (UK joined the ERM in October 1990.)

Answer 4

(a) Reasons for intervention:

(i) To defend a parity with a 'fixed' exchange rate system, the authorities must intervene.
(ii) To avert sharp fluctuations in exchange rates.
(iii) To achieve a desirable depreciation to improve export and competitiveness and/or curb imports.
(iv) To revalue currency to reduce import costs and the domestic inflation rate.

(b) (i) By direct intervention – buying/selling domestic currency.
(ii) By raising/lowering interest rates.

(c) Intervention would not succeed if:
- other fundamental factors, notably inflation and balance of payments performance were markedly adverse.
- By keeping domestic interest rates relatively high, could succeed for several years in preventing the adverse effects of inflation and balance of payments performance being reflected in a falling exchange rate.

Answer 5

- Advantages claimed from floating exchange rates:
  (i) A continuous and automatic adjustment of the balance of payments.
  (ii) Independent domestic economic policies can be pursued; no exchange rate target to defend.
  (iii) To insulate internal economy from 'imported' inflation; exchange rate moving in line with relative inflation rates. If low relative inflation, balance of payments improves, exchange rate rises and price of imports falls.
  (iv) A reduced need for official reserves.
- How far have the theoretical advantages of floating rates actually been achieved?
  (i) Automatic adjustment of the balance of payments, especially on current accounts, not a notable success; partly because exchange rates did not move in line with

relative inflation rates (purchasing power parity theory), and partly because of low elasticities, at least in the short run. Adjustment of current and capital accounts was not really automatic, but was rather via highly volatile short-term capital flows.

(ii) Although there were no specific exchange rate targets to defend, yet the strength of the US dollar (due to higher interest rates) has constrained the domestic economic policies of other countries.

(iii) Insulation against 'imported' inflation has not been achieved because relative exchange rates have not moved in line with relative inflation rates: low inflation countries (e.g. Germany and Japan) have been most vulnerable to 'imported' inflation.

(iv) 'Free floating' has in fact been 'managed' floating; therefore official interventions have been almost as expensive as under fixed exchange rates, and there is still the need for more official reserves.

(v) The fixed or semi-fixed exchange rate under the EMS means that 10 European currencies have **not** been 'floating'.

Answer 6

Any factors which affect the supply and demand for a currency will affect its exchange rate.

- Factors affecting supply and demand for a currency:
  - (i) The balance of payments position on current account; a deficit implies less demand and more supply of the currency and therefore lower exchange rates.
  - (ii) Interest rate differentials; these will affect the level and direction of capital transactions (and thus dividends, profits, interest).
  - (iii) Inflation rate differentials; these will influence relative cost structures, activate purchasing power parity theory and thus affect current accounts.
  - (iv) Political stability affects long-term capital flows.
  - (v) Possession of natural resources, e.g. oil, for which there is, in the short term, inelastic demand overseas.
  - (vi) Official intervention via exchange controls or intervention on the foreign exchange markets.
  - (vii) Changes in expectations; 'leads and lags' – traders advance payments in a currency which they expect to appreciate (to avoid capital loss) and delay payments in currencies they expect to depreciate (to make capital gain).

Answer 7

(a)
- Under floating rates there is no one simple yardstick for measuring currency performances.
- Therefore a basket of the currencies of the major trading partners of the country whose currency's performance is to be measured, is constructed.
- The importance, or weight, given to each currency in the basket depends upon the volume of trade conducted with each country in the basket.
- A currency's performance is then measured on an index basis against the basket.

(b)
- The fundamental factors affecting a currency's performance are:
  - (i) interest rate differentials between countries;
  - (ii) relative national inflation rates;
  - (iii) relative current account performances.

(c) • Factors responsible for the *appreciation* of the dollar were:
  (i) higher short-term interest rates to finance huge budget deficits and to contain inflationary pressures;
  (ii) purchase of dollar assets by the Japanese, after the relaxation of their exchange controls.
- Factors responsible for the *depreciation* of the dollar were:
  (i) US economy became less attractive to overseas investors (balance of payments deficits, slowing down of economic growth);
  (ii) short-term interest rates have begun to fall (Plaza Agreement);
  (iii) US official policy: reduce the value of the dollar to repair the damage done to the economy and industrial growth.

A tutor's answer

Make an answer plan for the following question, which is related to the outline answer 6 above, before looking at the answer plan and specimen answer below.

Question

In the absence of official intervention in the foreign exchange market, what factors are likely to influence changes in a country's exchange rate?

Answer plan:
Factors affecting the supply and demand for a currency:
1. The balance of payments position.
2. Relative inflation rates.
3. Relative interest rates.
4. Expectations.
5. The stance of fiscal and monetary policies.
6. Political stability.

Specimen answer

Any factor that can influence the supply of, and demand for, a currency can effect changes in the foreign exchange rate of that currency. The major factors, apart from official intervention, are outlined below, although the strength of each factor varies both between countries and over time.

1. The balance of payments position

A country experiencing a balance of payments surplus on current account will on this count alone experience upward pressure on the exchange rate of its currency; similarly, countries with a current account deficit will tend to experience 'weak' currencies, i.e. a downward pressure on their currencies' exchange rates. Although relative current account performance is widely seen as a key factor in influencing exchange rate movements, the significance of capital account movements should not be overlooked. If, for example, overseas investors have confidence that a country has a considerable development potential and political stability, then they may initiate large-scale capital inflows. These may be sufficient to offset the otherwise downward pressure on its currency of a current account deficit.

2. Relative inflation rates

A country with a high inflation rate relative to its major trading partners will tend to lose competitiveness. This would signal, other things being equal, a deterioration in its balance of payments, which, in turn, will normally cause a fall in the exchange rate of its currency; and vice versa.

3. Relative interest rates

In order to maximise the aggregate returns from his investment portfolio, an investor with a spread of investments in different currencies will seek to ensure that the returns he expects on the marginal investment in different currencies will be approximately equal. By definition, the expected return will be equal to the interest differentials plus the expected change in the exchange rate. Higher interest rates will raise the expected rate of return and lead to a higher demand to invest in the currency offering higher interest rates; this will lead to upward pressure on its exchange rate.

4. Expectations

Foreign exchange markets generally seek to anticipate changes in key economic variables, such as in a country's economic performance and in its level of interest rates. For example, if the markets expect a country's balance of payments to deteriorate, then the exchange rate of its currency may well move downward in anticipation. An expectation of a rise in interest rates for a currency may well move its exchange rate upward. The influence of expectations therefore is of central importance.

5. The stance of fiscal and monetary policy

A government's fiscal and monetary policy stance is seen by the foreign exchange market as a yardstick against which to judge exchange rate behaviour. For example, an increase in money supply, on account of an expansionary economic policy, will be seen by many, especially the monetarists, as inevitably leading to a fall in its exchange rate: high money supply growth leads to a high inflation rate and a weak balance of payments position, and hence a weak currency.

6. Political stability

Political stability, or instability, has a very important influence on long-term capital inflows, which will significantly influence the overall balance of payments position, and therefore the exchange rate.

A step further

The factors likely to influence exchange rate movements, under a floating exchange rate system, are assuming ever-increasing importance. Sharp changes in exchange rates are of particular concern to many bank customers and to banks themselves, especially their foreign exchange dealers. Although there is no definitive answer to the problems to which foreign exchange rates – whether fixed, floating or permutations in between – give rise, yet as a prospective banker you are expected to speak intelligently on the broad topic of foreign exchange rates. Try to keep abreast of changes in foreign exchange rates and their effects on the national and international economic scene. You can do this by reading the quality press, *Banking World*, the Bank of England *Quarterly Bulletins* and The Chartered Institute of Bankers' *Examiners' Reports* and *Updating Notes*. Pay especial attention to the developments in the EMS; the UK is a member of the EC and partly involved with the EMS. For a basic understanding of this topic, see the Banking Information Service publication *A Guide to International Financial Systems*.

Keep an eye on the effects of the UK's entry into the ERM of the EMS on the UK economy, inflation and interest rates. Also keep abreast of the moves towards a single European central bank and a single European currency, i.e. the full EMU.

CHAPTER 10

Supervision and Regulation

Syllabus requirements

- Supervision by the Bank of England under the 1987 Banking Act.
- Supervision and regulation by the international institutions.
- Prudential controls.
- Third World debt problem and banks' capital positions.
- Regulation of the investment industry under the 1986 Financial Services Act.
- Regulation and supervision of the building societies and insurance companies.

Getting started

This is a descriptive chapter setting out in some detail the provisions of the relevant acts and describing the legal powers and duties of the supervising and regulating institutions. The contents of this chapter provide a hinterland of useful knowledge relating to the supervision of the operations of the main types of financial institution in the UK. You are **not** expected to memorise the legal provisions of the enactments discussed in the MFS exams.

The 1987 Banking Act gives the Bank of England legal supervisory powers to ensure that only fit and proper institutions take deposits. The chief objective of the Act is to protect depositors. The Financial Services Act 1986 has as its main objective the protection of investors. To achieve this it has established the Securities Investment Board and Self-Regulating Organisations.

The directives of the European Community give guidance and freedom to the financial institutions of member states in order to harmonise the 'rules of play' and the 'playing fields'.

Since the building societies and insurance companies are outside the supervisory jurisdiction of the Bank of England, they are supervised by the Building Societies Commission and the Department of Trade and Industry under the Building Society Act 1986, and various acts relating to insurance business. The contents of this chapter have practical relevance to the UK's financial system, and you should keep that point in mind as you read and learn the information contained in this chapter. Due to the nature of the content, the sections 'Essential Principles' and 'Useful Applied Material' have been combined.

Essential principles and useful applied material

Banking Act 1987

Origin and aims

The 1984 Johnson Matthey Bankers (JMB) crisis pointed to the weaknesses of the 1979 Banking Act supervision regulations, under which the Bank of England oversaw the management of UK banks. These weaknesses were principally the ease with which JMB could lend the equivalent of their entire capital to a single, doubtful borrower, the failure of JMB auditors to spot the trouble, and the slowness with which the Bank responded to JMB's imprudence.

One of the central aims of the 1987 Act is to establish the Bank of England as the *legal* supervisory authority (something which was never fully formalised in statute before) and to strengthen its statutory powers to prevent financial institutions taking in illegal deposits. The basic concern of the Act is the protection of *depositors*; the protection of *investors* is the province of the 1986 Financial Services Act.

The Act brought about the following major amendments to 1979 legislation:

(a) A Board of Banking Supervisors consisting of Bank of England officials and outside experts has been established to advise the Bank on supervisory matters. The purpose of the Board, which will report separately to the Treasury, is to make the Bank more accountable for the way it carries out its supervisory responsibilities. The Board has the right to approach the Chancellor of the Exchequer directly if it feels that its advice to the Bank is being ignored.

(b) The two-tier system of authorisation under the 1979 Act ('recognised' and 'licensed' institutions) is replaced by a unified system with a single category of 'authorised' institutions.

(c) All authorised institutions have to meet statutory prudential requirements which, in brief, are that:
   (i) an institution's directors, controllers and managers are 'fit and proper' persons to hold their positions;
   (ii) the business is conducted properly – which covers, among other things, adequate capital and liquidity provisions (see below) for bad and doubtful debts, accounting and other records, and internal controls; and
   (iii) when authorisation is granted, the institution has net assets of not less than £1 million.

(d) A UK authorised institution will be permitted to use a banking name, provided it has at least £5 million paid-up share capital and/or undistributable reserves.

(e) For each authorised institution, an independent firm of accountants will make available to the Bank of England three separate annual reports: on its internal control system; on its accounting and other records; and on its prudential statistical returns.

(f) The Bank of England is empowered to intervene in the merger or acquisition of a bank on prudential grounds.

(g) Authorised institutions are required to report to the Bank of England loan exposurers of over 10 per cent of capital and to give *prior notice* of proposed transactions exposing them to the risk of losing over 25 per cent of capital.

(h) The Deposit Protection Scheme is extended to cover all authorised institutions: 75 per cent of the first £20,000 of sterling deposits made with an authorised institution is covered.

(j) The 'exempt' institutions (i.e. building societies, the National Savings Bank, the Banking Department of the Bank of England, insurance companies and pension funds) are excluded from the jurisdiction of the Act, because they are already satisfactorily regulated and supervised under separate legislation.

(k) The Treasury can amend the definition of 'deposit' and 'deposit-taker' to help it keep up with changes in the financial markets/services industry.

(l) The Bank of England has been granted greater information-gathering powers. In particular, the auditors of banks can inform on them without being in breach of their duties.

Thus the 1987 Banking Act provides a more elaborate supervision system backed by stronger statutory powers, including supervision at international level in order to achieve common standards for the UK and overseas banks on capital and liquidity adequacy (see below).

Capital measurement

Bank of England

In September 1980, the Bank of England produced a paper on the measurement of bank capital. This is an important area because, if the capital of a bank is not adequate, it may not be able to absorb the bad debts which it may create.

The Bank of England basically monitors two measures of capital:

(a) the gearing ratio: and
(b) the risk measurement.

Both start from a common capital base which includes share capital, loan stock of over five years, reserves and general bad debt provisions; specific provisions are excluded. For the purpose of the gearing ratio, deductions are made for equipment and other fixed assets, goodwill and investments in subsidiaries. This total is then compared to total non-capital liabilities.

The risk measurement entails comparing the capital base of the bank to an adjusted total of risk assets, reached by applying a series of weights to different categories of assets.

The Bank has avoided setting specific guidelines for how much each ratio should be. Instead, the capital position of each bank is discussed with it individually.

International agreement on capital measurement and adequacy

In July 1988, the central banks of the ten leading countries (the Group of Ten) agreed on a set of rules for how much capital banks must have in relation to the size and riskiness of their assets and off-balance-sheet exposure. The key features of the agreed set of rules (known as the Basle Agreement, because the Committee on Banking Regulations and Supervisory Practices of the Group of Ten meets at the Bank for International Settlements in Basle, Switzerland) are as follows:

(a) By the end of 1992, banks with significant international business must maintain capital equivalent to at least 8 per cent of assets weighted according to risk.
(b) At least half of the bank's capital base must consist of 'core capital' (equity, disclosed reserves and non-cumulative participating preference shares). The other half may consist of 'supplementary capital' (which may be revaluation of reserves; some unrealised capital gains on securities; general provisions; hidden reserves; hybrid (equity/debt) instruments; subordinated term debts (fixed maturities) subject to certain limits).
(c) In calculating the capital requirements, off-balance-sheet items will be taken into account by using credit conversion factors to establish their credit risk equivalent (see below).
(d) Assets and off-balance-sheet exposure must be given weightings of 0; 10; 20; 50; or 100 per cent which reflect their risk. For example, in the 100 per cent weighting category are all loans to the private sector; premises, fixed assets and investments. In the 0 per cent category are cash; claims on the central government and central banks of other countries, if they are funded and denominated in the currency of the country concerned.

    Claims on non-OECD governments which are not in national currency are weighted 100 per cent. Claims incorporated in the 24 member countries of the Organisation for Economic Co-operation and Development (OECD) are weighted 20 per cent, as are claims on non-OECD banks with less than one year to maturity; longer-term claims are weighted 100 per cent. Loans fully secured by mortgages on residential property for owner occupation or rental are weighted 50 per cent.

(e) An interim target date has been set at the end of 1990, when the minimum ratio will be 7.25 per cent but the definition of capital will be less strict than in the final rules. The countries in the Basle Agreement are Belgium, Canada, France, Italy, Japan, Luxembourg, the Netherlands, Sweden, Switzerland, West Germany, the UK and the USA.

Table 10.1 shows the transitional arrangements regarding capital adequacy from the end of 1987 to the end of 1992.

Table 10.1 *Transitional Arrangements*

	Initial	*End-1990*	*End-1992*
1. Minimum standard	The level prevailing at end-1987	7.25%	8.0%
2. Measurement formula	Core elements plus 100%	Core elements plus 100% (3.625% plus 3.625%)	Core elements plus 100% (4% plus 4%)
3. Supplementary elements included in core	Maximum 25% of total core	Maximum 10% of total core (i.e. 0.36%)	None
4. Limit on general loan loss reserves in supplementary elements*	No limit	1.5 percentage points, or exceptionally up to 2.0 percentage points	1.25 percentage points, or exceptionally and temporarily up to 2.0 percentage points
5. Limit on term subordinated debt in supplementary elements	No limit (at discretion)	No limit (at discretion)	Maximum of 50% of Tier 1
6. Deduction for goodwill	Deducted (at discretion)	Deducted (at discretion)	Deducted (at discretion)

* This limit would only apply in the event that no agreement is reached on a consistent basis for including unencumbered provisions or reserves in capital.

Source: Committee on Banking Regulation and Supervisory Practices, July 1988.

One effect of the new capital adequacy standards, which include off-balance sheet items, might be to encourage the *securitisation* process, which involves the sale of risk assets and a move from lending business to acting as a broker or guarantor between suppliers and users of capital. In the securitisation process the bank earns fee income without increasing its balance sheet exposure. The Bank views securitisation with caution, since some residual liability may rest with the banks involved, and has therefore advised them to allow for any such residual risk in their capital adequacy ratios.

Since all the 12 countries will be implementing the same rules, foreign banks in London will have no advantage or disadvantage (except that the risk asset ratios will be above the 8 per cent minimum) by operating in London. The additional cost due to higher ratios in London may be offset by increased cost of doing business in other financial centres with hitherto more liberal regimes, once they come into line with the supervised banks.

Liquidity adequacy

Cash flows

Banks have to be capable of meeting their obligations as and when they fall due. The Bank of England believes that in order that a bank should be able to meet its obligations, it should have sufficient cash and liquid assets, and also a future cash flow showing its position in the months ahead.

Banks have obligations to their depositors, whose money may be repayable at sight or at short notice. The banks must ensure that they hold cash and liquefiable assets to meet these demands. For each particular institution, the mix of maturing assets and cash will be different. Two points are important:

(a) The sole responsibility for a bank's liquidity rests with its management. For this reason the Bank of England does not seek to impose all-embracing liquidity ratios. The Bank will need to be satisfied, however, that banks have given adequate attention to liquidity and that their policies are prudent in this area. The Bank realises that every institution is different and it takes this into consideration when deciding what is prudent.

(b) The Bank of England has instigated a basis for bank liquidity measurement which relates to the total obligations of banks in the form of cash flows. A cash flow may be in the following format:

Table 10.2 *Cashflow format*

	Sight–8 days	*8 days–1 month*	*1–3 months*	*3–6 months*	*6–12 months*
Liabilities					
Deposits					
Commitments					
Less Assets					
Marketable					
Non-marketable					
Standby facilities available	______	______	______	______	______
Net position c/f	______	______	______	______	______
Net cumulative position	______	______	______	______	______

Weights are given to assets depending on how 'safe' they are. For example:

Nil discount	–	Treasury bills, eligible local authority bills, and eligible bank bills. Government and government-guaranteed marketable securities with less than 12 months to maturity.
5% discount	–	Other bills and CDs with less than six months to maturity. Other Government, government-guaranteed and local authority marketable securities with less than five years to maturity or at variable rates.
10% discount	–	Other bills and CDs and Floating Rate Notes with less than five years to maturity. Government, government-guaranteed and local authority marketable debt with more than five years to maturity.

Source: BEQB, July 1982.

Bank of England proposals

Primary liquid asset requirements

After 1985, the Bank issued a number of liquidity proposals. These proposals, among other things, incorporated a 'primary liquid asset requirement' for banks, comprising cash, bank balances at the Bank, Treasury bills, gilts *less than* one year to maturity, eligible bills *up to* 91 days, and money placed on a secured or unsecured basis *up to* one month with bill and gilt market-makers. The Bank applies a liquidity formula based on the level of primary liquid assets held, measured as a proportion of total sterling liabilities with a maturity of sight to eight days.

The level of primary liquidity has been set at approximately 12 per cent. The bank requires liquidity returns to be made quarterly, although banks are expected to maintain the liquidity requirement on a day-to-day basis.

Supervision/regulation by international institutions

European community

By the end of 1992, the remaining physical, technical and fiscal barriers to free movement of goods, services, capital and people will have been removed among the 12 member states of the European Community (EC), and a single market will be created. The single market will cater for over 320 million people – over 7 per cent of the world's population – with high disposable income.

The First Banking Directive in the EC (1977) achieved three things: the freedom of establishing banks and other credit institutions anywhere in the EC: the acceptance of common standards for granting banking licences, and the introduction of the basic principle of home-country control of the financial institutions established abroad in the EC.

The Second Banking Directive (1988) has established two new principles: that the home country of an institution will be responsible for regulation and supervision: and a mutual recognition by all member governments of each others' regulatory arrangements. Thus, the Second Directive has removed all remaining obstacles to freedom of establishment in the EC banking sector.

The implications of the Second Directive for UK banks are:

- easier cross-border banking business;
- international expansion via location in member states;
- cheaper location, because committed capital will not be required for foreign branches;
- no specific solvency ratios or large exposure limits on foreign branches; and
- the opportunity for a bank to undertake in other states whatever it is able to undertake in the home country.

The central issue for competing banks is *access* to potential customers and the creation of effective *delivery* systems for financial services. Access to customers in the EC states would be possible in the following ways:

- by establishing a network of branches;
- by mergers with institutions in other states;
- by acquiring subsidiaries in other EC countries;
- by developing cross-border business links with other institutions in the community;
- by successful marketing of banking services in other states.

With regard to delivery in the single market, a distinction needs to made between retail and wholesale banking, because the competitive conditions in these two types of banking business vary both within and between member states. The wholesale banking business tends to be large scale, with comparatively few, but large, customers. Therefore, delivery can be made without a network of branches. Retail banking, on the other hand, involves a large number of small accounts, and access *and* delivery are, usually, through a network of branches. Therefore, the future European integration is more likely to be strongly felt in the retail banking sector.

However, the impact within the UK retail banking sector may not be substantial, because in the UK deregulation (the 'Big Bang') of the financial industry and the presence of so many foreign banks in the City – banks of over 73 countries are operating in London – means that competitive conditions are already demanding for the UK retail banks. Furthermore, in the UK there is no exchange control; all major EC banks already have a presence in London; there are no restrictions on the range of business activities; and branches of retail banks are not required to have committed capital.

The unique strength of the UK banks, arising from their long experience and expertise in innovatory skills and financial strengths and acumen, will give them the opportunity both to compete with the EC banks with advantage and to shape banking in the European single market.

The EC's Investment Services Directive (ISD), December 1988, proposes that by 1 January 1993, *inter alia*, financial services (including banking, insurance, investment, pensions) will flow freely across EC member states borders. Except for a certain code of business conduct rules, the ISD does *not* apply to banking and credit institutions that already comply with the Second Banking Directive (see above), and therefore such institutions need not seek authorisation under the ISD to provide their *investment* services. This would give banks an advantage over securities and investment houses.

Prudential controls and banks' balance sheets

Liquidity adequacy of a bank shows the extent to which its liquid assets are sufficient to meet its obligations as they fall due, e.g. withdrawal from sight and time deposits, commitment to lend at a specific date, unforeseen demand for financing, unused overdraft facilities, daily interbank settlements. The components of a bank's balance sheet relevant to its liquidity adequacy (as under the liquidity adequacy requirement by the Bank of England) are notes and coins, operational deposits with the Bank of England, Treasury and eligible bills, secured on-call and short-notice lending to discount houses and GEMMS, short maturity government stocks (and the ability to borrow on the CDs and interbank markets). However, the bank has to be mindful that the 'quality' of its marketable assets can vary due to asset price fluctuations and changes in interest rates. It should also so manage its assets portfolio as to ensure appropriate cash flows from maturing assets, keeping in mind that defaults can occur. It must maintain a diversified deposit base and high standing in the markets so that it is able to attract new deposits without undue costs.

Although the Bank of England, in its supervisory role aims to ensure that individual banks follow prudent liquidity management policies, it leaves banks' managements free to choose what they consider to be the optimal combination of liquid assets vis-á-vis the liability structure in their balance sheets, their financial objectives, and the prevailing economic and financial circumstances.

Capital adequacy means the extent to which a bank's capital covers the risks inherent in its operations, as seen from its balance sheet. Clearly the risks of each bank will differ from the risks of other banks. Capital adequacy and liquidity are required under the 1987

Banking Act, but the banks under their own prudential practices need capital adequacy to withstand possible losses on operations, notably bad advances. A bank's capital adequacy ratio can be gauged from the ratio between its total assets or deposits and its capital in its balance sheet. If its capital adequacy ratio becomes unacceptable, it must either raise more capital (e.g. by rights issues) or reduce its operations.

Banks and the Third World debt problem

In March 1990, the UK clearing banks announced the huge £4.6 billion of Third World debt provisions in their 1989 accounts. Two banks have the unusual situation of having more in provisions now than they do in shareholders' funds. However, these colossal figures are really of historical interest because the clearers are now in a position to write most of the Third World debts off if they want to.

Individual banks have been, understandably, reluctant to give new loans, unless persuaded by the IMF or the US Treasury, and they have been content with debt rescheduling. So, the most striking feature of any table showing sources of finance for the LDCs during the 1980s has been a decline in private lending to LDCs. From a peak of $83 billion in 1982, this fell to $18 billion in 1987. The counterpart has been an increase in official lending – from 33 per cent of the total in 1982 to 43 per cent in 1987. Within this, the decline in IMF credits has partially reversed the increase in IBRD (International Bank for Reconstruction and Development) funding.

The banks' attitude towards the international financial market has changed from a philosophy of asset-growth towards improving profitability, in particular by improving the quality of assets, or by increasing fee-earning off-balance-sheet business. Deregulation, the creation of new financial instruments (FRNs – Floating Rate Notes and NIFs – Note Issue Facilities), and the process of securitisation, and disintermediation (avoiding the bank as intermediary) have required banks to turn their attention away from trade and project-lending and sovereign loans towards preserving their share of business with corporate customers and high-quality institutional borrowers in OECD countries. Hence, funds are recycled more between surplus and deficit OECD countries than between OPEC and LDCs. Indeed, OPEC's surplus has diminished during the 1980s as a result of the fall in real price of oil, and this process looks likely to continue for some time to come. The new surpluses are from Japan, Germany, and the Asian newly-industrialised economies.

There has, nevertheless, been a flood of innovations in financing instruments which bankers have invented to help with the problem of LDC debt. Financing in 1984–85 saw the use of certain financial instruments – e.g. interest-retiming, trade facilities, debt conversions. More recent schemes have included securitisation (bundling together a series of doubtful debts and selling the bundle to outside investors as a new asset in the secondary market at much less than their nominal value), debt buy-backs (as in the case of Bolivia), and Debt Equity Swaps (DESs).

In 1987, some $15 billion in DESs was traded and, in 1988, this amount was expected to double. DESs have certain advantages for banks and debtors: a country can turn a debt with a fixed stream of payments due into equity the dividends of which will depend on the profitability of the particular investment: the banks can use DESs as a way of tidying up their book, or for the smaller banks to leave the debt crisis altogether – removing these assets from their book and passing them to another bank or an industrialist who wishes to keep up long-term links with that country. There is also the advantage of opening up access to foreign investment, and thus to management skills and technology. DESs can mobilise for domestic investment those assets held by residents overseas – i.e. reversing the capital-flight problem.

For example, a company wishing to set up, say, a $10 million tyre factory in Mexico could buy $10 million of Mexican debt at the market price, around 33 cents in the dollar, in April 1989. The company would then sell the debt to the Mexican authorities for close to its face value and receive payment in pesos. In theory, everyone benefits from this transaction: banks – typically, small-and medium-sized regional banks – are able to unload their bad loans on the *secondary-debt market* (see below); Mexico reduces its debt and gains a tyre factory; and the traders make a profit on the difference between the buy and sell price of the loan.

The problem with swaps is that the debtor countries are encouraged to print their money to purchase debt, thereby worsening the already horrendous inflation problems in LCDs. Instead of printing more local currency, the debtor government may sell domestic debt instruments. The public-sector deficit may, thus, be higher if the cost to the government of this new debt is higher than the cost of servicing the old debt. Some LDCs have been more worried than others by these problems and they have wrapped their debt equity swap schemes in layers of restrictions which have limited their effectiveness. Others have acted as did Chile, which swapped $4 billion since 1985 and which plans swapping another $4 billion by 1990. A good DES is a useful tool but it will only make a marginal – if useful – contribution to easing the debt crisis of a debtor country.

Few of the cut-price investments (as in the example of tyre factory, above) can be proved to be genuinely additional investments. Most would have been made anyway, bringing desperately-needed hard currency into the developing country.

There is a flourishing re-sale, or secondary, market in Third-World debt, which has grown from zero to over $30 billion p.a. in the five years to 1980. Chile, with the help of the secondary market, has reduced its debt by 36 per cent in the past few years (1984–1988).

The secondary debt market, now a profitable sideline for at least a dozen international banks, is based on the willingness of some LDCs to buy back their debt in local currency or in company shares.

International banks with big debt portfolios also do direct debt-for-equity swaps, exchanging debts at favourable rates for shares, or full ownership, of companies in LDCs. The UK's Midland Bank, saddled with over $4 billion of debt, has been specially active in this way.

The secondary debt market has developed a dynamic of its own, at one stage removed from real supply and demand. The IBRD estimates that about $10 billion of debt was traded back to the Third-World countries in 1988. However, the volume of trading on the secondary debt market was over $30 billion. The debt claims, once sold by the original creditor, may be sold over and over again between traders profiting from the market fluctuations. The US government would like to see more such activity as part of its voluntary debt-reduction plan. So would the banks: but the debtor countries themselves are less enthusiastic. Countries of the secondary debt market say that this market preys on the suffering of the Third World. Bankers and traders say that it rationalises the chaotic portfolios of smaller banks and that it has helped to convert debt into productive investment in some LDCs.

Financial Services Act 1986

Regulation of investment business

The government's objectives in enacting the Financial Services Act (FSA) are to make the financial services industry of the UK *efficient*, *competitive* (domestically and internationally), inspiring *confidence*, and possessing *resilience*.

You will recall reading in Chapter 4, under section 'The Big Bang', the reason for the passing of the Financial Services Act 1986, and of some of the bodies created under the Act.

You will now see the main provisions of the Act, and a further discussion of the Securities Investment Board and the five Self-Regulating Organisations.

The provisions of the FSA are as follows:

I The Act empowers the Secretary of State for Trade and Industry to authorise and regulate the carrying on of investment business. The Secretary of State has transferred the majority of his powers to a Designated Agency, viz. the Securities Investment Board (SIB).

II SIB is not a government department; it is a private limited company. It will nevertheless have substantial regulatory powers under the Act.

The executive chairman and members of SIB are appointed jointly by the Secretary of State for Trade and Industry and the Governor of the Bank of England. Its members are practitioners from a wide variety of investment activities and independent 'lay' members representing both the users of financial services and the public at large. The Act has armed SIB with a formidable armoury of regulatory sanctions ranging from reprimands, private and public, through crucial actions to obtain restitution of investor funds, where appropriate, up to suspension and – the ultimate sanction – withdrawal of authorisation from an investment business. Despite the formidable, legally backed regulatory powers, SIB is to be financed entirely by the financial markets themselves, with no contributions from the public purse.

III The Act defines 'investments' and 'investment-businesses' and enables the Secretary of State to amend the definitions so that the definitions can be kept up-to-date when new forms of investment are developed.

1 *The main types of investment covered by the Act* are:

(a) Stocks and shares in UK or foreign companies.

(b) Debentures including debenture stock, loan stocks, bonds and certificates of deposit.

(c) Government and other public securities including gilt-edged stock, local authority bonds and bonds issued by foreign governments and international organisations.

(d) Warrants entitling the holder to subscribe for shares and bonds.

(e) Depository receipts for shares, bonds or warrants.

(f) Units in collective investment schemes including units in unit trust schemes and shares in an open-ended investment company.

(g) Options on currency, gold or silver and on any other investment.

(h) Futures contracts for commodities and other property.

(i) Contracts for differences whose value is linked to the value of any kind of property or to an index (e.g. a stock market index).

(j) Insurance policies which are investment – such as endowment and unit-linked policies – but not pure term insurance or policies which simply protect against risk, e.g. most permanent health and credit protection policies and general insurance such as fire and theft.

2 *Investment businesses*
A 'person' (i.e. any body or company with legal personality) will be carrying on investment business if, as a business, he/she:

(a) Buys and sells investments;
(b) Arranges for others to buy and sell investments;
(c) Manages investments belonging to others;
(d) Advises others on their investments; or
(e) Operates a collective investment scheme.

Exceptions
(a) A person who buys and sells investment for his/her own account *unless* he/she does so to make a market in them.
(b) Transactions within a group or a joint commercial enterprise.
(c) Trustees and personal representatives who manage or advise on investments *unless* they hold themselves out as providing professional investment services.
(d) A person who gives investment advice purely as a consequence of advice on non-investment matters – e.g. a tax consultant advising a client to sell shares for tax reasons.
(e) Advice included in a *bona fide* newspaper (but not a tipsheet).
(f) The administration of employee share schemes and the operation of 'share shops' set up to help employees to exchange shares in the company or group which employs them.
(g) Anything done to buy or sell more than 75 per cent of the shares in a private company where both the vendor and the purchaser satisfy conditions.
(h) An overseas person without a permanent place of business in the UK entering into investment transactions in the UK only with or through authorised or exempt persons, or if the only activities he/she carries on in the UK result either: (i) from an unsolicited approach made by a person in the UK on the overseas business; or (ii) from an approach made by the overseas person in the UK which did not contravene the provisions of the Act relating to 'cold-calling' or 'advertising' (see below); (iii) wholesale money market activities of those institutions which are admitted to a list maintained by the Bank of England and only those transactions which are above a specified monetary limit. The limit is £100,000 for debentures, loan stocks, etc. and an underlying contract value of £500,000 for currency options, futures, etc. Transactions below this limit are, however, permitted with established wholesale customers.

IV *Compensation of investors.* A Compensation of Unpaid Investors Scheme is set out which is, under the Act, subject to future consultation with those SROs who will be required to join it. It proposes that investment businesses contribute to the cost of compensation on the basis of equal proportions of gross revenue of each firm, up to a limit in any one year (the limit proposed being £100 million from all contributors *as a group* in any one year). Members of one SRO may be required to contribute up to the maximum in respect of claims against one of their fellows, and members of other SROs only, thereafter. The indications are that compensation under the scheme would be limited to private investors who lose money through an investment business's fraud, negligence or failure to comply with the rules. The maximum compensation, it is hoped, will be in the region of £30,000 to £50,000 in individual cases.

Where a participant firm has become insolvent and an investor satisfies the Compensation of Investors Schemes Manager that the firm is unable to satisfy his claim, the Scheme Manager shall pay to the investor out of the Compensation Fund the amount of the unsatisfied claim subject to the following limitations:

1. 100 per cent of valid claims of losses up to £30,000.
2. 90 per cent of losses on a further £20,000 to an effective limit of £48,000.
3. The maximum amount paid out in claims cannot exceed a ceiling of £100 million in any one year.

Claims from the Scheme will only be met when no further redress can be secured from the defaulting firm, in other words, when the firm is bankrupt or otherwise unable to meet its obligations. Professional investors are not eligible and investors who have opted out of the protection of their client money will not be eligible to claim for loss of such money. An investor's claim for compensation shall be rejected if submitted more than six months after the investor became aware of the insolvency of the firm, unless the Scheme Manager considers that it ought in the circumstances to be allowed. The scheme came into operation on 27 August 1988 and it is not retroactive.

V *Auditors.* Provision is made to facilitate communication between the auditors of an authorised person and that person's supervisors. The SIB can require a directly authorised business to appoint an auditor (if it is not already required to do so by other statutes such as the Companies Act); accounts or other information reported by an auditor may be required to be submitted for a second examination by another qualified person; and no duty to which an auditor may be subject is to be regarded as being contravened if he/she reports to the supervisor of an authorised business in good faith any matter which is relevant to that supervisor's function. The circumstances in which such reports should be made are expected to be laid down in professional guidance, but, in the event that some auditors are not subject to satisfactory guidance, the Secretary of State will have power to specify the circumstances in regulations.

VI *Insider dealing.* In broad terms it means dealing in securities of a company by persons 'connected' with that company whilst in possession of unpublished price-sensitive information. Connected persons do not only include directors and senior officials but also auditors, solicitors, merchant bankers and other professional persons acting on the company's behalf. The Act empowers the Secretary of State to appoint inspectors to investigate possible insider dealing. The inspector will be able to question connected people on oath and require papers and documents to be produced. The Act also extends this offence of inside dealing by Crown servants and to other public servants.

Securities investment board and self-regulating organisations

The Financial Services Act 1986 (FSA) empowers the Secretary for Trade and Industry to authorise and regulate the carrying on of investment business. The majority of these powers have been transferred to the Securities Investment Board (SIB), which is not a government department but a private limited company. The FSA has armed the SIB with formidable regulatory sanctions, ranging from reprimands, private and public, where appropriate, up to suspension and – the ultimate sanction – withdrawal of authorisation from an investment business. Despite the formidable legally-backed regulatory powers, the SIB is financed by the financial markets themselves.

The SIB has recognised five self-regulating organisations (SROs). A recognised SRO is a practitioner-based body set up to provide proper regulations (to achieve investor protection standards laid down by the SIB) of the investment companies under its jurisdiction. Each SRO has to demonstrate to the SIB that its rules are equivalent to those of the SIB and that it is able to ensure compliance with those rules by the member firms.

The five SROs which, in broad terms, cover the following investment areas, are:

(a) *Association of Futures Brokers and Dealers* (AFBD) – Its member firms deal in arranging and advising on deals in futures, options and contracts for differences, and managing portfolios of these types of investments.

(b) *Financial Intermediaries, Managers and Brokers Regulatory Association* (FIMBRA) – Member firms advise and arrange deals in life assurance and units in authorised unit trusts and similar collective investment schemes, and provide investment advisory and management services.

(c) *Investment Management Regulatory Organisations* (IMRO) – IMRO member firms are engaged in investment management, management and operation of collective investment schemes, acting as trustees of unit trusts and pension funds, and advising corporate customers on investment matters.

(d) *Life Assurance and Unit Trust Regulatory Organisation* (LAUTRO) – Its member firms are insurance companies and friendly societies engaged in retail marketing of life assurance products and units in collective investment schemes.

(e) *The Securities Association* (TSA) – TSA member firms arrange deals in shares, debentures, gilts, warrants, financial futures and options on securities and foreign currencies, and manage and advise on transactions in life assurance and collective investment schemes.

The Financial Services Act (FSA) provides for a **compensation scheme** for investors with valid claims, and establishes a framework for investor protection, which includes wide-ranging statutory powers and new criminal offences. In summary the investor protection provisions under the FSA (and the Securities and Investment Board rules drafted under the FSA) are as follows:

(a) The appropriate self-regulating organisation (SRO) has the power to arrange spot checks of the financial and other records of authorised investment firms under its jurisdiction and to impose disciplinary measures where appropriate. An investment firm operating without authorisation or exemption under FSA, is committing a *criminal* offence.

(b) Only 'fit and proper' firms can carry out investment business: it must have adequate financial resources and its officers' previous records must be fit and proper.

(c) A firm must subordinate its own interests to the best interest of its clients in any advice given, which must be the best for each client's circumstances.

(d) Firms must set out the basis of their relationship with their clients in agreement letters stating the services they are to provide, their responsibilities and charges.

(e) Firms must adhere to proper complaints procedure, fully investigating and dealing with clients' complaints and keeping records of complaints and produce them for a subsequent inquiry by the SRO, if required.

(f) Ordinary investors are entitled to the full protection of the Act, but professional and experienced investors do not have the same degree of protection.

(g) Unsolicited visits and telephone calls to sell investments are, for the most part, banned. The customer has a 14-day 'cooling-off' period during which to reconsider the transaction entered into.

(h) A much wider disclosure of information relevant to life assurance must be given by investment firms, enabling the customers to know surrender values, commission levels and the status of persons selling assurance products.

(i) All kinds of advertisement material must give clear warnings about matters such as the volatility or the marketability of the product advertised.

(j) All published recommendations must be fully researched and be capable of substantiation.

(k) Investment firms must make proper arrangements for the segregation of clients' money.

(l) There must be compensation arrangements in all sectors of the investment industry to protect clients' funds, up to defined limits, in the event of the collapse of the investment firms.

Regulation of building societies, insurance companies, and unit and investment trusts

Building Societies Act 1986

This Act came into effect on 1 January 1987. It provides a further spur to competition between banks and building societies. It has also opened up the possibility that some building societies may opt to become banks, in which case they will come under the supervisory regime of the Bank of England under the 1987 Banking Act. The Financial Services Act 1986 (FSA) will also create a number of challenges for building societies. The prime objective of FSA is to regulate any person who conducts investment business. As many building societies and their subsidiaries may carry out ancillary services of an investment nature for their customers they too fall under the FSA jurisdiction.

The main investment activities of the societies which will come under the requirements of FSA include:

1. Arranging for the provision of, and advising on, life insurance, including endowment policies linked to mortgages.
2. Establishing and managing of unit trusts.
3. Providing of personal pensions.
4. Establishing and managing of personal equity plans.
5. Arranging for the provision of services in connection with stocks and shares.

It will be a criminal offence to engage in investment activities of this nature without authorisation. Societies can obtain authorisation from either SIB or from one or more of the SROs, depending upon the breadth and mix of investment business activities undertaken.

Whether or not a society requires authorisation depends on its activities and the manner in which they are undertaken. Each society therefore will need to:

1. Determine whether any of its current or proposed activities constitute investment business; if not, it does not require authorisation.
2. Decide its policy on whether it will be an introducer or a representative; introducers (who restrict their investment service to introducing customers to authorised independent intermediaries on a commission basis), and representatives (who represent a single authorised life office or unit trust operator for a fee), do not require authorisation.
3. Choose to become independent investment intermediary or manager, then it will need authorisation from appropriate SRO(s) or SIB.

Investor protection in building societies

Prudential requirements

1. The law and regulations under which societies currently operate require that at least 90 per cent of their total commercial assets (i.e. total assets less liquid and fixed assets) be in the form of loans for house purchase to individuals which are secured by first mortgage. Societies may not lend more than 100 per cent of the valuation of the property.

Residential property has generally risen in value. Consequently, losses as a result of bad debts are minimal, at the end of 1985 provisions for mortgage losses accounted for only 0.012 per cent of mortgage assets of about £97,000 million.
2. The size of the societies' liquid funds and the manner in which these funds can be invested are closely controlled by regulations made by the Building Societies Commission (set up under the Building Societies Act 1986), the government body responsible for the prudential supervision of societies. Broadly speaking, societies can invest their liquid funds only in authorised banks and government and government-guaranteed securities. A proportion of liquid funds must be in short-term securities and in practice most investments are held on a fairly short-term basis.
3. Societies are required, for the prudent operation of their business, to maintain adequate reserves and comprehensive accounting records and internal control systems.

Monitoring of building society activities
The Building Societies Commission monitors very closely the activities of building societies. Societies are required to complete detailed monthly, quarterly and annual returns on their activities to identify any potential difficulties at an early stage.

The statutory investor protection scheme
The Building Societies Act 1986 provides a new legislative framework for building societies and includes provision for a statutory *Investor Protection Scheme*. This replaces the voluntary scheme set up by the Building Societies Association in April 1982 and covers all 'authorised' building societies: 123 societies, out of a total of 131, at the time of writing. The statutory scheme is along similar lines to that which exists for the banks, with two important differences:

1. Unlike the banks' scheme, the building society Investor Protection Scheme does not have a permanent fund of money. The reason given for this by the Treasury is that 'experience suggests that calls on the scheme are likely to be much less frequent than those on behalf of depositors with small licensed deposit takers under the Banking Act Scheme'.
2. The level of protection is 90 per cent of amounts up to £20,000. Hence an individual investor would be guaranteed a maximum of 90 per cent of £20,000 regardless of how many accounts are held in the society. (Depositors of larger amounts than £20,000 can of course split their funds between two or more societies, but then they will lose out on the increasingly popular high interest accounts with a £20,000 minimum.)

When the investor/depositor protection provisions under the Banking Act 1987 and the Building Societies Act 1986 are compared, building societies appear to provide greater protection: for example, the maximum fund which could be raised under the Banking Act would not be nearly sufficient to repay the depositors of any one of the big four clearing banks, in the unlikely event of a bank losing all its funds.

Regulating insurance industry

The group banking structure often includes insurance business. Therefore it is relevant for you to know the main provisions of the enactments under which insurance industry in the UK is regulated and supervised.

1. *Insurance Companies Act 1974*

(a) Any salesman or agent selling insurance policies, whether for protection or investment, must reveal his connection with the insurance company whose policies he is selling to the customer.
(b) The Act protects the interests of investors who purchased insurance investment products from press advertisements, salesmen, brokers or on the recommendation of investment advisers.
(c) It is a criminal offence to make misleading, false or deceptive statements, orally or by advertisements.
(d) The DTI is empowered to regulate the content of insurance companies advertisements, so that no misleading and false statements are made.
(e) The insurance companies must issue a statutory notice detailing the terms of the insurance contracts, and giving the proposers (the customers) a cooling-off period, within which they can cancel, without obligation, the contracts that they previously signed.

2. *Policyholders Protection Act 1975*

(a) The Policyholders Protection Board, set up under the Act, can impose a levy on failed insurance companies of up to 1 per cent of their premium income, and also on the insurance brokers and agents up to a proportion of their commission earnings from the sale of failed companies' business to ensure that their policyholders receive 90 per cent of the anticipated maturity value of their policies.
(b) Investment advisers who recommend insurance products, act as 'accountable intermediaries'.

3. *Insurance Brokers (Registration) Act 1977*

All those calling themselves insurance brokers must be registered with the Insurance Brokers Registration Council; which lays down the code of professional conduct for its members. It is a criminal offence for a person to describe himself as an insurance broker unless he is registered with the Council (FSA imposes further restrictions).

4. *Insurance Companies Act 1982*

This Act is now the definitive legislation on the subject of regulation of insurance industry, and its main provisions are as follows:

(a) Before a company can write insurance business, it must be authorised by the DTI. To obtain DTI authorisation, it must:

(i) comply with the solvency regulations;
(ii) possess sufficient financial resources to meet its needs;
(iii) have controllers, directors, managers and underwriting agents who are 'fit and proper persons'; and
(iv) submit to the DTI a detailed plan of its business projections for some years (normally five) hence, setting out the type of business that it proposes to underwrite, the premium rates to be charged, the reinsurance arrangements and so on.

Authorisation is granted for specific classes of business. The Act breaks down the classes of business into long-term (e.g. life business), of which there are seven classes, and general (e.g. non-life business), which comprises 17 classes.

(b) No new authorisations will be given for companies to write both general and long-term business, other than reinsurance basis, although existing composite companies may continue writing both classes of business.
(c) Insurance companies are prohibited from carrying out non-insurance business anywhere in the world – although they can establish subsidiaries to transact other type of business.
(d) In terms of requirement for trading, the Act defines, at present, three categories of insurance company.

  (i) *External companies*. These have their head offices outside the EC, and are subject to extremely stringent controls. They must appoint a person, or a company, resident in the UK to act on their behalf and this representative, and its relevant executives and main underwriting agents must be 'fit and proper persons'; additionally they must keep assets of a prescribed value within the UK, as well as placing a deposit with the High Court.
  (ii) *Community companies*. These have head offices in EC countries, other than the UK. They have to satisfy the authorisation requirements of the member country in which they have their head offices, and they are governed by what are called matching and localisation provisions of the Act.
  (iii) *United Kingdom companies*. These are indigenous UK companies, with UK head offices, formed under various companies acts, Royal Charter, Acts of Parliament, or are registered friendly societies. They will be subject to the full weight of the 1982 regulations.

(e) As the codifying Act, the 1982 Act also covers matters provided for in earlier legislation (see above). For example, it covers matters relating to the conduct of business within the insurance industry, for the protection and benefit of the insuring public, and relates to such things as advertising, misleading statements, connected intermediaries and the issue of 'cooling-off' notices which allow a proposer to withdraw from a long-term contract of life assurance.
(f) The Act lays down restrictions on companies transferring business to other insurers, including Lloyds. If it is the general business which is to be transferred then the approval of the Secretary of State (DTI) is required, and details must be sent to the affected policy holders, whilst with long-term business the sanction of the High Court, or the Court of Session in Scotland, is required.

DTI: the major watchdog

The DTI keeps a very tight control over insurance companies' activities. It checks on their solvency and management generally, as per the 1982 Act, which requires that all companies must deposit detailed accounts with the DTI each year, together with other information relating to premiums, claims analyses and reinsurance arrangements. Companies transacting long-term business are also required to carry out an annual valuation of the assets and liability of their life fund, or funds, details of which must be submitted to the DTI for checking.

Should an insurer fail to comply with the requirements of the 1982 Act, the Secretary of State may intervene; should there be any concern over an insurance company's activities, the DTI can invoke its powers of intervention: these powers would be used in the following main areas:

(a) To protect existing or potential policy holders against the risk of the company becoming insolvent, or unable to meet the expectations of its long term policy holders.
(b) If the company, or its parent or subsidiary, fails to meet any of the obligations of the 1982 Act, submits misleading information, or if any grounds exist that would prevent the Secretary of State from granting authorisation, or its authorisation has been withdrawn in another EC member state, the DTI will intervene.
(c) There seems to be an open power of intervention by the DTI within five years of an authorisation to trade is given, or a person who is unapproved becoming a controller of a company.

The Secretary of State can, in such circumstances, take whatever action he considers necessary, by specifically ordering the company:

(i) not to make or realise investments of a specified class;
(ii) to maintain adequate assets in the UK to cover liabilities;
(iii) to deposit such assets with an approved person;
(iv) to limit premium income to a specific amount;
(v) to carry out a special valuation of its long-term business;
(vi) to liquidate certain investments;
(vii) to stop the office taking new business or even renewals;
(viii) to produce its accounting returns more speedily;
(ix) to produce specified information, books, documents;
(x) to prohibit the appointment of certain persons as directors or senior controllers of the company;
(xi) to instruct an insurance company to reduce its bonus rate applicable to with-profit life contracts.

An insurance company can be wound up under the normal Companies Acts rules, but also by the DTI if the company cannot comply with the provisions of the 1982 Act, or if it is felt that to wind it would be in the public interest.

Examination questions

The contents of this and of the next chapter are new, post-Wilkinson additions, therefore there are, as yet, no exam questions and answers which cover these topics. The following *specimen* questions and answers are intended to pinpoint specific information from a long chapter. **Note**: The MFS exam questions on this topic will be much more general, for example: Examine the impact on banks' balance sheets of: (i) the LDC debt problem; (ii) international agreement on capital adequacy; (iii) the need for liquidity.

Question 1

What are the provisions for the unpaid depositor/investor under the:
(a) Financial Services Act 1986?
(b) Building Societies Act 1986?
(c) Banking Act 1987?

Question 2

What are the requirements of the Insurance Companies Act 1982, of which a banking group, with an insurance subsidiary company, should be aware?

Question 3

What is the 'Basle Agreement', and what are its provisions?

Question 4

What are the implications of the Second Banking Directive of the European Community (1988) for the UK banks?

Outline answers

Answer 1

(a) *Financial Services Act, 1986*
Compensation of Unpaid Investor's Scheme:
- Investment industry to contribute to meet the cost of compensation.
- Each investment firm to contribute in proportion to its gross revenue.
- Members of the appropriate SRO to contribute, as a group up to £100 million in any one year, in respect of claims against one of their fellows.
- Members of the other SROs to contribute only thereafter.

(b) *Building Societies Act, 1986*
Investor Protection Scheme:
- The level of protection is 90 per cent of amounts up to £20,000; individual investor is guaranteed this amount regardless of the number of accounts he holds with the building society.
- With joint accounts, each individual is guaranteed a maximum of 90 per cent of up to £20,000.

(c) *Banking Act, 1987*
Banking Deposit Protection Scheme:
- All 'authorised' institutions, including overseas banks, are required to participate in the scheme.
- The level of protection is 75 per cent of the first £20,000 of sterling deposits made with an authorised institution's UK offices.

Answer 2

The requirements of the Insurance Companies Act 1982

- Before the company can write insurance business, it must be authorised by the DTI; authorisation is given only after the company has met strict conditions.
- No new authorisation to write both 'general' and 'long-term' business, other than reinsurance business.
- The company cannot do non-insurance business itself, but can do it via a subsidiary.

- The Act recognises three categories of insurance company: External companies (head offices outside EC states, subject to stringent controls); Community companies (head offices in EC states, must satisfy the authorisation requirements of the state in which head office is located); and UK companies (indigenous UK companies, subject to the 1982 Act).
- Matters such as conduct of business rules, protection of policyholders, misleading advertising and oral statements, cooling-off period, are covered.
- Restrictions on transferring business to other insurers.

Answer 3

In July 1988, 12 most developed countries agreed on a set of rules on capital adequacy for banks in each country. The key features of the agreed rules are known as Basle Agreement, because it was agreed at the Bank for International Settlements in Basle, Switzerland. The agreed set of rules are as follows:

- By the end of 1992, banks with significant international exposure, must maintain capital equivalent to at least 8 per cent assets, weighted according to risk.
- At least half of the bank's capital must consist of 'core capital', and the other half 'supplementary capital'.
- In calculating capital adequacy, off-balance-sheet items will be taken into account, according to specified weightings.
- An interim target date is the end of 1990, when the minimum capital adequacy ratio will be 7.25 per cent.

Answer 4

The implications of the Second Directive for UK banks:

- easier cross-border banking;
- international expansion via location in EC member states;
- cheaper location because no committed capital is required for foreign branches;
- no specific solvency ratios or large exposure limits on foreign branches;
- opportunity for a bank to undertake in other states whatever it is able to undertake in the UK;
- central issue for UK competing banks:
  - access to potential customers;
  - efficient delivery systems for financial services.

A tutor's answer

The following question, which seeks to examine your understanding of two important issues discussed in this chapter, was asked recently in the CIB exams. Try to answer it from the knowledge you have obtained from the study of this chapter, before looking at the outline answer provided below.

Question

(a) Explain why each of the following is important to a commercial bank:

(i) Capital adequacy;
(ii) Liquidity;
(iii) Profitability.

(b) With reference to the structure and components of a bank's balance sheet, discuss how a bank provides for capital adequacy, liquidity and profitability.

Specimen answer

(a) (i) *Capital adequacy* is essential for a bank to withstand:
- possible losses on operations;
- bad advances; and
- loss on investments.

● As an official requirement under the:
- Banking Act 1987, and
- Basle Agreement.

(ii) *Liquidity* is significant for a bank to meet:
- cash withdrawals;
- daily inter-bank settlements;
- unforeseen demand for financing;
- interruptions to cash flow.

(iii) *Profitability* is important to a bank to provide:
- a return to shareholders;
- for a build-up of reserves (to maintain capital adequacy); and,
- for financing future expansion.

(b) (i) Balance sheet shows capital and total assets and deposits, giving ratios which are used to gauge *capital adequacy*.

(ii) Balance sheet components which are relevant to *liquidity* include: notes and coins, operational deposits with the Bank of England, Treasury bills, eligible bills, secured call money and short-notice money with the discount houses, short-dated local and central government stocks.

(iii) Balance sheet structure shows a trade-off between *most profitable* (therefore least liquid) assets and liquidity.

A step further

Your best sources of keeping up-to-date with the requirements of this topic are the quality financial press, articles in *Banking World*; especially watch out for updating articles by the Chief Examiner. The Bank of England's *Quarterly Bulletin* must remain your most authoritative source for guidance on relevant legislation on regulation and supervision of commercial banks.

CHAPTER 11

Corporate Finance and Risk Management

Syllabus requirements

- Reasons for hedging.
- Hedging instruments.
- Corporate short-term finance.
- Corporate long-term finance.
- Role of equities in corporate finance.

Getting started

Hedging reduces exchange rate and interest rate risks. In the context of this chapter, hedging means using the financial machinery, via hedging instruments, to gain protection against loss arising through fluctuations in the exchange rates and interest rates. A financial intermediary, say, a bank, can do the matching of two or more offsetting transactions entered into by hedgers.

The growth in the use of hedging instruments is generally thought to have been caused by the volatility which followed the collapse of the Bretton Woods fixed exchange rate agreements. It is also attributed to the widespread exploitation of arbitrage opportunities between different financial markets, where the interest rates and exchange rates had gone out of alignment. However, the financial (hedging) instrument market has now grown to such an extent that it is probably capable of generating its own volatility, which in turn requires further use of more and varied instruments. These factors have resulted in the development of many ways of risk management by which risks may be transferred between different participants in the financial markets.

You are, however, expected only to be **aware** of the hedging instruments, and **not** with their technical details.

The corporate finance part of this chapter deals with the financial instruments which are used in obtaining short-and long-term finance by the companies, including venture capital providing new equity funds for them.

Short-term finance means making available funds for short periods of time; money borrowed for periods up to one year may be termed short-term finance. There are no definite dividing lines between short-term, medium-term, and long-term finance, but one-year to five-year borrowing is termed medium-term, and borrowing over five years may be called long-term.

Essential principles

The following are the main hedging and corporate financing instruments.

1. **Hedging instruments: exchange rate risks protection**
   (a) *Foreign currency options (FCOs)*
   An FCO is a contract between a buyer and a seller of a foreign currency which gives the option buyer (say, a bank's customer) the right, but not the obligation, to buy (a call FCO) or to sell (a put FCO) a specific amount of one currency for another currency at a predetermined price (the exercise or strike price) on or until a certain future date (the exercise period or date). An FCO has a predetermined maturity date; and if it can be exercised at any time between the date that it was written and the date of its maturity it is called an American option; if it can be exercised only at maturity date it is known as a European option.
   The customer, on purchasing an FCO on payment of a premium, obtains complete hedge against adverse exchange rate movements, but is still able to benefit from favourable movements. Taking out an FCO is therefore not just a hedging operation.
   (b) *Forward foreign exchange contract (forward cover)*
   A forward cover is a **binding** deal between two parties (say, a bank and its customer) to buy or sell a fixed amount of one currency for a fixed amount of another currency either on a specific future date (fixed forward cover) or on any day during the specific period (option forward cover). The rate at which the exchange is agreed between the two currencies by the parties to the forward deal, is called the forward exchange rate. Like the FCO, a forward cover is a hedging operation, and the main difference between the two is that whereas with a forward cover the exchange rate is always quoted from the bank's own point of view – the bank buys and the bank sells – with an FCO it is the customer who buys the *right* to buy or sell, from or to, the bank an underlying foreign currency at a specified rate of exchange; with an FCO a customer can 'walk away' if the actual rate of exchange on the day the currency is to be bought or sold becomes unfavourable, losing only the premium. With a forward cover he cannot 'walk away' even if he is unable to comply with the terms of the binding contract.
   (c) *Currency swap*
   A bank and its customer agree to exchange specified amounts of two different currencies for a specified period, usually between five to ten years. At the end of the agreed period the parties re-exchange the same amounts of currencies regardless of the exchange rate ruling at the time. Usually, during the swap period the two parties exchange a series of interest rate payments based on the amount exchanged. Currency swapping often occurs across national boundaries, and enables the parties to borrow the currency they desire at a cheaper rate than otherwise would be possible, whilst at the same time the parties are covered against a future currency exchange risk.

2. **Hedging instruments: interest rate risk protection**
   (a) *Interest rate swap*
   This involves a swapping of interest rate payments, and normally involves one company raising fixed rate borrowing and another raising floating rate borrowing. This arrangement enables both companies to achieve the type of interest rate each desires, at a cheaper rate than is otherwise possible.
   (b) *Interest rate cap*
   This agreement places an upper limit on the rate of interest payable on a variable rate borrowing linked to the base rate or LIBOR. Interest rate caps can be traded quite separately from the borrowing to which they relate.

(c) *Interest rate option*
This contract is basically similar to a foreign currency option contract except that instead of a currency, a specified financial arrangement is bought (call option) or sold (put option) at a predetermined price (exercise or strike price) on or until a future date (exercise period or date). The buyer of the option will exercise his right only if he sees an interest rate advantage over the current interest rates.

(d) *Forward rate agreement*
This is a contract between, say, a bank and a customer under which each party agrees to compensate the other party for the effect of movements in the LIBOR upon a notional borrowing over a predetermined contract period (settlement date). The seller agrees to compensate the purchaser for any increase that occurs in the intervening period, and the purchaser in turn agrees to pay over to the seller the difference between the agreed and the prevailing rate if the rate falls.

Euro Currency Unit (ECU)
ECU provides hedge against both exchange rate and interest rate risks. Therefore business companies trading in Europe and seeking protection against these risks should consider using ECU-denominated arrangements.

Although ECU was created to facilitate payment of debts between member states of the EC, it is being used increasingly by the private sector throughout Europe. For business companies it provides two distinct advantages: (1) Interest and exchange rates fluctuations of its 12 component currencies are smoothed out, thus providing relative stability, even when, for example, the pound sterling is moving quite sharply against certain other EC currencies. (2) It provides protection or hedging opportunities for exporters and importers. ECU enables businesses to take out protection against exchange risk in a *single* transaction rather than a range of separate transactions, which means it is both simpler and cheaper.

Transaction and translation risks

Transaction risks are inherent in most business ventures. Suppose a developer borrows £10 million to set up a shopping centre, and expects to recoup his investment *plus* profit from the rental stream. If the rental stream gets partially silted due to fall in retail sales (recession, credit squeeze, rising unemployment), he may not be able to recoup his investment due to the transaction risk. It is very difficult to hedge a transaction risk.

Translation risks relate to the translation, or conversion, of assets in currencies other than sterling. Suppose a company has assets worth DM2 million, in Germany, and the rate of exchange is £1 = DM2.60. If the sterling's exchange rate improves against DM to, say, £1 = DM3.00, the company's translation loss will be DM800,000, or £266,666.66. Like the transaction risk, it is very difficult to hedge a translation risk.

Corporate financing instruments

Corporate finance involves provision of funds to incorporated bodies, e.g. business companies and other businesses, for varying periods of time, viz. short term, medium term and long term.

1. **Short-term financing techniques**

(a) *LIBOR-linked lending*
The London Inter-Bank Offered Rate (LIBOR) is a true reflection of the cost of funds to the banks, and it is logical to use it as a true base rate when lending to

other banks and to sophisticated non-bank businesses. A LIBOR-linked loan is a facility by the bank, whereby the customer borrows wholesale funds at market rates, for periods between one and 12 months, usually at lower rates than the overdraft rate, which is linked to the bank's base rate.

(b) *Base rate-linked advances (overdraft)*
The base rate is the basic lending rate of a bank or financial institution, on which its lending (and deposit) rates are founded. Base rate-linked advances may be fixed rate or floating rate lending. The advance period is usually up to one year. With the volatility of interest rates, some banks split their base rate-linked advances into two, one advance with a fixed rate of interest, the other with a floating rate. If the base rate goes down, the customer gains on floating rate – and if the base rate goes up, the customer is protected on the fixed half.

(c) *Acceptance credit*
This is a facility whereby the customer (usually larger businesses) draws a bill of exchange on the bank, up to an agreed limit, payable at a stipulated future date. The bank accepts the bill and arranges for it to be discounted. Acceptance credit can be arranged from a period of one week to over six months. This facility is not as flexible as an overdraft, but it offers the advantage of cheaper borrowing; a reputable bank's acceptance attracts the lowest discounts from the bank, and certainty of cost; the customer is informed by the bank of the exact cost of his borrowing, i.e. acceptance commission and the discount he can obtain.

(d) *Sterling commercial paper (SCP)*
SCP comprises sterling promissory notes of maturity periods between seven and 364 days issued by corporate borrowers direct to investors, thereby by-passing traditional bank lending (this process is known as 'disintermediation'). This source of finance is available to company customers with a listing on the International Stock Exchange and with minimum surplus resources of £25 million, and borrowing a minimum of £100,000.

2. **Medium-term finance**

All major banks provide variations of the following loans to businesses.

(a) *Business loans*
The customer borrows at a fixed rate of interest and repays, in monthly instalments the loan over a number of years, or early, at any time, with no penalty. In many cases the loan can be unsecured. The fixed interest means that the customer knows, in advance, exactly what his monthly commitment is, which assists him to forecast his cashflow more accurately. The period of business loan is usually between one and five years.

(b) *Flexible business loans*
For borrowing larger amounts than under business loans, say, for purchasing an expensive asset, a business, or for providing working capital, a company may seek a flexible business loan, borrowing a single lump sum or borrowing sums in stages as needed, paying interest only on what has been borrowed. Borrowers can choose either a fixed or a floating rate at the start and can switch between them during the loan period, which may be up to five years, but can be up to 20 years. Repayments can be monthly or quarterly spread over the full term. If the borrower chooses, he can enjoy no capital repayment for up to two years, but repaying only interest, thus reducing pressures on his cashflow early on. Flexible business loans can be tailored to borrowers' needs.

3. Long-term finance

(a) *Debenture stock*

A company may issue debenture bonds to borrow long-term funds. A debenture bond is an acknowledgement by the issuing company of its debt to the debenture bondholders. Debenture stock (the total of issued debentures) may be secured by a *fixed charge* over a fixed asset, e.g. land, premises, machinery by the issuing company, and the company must keep the mortgaged asset intact, i.e. it must not be sold, exchanged or other charge created against it. The secured charge may be a *floating charge*, applying to all assets, not already mortgaged, which normally can be traded. Therefore, debentures with a fixed charge are more secure than those with a floating charge.

Debenture stock carries a fixed rate of interest and normally a guarantee of repayment in full by a specified date. Payments of debenture interest rank ahead of dividend payments to preference and ordinary shareholders. If the issuing company is being wound up, debenture-holders rank before preferential creditors (e.g. unpaid wages, taxes, etc.) and before preference and ordinary shareholders, for repayment of capital from the sales proceeds of its assets. Not all indebtedness of a company can be described as a debenture stock; the loan must have some permanence, say ten years or more, to be classed as debenture stock.

Banks lending via purchases of debenture stock of a company pay particular attention to the following aspects of the company: (a) Interest cover – the extent by which its gross profits exceed its interest obligations; (b) Liquidity – the extent by which its cash inflow exceeds its cash outflow; (c) Debt redemption provision, if any; (d) Marketability of debentures – marketing will be restricted if the issuing company is not a 'blue chip' company.

(b) *Fixed and variable rate loans*

Flexible business loans, discussed under 'medium-term finance', can be geared to provide long-term finance, of up to 20 years.

(c) *Equity finance*

The larger commercial banks provide finance to businesses to buy-in the shares of retiring directors (management buy-outs), or other shareholders who wish to realise their holdings (another form of management buy-out). They also provide development capital where a business expansion may be limited by the fact that it is nearing the limit of what it can raise by other conventional means. The bank makes available the necessary finance (normally upwards of £150,000) to the business in return for minority shareholding in the business. Thus by providing a percentage of equity capital, the bank is injecting long-term funding and an equity subscription, in return for a proportion of the ordinary equity, usually 15–40 per cent. The bank will normally seek to appoint a member of its staff as a non-executive director. This means that although a shareholder the bank does not expect the board of directors of the business to alter their on-going successful business strategy, nor does it expect to interfere with the day-to-day management of the business. The role of the bank's non-executive director is to assist in an advisory capacity in the development of future business plans and to give financial guidance. For smaller amounts of capital injection (£100,000 or more), the bank may seek a mix of preference share capital and ordinary equity; the proportion of equity is normally 10–20 per cent. The bank, in such a mix, will not expect board representations but will expect a guaranteed preference dividend.

(d) *Venture capital*
A larger private company or a smaller public company may wish to raise new capital for investment in a specific project or for expansion, in which there is a risk. Fixed interest capital, even if available, is not suitable. The capital required is called 'venture capital'; the provider of this capital is being asked to share in the risks. The critical stage which determines whether a company will succeed in growing into a large company is rather like the chrysalis stage when a caterpillar turns into a beautiful butterfly; there is apparently not much happening on the outside, but inside a major transformation may be underway. Companies in the chrysalis stage need help. Venture capitalists can provide help. Control often needs to move from the entrepreneur who *started* the business to a management team who will help it *grow*. The high street banks usually provide the venture capital by lending up to about £100,000.

(e) *Invoice discounting (factoring)*
The bank purchases a business's book debts on a continuous (therefore, long-term) basis, and provides the business customer with an immediate cash advance of up to 80 per cent of the value of invoices. This prepayment of invoices assists customers to sustain their cashflows, and to cut their overdrafts.

(f) *Eurobonds*
Eurobonds are an extension of eurocurrency markets' short-term lending and borrowing. They are sold in more than one country simultaneously, usually through an international syndicate of bankers, who may also agree to underwrite the issue. They are issued at fixed rates, as well as variable rates (then they are known as floating rate notes); the interest rate is fixed usually every six months in line with the changes in six-month eurodollar interest rate. Thus the interest rate on medium- and long-term bonds – average maturities are between 10 to 15 years – can be brought into line with the short-term interest rates. The currencies of issue are usually dollar, deutschemark, Swiss franc, and also sometimes pound sterling and ECU. Most bonds are payable to bearers and all are paid without deduction of tax. The amounts involved are large and therefore eurobonds are suitable for the needs of multinationals, local and national governments, and public corporate bodies.

Useful applied material

In this section we shall look at the practical aspects of hedging instruments and corporate finance techniques.

Hedging instruments

(a) *Forward exchange contract (forward cover)*
These contracts provide a cheap and simple means of reducing businesses' exposure to exchange rate changes, because a forward cover is a contract between the customer and the bank to exchange a specified amount of a currency for another at a *future* date but at the rate of exchange between the two currencies set *now*. Thus a forward cover provides businessmen with *certainty* about the exchange rate at which the future transaction will take place. The future date may be as far away as five years, and even longer in some cases, and the currencies in which forward cover contracts are available may be as many as 40. Forward covers are available in large and small amounts, and therefore are particularly suitable for smaller businesses seeking exchange rate cover.

Suppose a company signs a contract to supply goods for \$100,000 when the dollar/sterling exchange rate is \$1.70, but on supply of goods and on receipt of payment the pound has risen to \$2. The amount the exporting company would receive drops from nearly £59,000 to £50,000 – which could wipe out most or all of its profit on the transaction. However, this would not happen if the company had taken out a forward cover contract with a bank: its profit margin in sterling will remain unaffected by exchange rate movements during the *lifetime* of the contract.

(b) *Foreign currency options (FCOs)*

FCOs allow bank customers to take advantage of favourable exchange rate movements while protecting them against adverse changes.

Suppose X PLC invoiced their American customers for \$5.1 million, for payment in 90 days. X PLC estimated that at existing rate of \$1.70 there was a 20 per cent profit on the deal, and if the pound fell the profit would be even more. Nevertheless, X PLC in order to protect their profit margin to at least 15 per cent, took out an FCO to convert their dollar proceeds back into sterling at \$1.78 in three months' time. As it turned out, the pound rose and the exchange rate moved to \$1.85! X PLC were glad to exercise their option at \$1.78 and protect their profit margin. The premium paid in advance, of around 0.65 per cent was well worth it to X PLC.

(c) *Interest rate swaps*

Suppose Company X borrows from Y a notional sum of £10 million, which will never actually be exchanged, on a floating rate basis of LIBOR plus ¾ per cent; the rate is to be refixed every six months for the life of the deal. (Company X could have borrowed at a fixed rate of 12 per cent for a five-year period).

Company X entered into an interest swap agreement with its bank, under which the company pays a fixed sum on six-monthly intervals on the same days as the rollover dates for the LIBOR-linked £10 million borrowing. The six-month LIBOR received from the bank normally equals the six-month LIBOR paid out to Y.

Interest payments by Company X are therefore fixed as follows, assuming the LIBOR at 10 per cent:

10% + ¾% paid to bank (10% LIBOR received from bank and paid over to Y)
+ ¾% paid to X
11½%

As Company X could have borrowed at 12 per cent fixed, it is saving ½ per cent of the interest cost.

The swap arrangements are normally available to larger companies who can fix interest rate exposure. Normally the minimum amount is £1 million and the minimum and maximum terms are two years and 10 years respectively.

(d) *Currency swap*

Under currency swaps, unlike under interest rate swaps, there is the exchange of principal borrowed as well as interest.

Suppose Company X borrows from Y \$16 million, and then enters into a currency swap with its bank to receive sterling in exchange, at the exchange rate of £1 = \$1.60.

	Y lends \$16 million to Company X.
Day 1	Company X transfers \$16 million over to bank.
	Bank returns £10 million to Company X.

Interest payments	Company X pays interest in dollars to Y, on \$16 million. Company X pays interest in sterling to bank, on £10 million. Bank pay interest in dollars to Company X, on \$16 million.
Last day	Company X pays back £10 million to bank. Bank pays back \$16 million to Company X. Company X repays \$16 million to Y.

Currency swaps are normally available to companies who can borrow in a currency in which they have a competitive advantage but no cash inflow and benefit from exchange cover when the forward market is 'thin'. Minimum amount of currency swaps is £5 million or its equivalent, and the term ranges from two to 10 years. Currency swaps are not commonly seen.

(e) *Interest rate caps*
These caps, on base rates or LIBOR, limit borrowers' interest rate costs to a specified level for a specified period of time. But, at the same time, they enable borrowers to benefit from a fall in rates.

Suppose LIBOR/Base Interest Rate = 11 per cent. The bank is willing to lend to the customer at 2 per cent over LIBOR/Base Rate. The customer does not wish to pay more than 13 per cent (including the 2 per cent margin), i.e. he wishes to cap the LIBOR/Base Rate at 11 per cent. If interest rates rise to a figure in excess of 11 per cent, the bank will reimburse the difference to the customer.

Suppose the underlying cap amount is £1 million, and that the interest rates rose immediately after the interest rate cap agreement to 12 per cent for the year, the customer would be paid 1 per cent (difference between Cap rate at 11 per cent and interest rate at 12 per cent) on £1 million for 1 year = £10,000.

The minimum and maximum limits usually for LIBOR Caps are £5 million and £100 million, and for the Base Rate Caps £250,000 to £10 million. The LIBOR Cap terms tends to be up to five years, and for the Base Rate Cap, one or two years.

(f) *Interest rate options*
These are similar in character and purpose to FCOs (see above), in that a customer having paid a single premium in advance, has the right to fix the rate, for a specified period, on a future notional loan, deposit or investment, but he is under no obligation to take up that right. Suppose he fixes a future loan rate at 15 per cent for a period up to two years. Afterwards, interest rates fall sharply to say 11 per cent, he can simply walk away from the option and borrow instead cheaply at the lower prevailing market rate. If, on the other hand, interest rates rose sharply to, say, 18 per cent, he will be glad of being able to borrow at 15 per cent. These options are of particular interest to those businesses whose large customers do not pay on time!

(g) *Forward rate agreement (FRA)*
These agreements between corporate customers and their banks enable customers to borrow or lend a specified notional amount in the future at a fixed rate, fixed at the time of the agreement.

Suppose Company A has a seasonal borrowing requirement at £1 million for a three-month period commencing 5 January. In September LIBOR rate is 10 per cent, and the company purchases an FRA in September, for January–March at 10½ per cent. LIBOR on 5 January is 11 per cent. Bank pays ½ per cent on the underlying contract of £1 million for contract period of three months, i.e. £1,250.

Company borrows at 11 per cent in the market, but with receipt of £1,250 the interest costs net 10½ per cent. However, if on 5 January, the LIBOR had been 10 per cent the Company would pay to the Bank £1,250.

The amount of FRAs ranges between £1 million and £50 million, and the term ranges between one month and six months.

Corporate financing techniques

(a) *Short-term LIBOR-linked loans*
These loans are normally available to companies needing working capital facilities or short-term finance for specific projects. The main advantages to borrowers include a loan facility 'committed' as to availability of funds at money market related interest rates which are usually cheaper than overdraft rates, and the borrowing costs are constant for the loan period. The actual interest rates charged will reflect the financial standing of the customer. Fixture periods (terms) range from one month to 12 months, although banks prefer fixture periods of three months or more. A fee may be charged from borrowers for early repayments or for the non-utilisation of the loan facility. All drawings are repayable on demand because it is a loan facility 'committed' as to availability of funds. Nevertheless, it gives companies another funding option with a minimum limit of £250,000, and with no upper limit.

(b) *Sterling commercial paper (SCP)*
These are unsecured sterling bearer promissory notes issued direct to the investor through a 'dealer' and administered by an 'issuing and paying agent'. The dealer is responsible for quoting rates to authorised issuer, i.e. corporate customers with a full listing on the International Stock Exchange and with minimum surplus resources of £25 million. The dealer is also responsible for finding investors for the SCP issue. Normally the issuers announce a programme indicating the maximum volume of SCP that could be outstanding at any one time. Minimum issue is £100,000. The issuing and paying agent arranges for the initial payment to the issuer and on maturity repaying investors. Interest rates will reflect the financial standing of the issuer, and will normally be linked to LIBOR/LIBID (London Inter-bank Bid Rate). The benefits of SCP to the issuer include cheap source of short-term (up to 364 days) funds, costs are fixed for the period of the paper, flexibility of maturity, ability to tap wider investor market, and advantages of comparative rates.

(c) *Acceptance credits*
This is a short-term credit facility made available by banks to corporate trading customers. Banks accept bills of exchange drawn upon them by customers who can then get these acceptances discounted by the issuing bank or in the London Discount Market at very low rates of discount. At maturity the customers provide the banks with sufficient funds to pay the bills on presentation – these funds can be provided by drawing a new bill of exchange. Banks charge from the customers the accepting commission, which is the fee for accepting the bill and lending their name to its strength.

Acceptance credit is usually cheaper than overdraft borrowing, and the finance costs are fixed at the outset of each transaction. The minimum facility is for £100,000, there is no maximum. Each individual bill should have a minimum value of £25,000 and a maximum value of £1 million. For individual bills the minimum term is 30 days and the maximum is 180 days. The main purpose for acceptance credits is to obtain short-term financing for corporate trading.

The following example shows that although the customer would receive £97,250 immediately, he will need to repay £100,000 in three months' time. Thus the cost of his finance has been paid in *advance* rather than, as is usual on overdraft, in arrears. The true rate of interest is therefore higher than the quoted discount rate.

Suppose:

Face value of the bill		£100,000
Tenor		90 days
Acceptance commission		1% p.a.
Discount rate		10% p.a.

Therefore:

Face value of the bill		£100,000
Less commission (1% p.a. × $\frac{3}{12}$)	£250	
Less discount (10% p.a. × $\frac{3}{12}$)	£2,500	£2,750
Borrower receives		£97,250

(d) *Debenture loan stock*

A company has benefit and drawback in raising the required finance via the issue of debentures instead of issuing more ordinary shares (equity capital) via a rights issue to existing ordinary shareholders.

Benefit

Corporation tax on a company's profits is charged *after* interest on loan stock, but *before* dividends to any class of shareholder: preference or ordinary.

Suppose Comnpany Z has:	£
(a) Profits before tax	1,000,000
less interest on loan stock (assumed)	100,000
	900,000
less corporation tax at, say, 35%	315,000
Profits available for ordinary shareholders	585,000
(b) Profits before tax	1,000,000
less corporation tax at 35%	350,000
	650,000
less preference share dividend (assumed)	100,000
Profits available for ordinary shareholders	550,000

Thus under (a) there is a tax saving to the company of £35,000 (£585,000–£550,000), and the true cost of the interest to the company is £65,000 (£100,000–£35,000). A 10 per cent loan stock, say, in debentures would cost the company, only £6.5 per cent $\left(10 \times \frac{100 - 35}{100}\right)$.

Company Z can raise loan stock in the capital market when it is short of funds, and it can buy its own stock back when it has surplus funds. This provides the company with flexible means to adjust its liquidity.

The higher the loan capital, the higher the proportion of trading income allotted to meet the loan interest charge. But however much it may be, it is a *fixed* sum, and therefore any increase in trading income has a more than proportionate effect (gearing) on the surplus available for net profit.

Drawback
The drawback arises out of the fixed and committed claim of loan stock interest against a company's trading profits, which is also backed by a fixed (or floating) charge against its assets. Should there be a serious drop in the company's trading income, it must pay in full the loan interest, or risk losing its charged or mortgaged assets.

Specimen questions

There are no exam questions, as yet, on this topic because it is a new, post-Wilkinson addition. The following specimen questions and their outline answers are intended to assist you in picking out required information from the contents of the chapter.

Note: The MFS exam questions from this topic will be much more general, for example: (a) outline the main ways in which a large company can raise short-term finance. (b) What is meant by the term 'disintermediation'? (c) Indicate which methods of borrowing discussed in part (a) are examples of disintermediation.

Question 1

(a) What is meant by 'hedging' operations?
(b) What are the particulars of interest rate hedging instruments?

Question 2

(a) 'Acceptance credits are a way for larger businesses to raise sums over £500,000, more cheaply than by overdraft'. Explain.
(b) Are acceptance credits always less costly than overdrafts?

Question 3

What are the advantages and disadvantages of debenture bonds to:
(a) the issuing company;
(b) the purchasers of debenture bond; and
(c) the company's ordinary shareholders?

Question 4

(a) Define Interest Rate Swaps and Currency Swaps.
(b) Explain how each of these would be of benefit to a company in risk management.

Question 5

(a) Distinguish between Interest Rate Caps and Forward rate agreements.
(b) Describe how each of these operates.

Outline answers

Answer 1

(a) *Hedging operation*
Using the financial machinery to gain reduction in loss arising through fluctuations in the exchange and interest rates.

(b)
- *Interest rate swaps.* Two parties agree to pay each other interest on a notional amount over a defined period but calculated according to different interest bases. At no time is the notional amount actually exchanged. Customers can fix interest rate exposure from two-to 10-year terms, for a minimum of £1 million but with no maximum limit.
- *Interest rate caps.* This agreement limits a borrower's interest rate costs to a specified level for a specified period of time. It allows borrowers not only to limit interest costs but also to benefit from a fall in interest rates. The term is from one year up to five years, and the minimum and maximum amounts for rate caps are £250,000 to £100 million.
- *Interest rate options.* A contract which gives the borrower a guarantee against the unexpected, i.e. interest rates actually rising when the borrower expected them to fall but without eliminating his chance to borrow should the rates fall.
- *Forward rate agreement.* A contract to borrow or lend an agreed notional amount in the future at a fixed rate which is agreed at the time of the agreement. Terms range from one month to six months, for amounts between £1 million and £50 million.

Answer 2

(a)
- Acceptance credits are easy to arrange and simple to operate.
- Minimum for each individual bill of exchange is £50,000.
- While not as flexible as overdrafts, they offer cheaper borrowing, certainty of cost, a continuous source of funds, and funds in a wide variety of foreign currencies.

(b)
- The customer receives the *discounted* amount immediately.
- The cost of his finance has therefore been paid in *advance* rather than, as is usual on overdraft, in arrears.
- The true rate of interest is therefore higher than the quoted discount rate.

Answer 3

(a)
- Advantages to the *issuing company*
  - saving on corporation tax;
  - ability to adjust liquidity conveniently.
- *Disadvantages*
  - interest costs are fixed and must be paid annually;
  - assets charged can be sold if the interest is not paid.

(b)
- *Advantages* to *purchasers* of debentures
  - fixed rate of return guaranteed for the whole term;
  - repayment of the principal normally in full at maturity;
  - security of charged assets.

- *Disadvantages*
  - interest rates rise after the debenture stock has been subscribed;
  - market value of charged assets may fall.

(c)
- *advantages* to *ordinary shareholders*
  - advantages of gearing;
  - higher dividends due to savings in corporation tax.
- *Disadvantages*
  - if interest not paid regularly, their company's assets may be sold;
  - disadvantages of over-gearing.

Answer 4

(a)
- *Interest rate swaps*. See Answer 1(a) above.
- *Currency swaps*. An agreement between two parties to exchange one currency for another now and to re-exchange the same currencies sometime in the future and in the intervening period each party agrees to pay the interest costs to the other. Unlike with interest rate swaps, with a currency swap the exchange of the principal as well as of the interest takes place.

(b)
- *Interest rate swaps* enable customers to fix interest exposure.
  - enables customers to achieve the type of interest rate they desire at a cheaper rate.
- *Currency swaps* enable customers to borrow the currency they desire at a cheaper rate.
  - at the same time covering a future currency exchange risk.

Answer 5

(a)
- With *interest rate caps*, borrowers limit interest rate costs to a specified level. If interest rates rise above that level, the bank will reimburse them with the difference.
- *Forward rate agreements* enable customers to borrow or lend a specified *notional* amount in the future at a fixed rate, fixed at the time of agreement.

(b)
- *Interest rate cap operation*. Suppose:
  - base rate is at 11 per cent;
  - bank is willing to lend at 2 per cent above the base rate;
  - customer agrees, but does not wish to pay more than 13 per cent, i.e. wishes to cap the base rate at 11 per cent;
  - if interest rate rises above 11 per cent bank reimburses customer.
- *Forward rate agreement operation*:
  - the amount to be borrowed or lent in the future at the agreed interest rate, is notional;
  - the bank reimburses customer if the rate on the contract-commencing day is higher than agreed;
  - customer borrows at higher rate in the market but is cushioned by the reimbursement amount;
  - if on the agreed day, interest rate is below the agreed rate, the customer reimburses the bank with the difference.

A tutor's answer

The following question deals with the two hedging instruments, protecting customers against exchange rate fluctuation risks. Spend a few minutes working out the possible answer before looking at the answer given below.

Question

Define, and contrast:

(i) Foreign currency options; and
(ii) Forward exchange contracts (forward covers).

Specimen answer

Foreign currency option (FCO)
This is a contract between a buyer and a seller giving the buyer of the option *the right, but not the obligation*, to buy (call) or sell (put) a specific amount of one currency at a predetermined price (the exercise or strike price) on or until a certain future date (the exercise period or date).

The option extends from the date it is written to a predetermined expiry or maturity date. If the option can be exercised at any time between the date of writing and maturity it is termed an American option. An option that can be exercised only at maturity is known as a European option.

Forward exchange contract (forward cover)
This is an agreement between two parties to exchange an amount of one currency for an amount of another on a specific future date. The rate at which the exchange is made on a forward deal is called the forward exchange rate. Under a forward cover contract, both parties *have the right and obligation* to fulfil their part of the deal.

Suppose a UK company is considering purchasing during the next three months a machine costing \$300,000. The decision has not yet been made but, due to the fluctuating exchange rates at the time, the company buys a call FCO to purchase dollars against pound sterling at a strike price of £1 = \$1.60, for a three-month period. The following are the possible outcomes:

(a) Machine purchased:
   (i) Spot dollar rate = \$1.70
   Company will let the FCO lapse and buy dollars at spot: cost of machine = $\frac{300{,}000}{1.70}$ = £176,470
   (ii) Spot dollar rate = \$1.50
   Company will exercise the option, and the cost of the machine will be £187,500 $\left(\frac{300{,}000}{1.60}\right)$.

   Under (a), the company will lose the option premium.

(b) Machine not purchased
   (i) Spot dollar rate = \$1.70
   Company allows the option to lapse and loses the option premium cost.
   (ii) Spot dollar rate = \$1.50
   Company re-sells the 10 cents advantage for a cash payment.

Whenever there is doubt about foreign currency receivables or payables, an FCO is a suitable method of covering the foreign exchange exposure.

Suppose that in the above example, the company had decided to purchase the machine and had therefore taken out a forward cover contract to buy $300,000 at the price quoted by the bank of, say, $1.60, three months hence, and during that period the dollar weakened; and on the fixed date the dollar spot was $1.70, the company could not have, as under the FCO deal, simply walked away and taken advantage of the more favourable $1.70 spot, but had to purchase the $300,000 at the agreed price of $1.60. On the other hand, the cost to the company of covering forward would have been lower than the cost of premium of purchasing an FCO, because with an FCO deal the bank is taking all the risks. Thus a forward cover provides *certainty* of price, at a cheaper cost, at which a future transaction will take place.

A step further

The most appropriate source for updating your knowledge of the contents of this chapter are the publications of your banks dealing with the financial risk management and corporate finance. Study these publications carefully and you will get to understand the strategy of your bank in this profitable area of its activity. I am indebted to the risk management and corporate finance literature issued by Barclays Bank and NatWest Bank in writing this chapter.

No doubt *Signpost* articles will appear in *Banking World*, giving guidance on the parts of the syllabus covered in this and the previous chapters; you must of course look out for these articles.

Index